TEST MATCH SPECIAL
50 NOT OUT

The Official History of a National Sporting Treasure

TEST MATCH SPECIAL

50 NOT OUT

Edited by Peter Baxter

With contributions from

Jonathan Agnew

Harsha Bhogle

Henry Blofeld

Tony Cozier

Angus Fraser

Bill Frindall

Gerald de Kock

Simon Mann

Vic Marks

Christopher Martin-Jenkins

Jim Maxwell

Shilpa Patel

Mike Selvey

Donna Symmonds

and Bryan Waddle

BBC

BOOKS

A VIEW FROM THE COMMENTARY BOX

Past and present

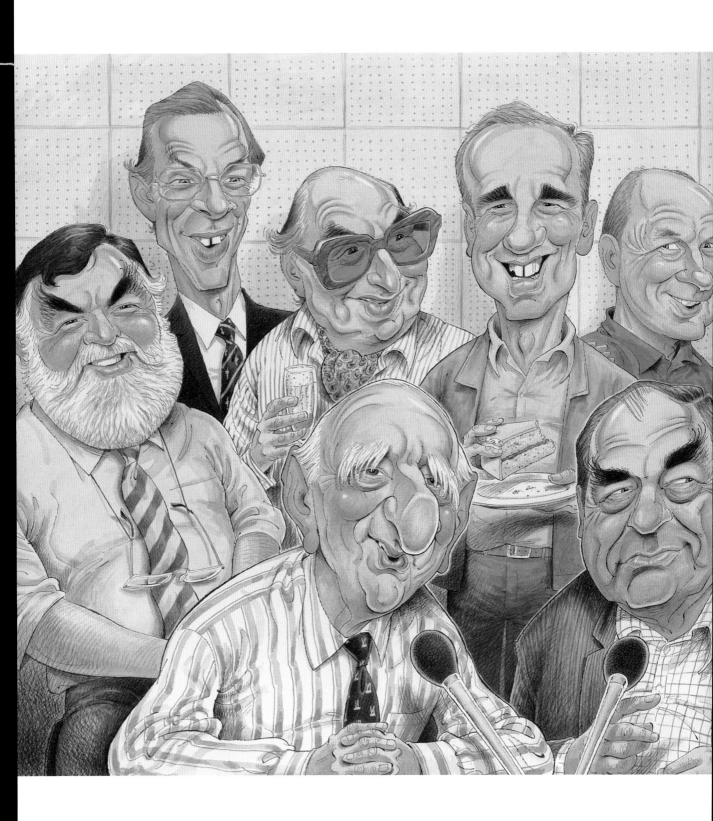

IRELAND

Bill Frindall

Christopher
Martin-Jenkins

Henry Blofeld

Jonathan Agnew

Vic Marks

Peter Baxter

Mike Selvey

Brian Johnston

John Arlott

10 9 8 7 6 5 4 3 2 1

Published in 2007 by BBC Books, an imprint of **Ebury Publishing**
A Random House Group Company

Copyright © Woodlands Books Ltd 2007

The Random House Group Limited Reg. No. 954009

Addresses for companies within the Random House Group
can be found at **www.randomhouse.co.uk**

A CIP catalogue record for this book is available from
the British Library

ISBN 978 0 563 53906 3

The Random House Group Limited makes every effort to ensure
that the papers used in our books are made from trees that
have been legally sourced from well-managed and credibly
certified forests. Our paper procurement policy can be found
at **www.randomhouse.co.uk**

Commissioning editor: **Vivien Bowler**
Managing editor: **Christopher Tinker**
Produced for BBC Books by **Butler and Tanner Ltd**, Frome
Project editor and picture researcher: **Julian Flanders**
Designers: **Kathie Wilson** and **Craig Stevens**
Production controller: **David Brimble**
Index: **Indexing Specialists (UK) Ltd**
Printed and bound in Great Britain by **Butler and Tanner Ltd**, Frome

Contents

A live programme is only as good as the people who take part in
it – the *TMS* team on the day of Aggers' debut, Headingley, 1991:
(left to right) Bill Frindall, Christopher Martin-Jenkins, Don Mosey,
Fred Trueman, Tony Cozier, Brian Johnston, Trevor Bailey,
Jonathan Agnew, Vic Marks, Peter Baxter and Mike Selvey.

Introduction

This book is a celebration of the golden jubilee of a radio programme.

Cricket commentary has been going much longer than 50 years, but what happened in 1957 created something of an institution around the name of that programme – *Test Match Special*.

In the following pages is the story of how it came about. A live programme can only be as good as the people who take part in it and we have reflected on a half-century of such characters. The list of voices has been necessarily restricted to those who have taken part within England. It would have doubled in length had we included all those who joined in on overseas tours. That self-imposed rule has deprived us of Michael Carey, Ralph Dellor and even David Gower (who earned a *Test Match Special* commentator's tie on a tour of the West Indies and was then promptly called into the England touring squad) and several others. I have also left out those who have only commentated on one-day matches and never done a Test Match. That list would have included no less a presence than Sir Tim Rice, who joined us during the World Cup of 1987 in India and Pakistan. His second match – in Pune – was between England and Sri Lanka, with whose players we were less familiar then than we are these days. Faced with an array of tongue-twisters, he opted for safety and listeners might have been surprised how often Vinothen John fielded the ball. 'The burly John' popped up at long-on and deep third man, sometimes in the same over. A future version of this book might yet include Tim, as, with typical enthusiasm, he always greets me with, 'Still available!'

We have told the story of how the programme – whose threatened demise once prompted questions in the House of Commons – came into being. At one stage in its history, indeed, such a sword of Damocles seemed regularly to hang over us as changes to radio networks gave planners nightmares which always appeared to bring them up against the great stumbling block that was *TMS*. Also included are the memories of many of the current habitués of the commentary box, from home and abroad.

Our listeners and our guests, from the highest to the lowest in the land, also have their place. Could any other game than cricket have thrown up such a programme? It seems very unlikely. Its pace, its structure, its history, its drama and its aesthetic qualities are the essential ingredients in the making of *Test Match Special*.

A former network controller once called *TMS* 'an art form'. John Arlott called it 'Folk'. Brian Johnston, in his own inimitable way, used to say, 'We're just a bunch of friends going to a cricket match and talking about it.' That'll do for me.

Peter Baxter
Soulbury, January 2007

1

THE BIRTH OF CRICKET COMMENTARY

There is no evidence to suggest that the Reverend Frank Gillingham was aware of his place in broadcasting history when – in May 1927 – he became the first cricket commentator. Although in fact 'commentator' is not really the word, because it was believed that ball-by-ball description of cricket was simply not possible.

Five years earlier in Australia, cricket commentary had been done for a state game and tried for Test cricket a couple of years after that. But the BBC in London had largely ignored those early steps in the far-off colonies. However, *Radio Times* made much of the groundbreaking significance of the Corporation's coverage of Essex's match against the New Zealand touring team at Leyton in May, because they published a full-page article under the heading, 'Cricket on the Hearth', in which, after stating that description of every ball was clearly not possible, they explained, 'What will be done is this. A microphone will be installed in the pavilion at Leyton and the BBC's narrator will watch the whole of Saturday's play from there. At fixed times [between

dance band music] he will broadcast an account of the state of the game.'

So, in between waltzes and foxtrots, Gillingham, a former Essex player himself and a stirring preacher, delivered his 'eyewitness accounts' of the game. These were not the 30-second reports which we are used to today, but five minutes or so on each occasion, so it is probable that he did get close to describing some live action as it happened.

Live sports commentary on the radio had started earlier that year, when Captain Teddy Wakelam had covered the England v Wales rugby international at Twickenham. Soon there was soccer from Highbury and the Oxford v Cambridge Boat Race, which was a tremendous technical undertaking. Several county matches, covered in the same style, followed that summer. Pelham Warner made the first broadcast from Lord's in June and later, it is recorded, Gillingham seriously blotted his copybook by filling a rain break at the Oval by reading out the advertising hoardings. The great C.B. Fry also added radio reporting to his already remarkable CV that year.

But live sports broadcasts were not to everyone's taste. Teddy Wakelam, who was regarded as the principal commentator on any sport, reported, after a difficult day at the Oval, that ball-by-ball

—CRICKET ON THE HEARTH.

Essex *v.* New Zealand   Saturday, May 14.

THE first few weeks of the cricket season have always, for the follower of the game, a peculiar charm. Complete familiarity has not yet set in ; the joy of sitting once again on a bench in the sun before the green oval, dotted with white—the crack of bat on ball, the sudden shout of ' How's that ?' the occasional, decorous applause—all these sensations are still keen and conscious whilst the memory of a winter's exile lasts.

And nowadays every cricket season has its extra attraction—some visiting team to arouse curiosity and add a fresh interest to the game. This year we have no Australians to watch, fearfully, trembling for our laurels ; but instead there will be the first visit to this country ever made by a New Zealand team. On the Rugger field, of course, we know the New Zealanders well, but their cricket form is new to us, and this match with Essex, their first against a county team, will be followed with particular interest by cricketers all over the country.

And, this year, broadcasting is not going to give cricket a miss. The B.B.C. will be there, and any listeners who wish may share in the feelings of those fortunate ones who are sitting on the Leyton ground. Broadcasting cricket is, of course, a new departure—an experiment, and something of an adventure. Cricket is one of the slowest games in the world ; it spreads over three days the incidents that in a football match are crowded into an hour and a half. To foreigners it seems not only leisurely but dull. The interest of it lies often more in the sheer skill of attack and defence than in violent fluctuations of fortune—though cricket can on occasion provide as thrilling a finish as any other game.

Obviously, to broadcast a running commentary on a cricket match by the method used for Rugger Internationals, the Cup Final, the Boat Race or the Grand National would be impossible. What will be done is this. A microphone will be installed in the pavilion at Leyton, and the B.B.C.'s narrator will watch the whole of Saturday's play from there. At fixed times, beginning with the resumption of play after the lunch interval, and thereafter for a few minutes every hour, he will broadcast an account of the state of the game, and after the close of play he will give a general description of the match. At other times, if anything happens worthy of special notice, his story will be 'faded into' the afternoon programme from the studio, that will be going on all the rest of the time.

In this way, it is hoped, listeners will be given the gist—not to say the cream—of the match. They will not have to sit through descrip-

Cricket as they played it in 1787, at ' the celebrated Cricket Field near White Conduit House ' ; from an old print now in the possession of W. T. Spencer, of 27, New Oxford Street. Those were the days of curved bats and stumps without bails.

tions of maiden overs and wait whilst the batsman sends in to the pavilion for his cap, but they will be able to listen every hour and hear the very latest score and any notable incidents of the last hour's play. Anybody who has spent his nights wondering what happened since the last edition will appreciate what this means.

And, of course, if any really thrilling occasion occurs in the course of the afternoon's play, listeners will be let in on it. Such occasions, it is true, are not too frequent on Saturdays, the day when first-class matches begin, and, owing to the way in which ordinary programmes are arranged, the most suitable day for broadcasting cricket. But if T. C. Lowry, the New Zealand captain (who is well

remembered over here as a lusty hitter for the Light Blues) should be on the point of rivalling the quick-scoring feats of G. L. Jessop, one of which Mr. Stacy Aumonier recalls in his article on the previous page ; or if J. W. H. T. Douglas threatens to pull off the hat-trick for Essex—then the London Station will ' go over ' to Leyton and tell the world what happens next.

The B.B.C.'s narrator, for this match, is a cricketer especially well known on the Essex grounds. The Rev. F. H. Gillingham (he is now Rector of St. Margaret's, Lee) first played for Essex in 1903, and has headed their batting averages in three seasons since then. He has long been one of the foremost amateur batsmen, and he played for the Gentlemen against the Players in 1908, 1919, and 1920. His long experience of the game, and his particular knowledge of Essex cricket, make him especially fitted to put listeners all over the country into real contact with the match.

And so for the first time the joys of cricket will go out on the air to all the radio population. It is a strange thought that the game of the *cognoscenti*, the life-long interest of the experts, should thus become the concern of everyone who has a wireless set. In the last few years, it is true, the game, like all forms of sport, has increased its public by leaps and bounds. The days when Test Matches were played to grounds only comfortably full have gone for ever. As the picture on this page shows, a big match nowadays is as much an event as a Cup-tie. But there is still a well-defined class of match-goer—the plump clergyman and the young men out from the office whom Mr. Stacy Aumonier recalls in his article on the opposite page are yet very typical of the crowd on an ordinary County ground.

Now all this can be changed. People who have never been to cricket matches because they didn't understand the game will be able to hear it described and explained by experts as it is being played, and after they have listened to one or two exciting incidents it will not be surprising if they begin to wonder whether it wouldn't be a good way of passing a Saturday afternoon to spend a shilling at the turnstiles of their local cricket-ground. Cricket-lovers living in the country will no longer have to depend upon morning-after accounts in the papers, and occasional visits to London in summer, for their contact with the game.

Cricket has long been the national summer game ; in the new era it may become so in a truer sense. Nothing, of course, could make real cricket lovers love cricket more, but broadcasting may bring the light to many who now languish in the outer dark.

Cricket as it is today—the national summer game. This picture, showing the excited crowds rushing on to the field at the close of the final Test Match at the Oval last year, to celebrate England's recovery of the Ashes, makes a striking contrast with the leisurely scene reproduced in the old print above.

commentary on cricket was not possible. And there was a further setback when Lance Sievking, the Head of Outside Broadcasts, who had conceived the idea of live sports coverage, was moved to Drama. It seemed that the right man to blow the spark into a flame was yet to arrive at the BBC.

Happily in the early 1930s a great partnership was to launch real cricket commentary. Seymour de Lotbinière, first as producer and then as an imaginative Head of Outside Broadcasts in the footsteps of Sievking, perceived that with the right broadcaster ball-by-ball commentary of cricket could indeed be done. The rhythm of the game, he recognised, far from being impossible for radio,

made it ideal. There was the build-up to a moment of violent action as the ball was bowled and then the time for reflection before the next release of action and that predictable pattern set a perfect template. De Lotbinière ('Lobby' to all who worked with him) had the genius to recognise the man and the sport as the perfect combination for radio description. 'Paint a picture and keep it the right way up,' was the instruction.

The means to convey the game to a radio audience came to de Lotbinière in the person of Howard Marshall. Gillingham, Warner and Wakelam may have gone before, but Marshall was the true father of ball-by-ball cricket commentary in a manner that

would not be out of place today. He had joined the BBC in his late twenties, with a rugby blue from Oxford and training in journalism behind him.

There were still some who believed that serious cricket on the radio would be too dull, and that village cricket – this theory ran – might be more entertaining. Tommy Woodruffe, who was to earn greater fame for his description of the Spithead Royal Navy review with the less than entirely sober exclamation, 'The fleet's lit up!', was despatched to Tilford in Surrey, where he was to have – more prosaically – Eddie the fast bowler from the Church Farm end with the sound not only of ducks quacking, but of a tractor revving up in the background. Woodruffe, perhaps years ahead of his time with regard to *Test Match Special*, informed the listeners that the players had enjoyed a very good tea. 'I had time to have some myself, as a matter of fact,' he said. Giving the score – and he seemed to imply that that detail was fairly unimportant – was very difficult because they were playing in steady drizzle and, 'The small boy who is looking after the scoreboard doesn't want to go out in the rain.'

It was one of those sorts of ideas that programme planners still have, while overlooking the fact that for something like that to work, the audience has to know a great deal more about the characters involved. They need to care about the individual and collective fates of players and teams.

The earliest recording of cricket commentary in the BBC archives is from 1934 – a famous game, because it was the only time that England beat Australia in a Test Match at Lord's in the 20th century. On the final day of the three-day match, the Yorkshire

Opposite Teddy Wakelam was BBC Radio's first sports commentator. He covered all major sports, including cricket, football, rugby and Wimbledon – where he once famously set his papers alight, on-air. He convinced that ball-by-ball commentary was not the way forward for cricket broadcasting.

Above The dream team. Head of Outside Broadcasts at the BBC Seymour de Lotbinière (left) and commentator Howard Marshall. Lobby recognised that cricket had the perfect tempo for radio broadcasting and knew that Marshall was the man to deliver the appropriate descriptions.

Arthur Wrigley
by Bill Frindall

Arthur Wrigley pioneered a role born out of Hedley Verity's phenomenal bowling performance against Australia at Lord's in 1934. In those early days of cricket broadcasting, Test Matches were covered by a lone reporter accompanied by an engineer with all his gear housed in a haversack. With the pitch uncovered, heavy rain on the rest day produced a 'sticky dog' and Verity's left-arm spin was virtually unplayable. He took 14 wickets for 80 runs on that third day as Australia were dismissed for 284 and 118. During the final hour, when Verity took the last six wickets, Howard Marshall's reports were in constant demand. He was compelled to provide virtually ball-by-ball commentary without a scorer and with only a primitive scoreboard visible. He had no idea what Verity's figures were. It was to be England's only Ashes victory at Lord's in the 20th century.

When Marshall returned to Broadcasting House he asked for a scorer for the Third Test at Old Trafford. He was flatly refused and advised to bribe a ground staff boy with a two-guinea match fee. Marshall went to the office of the Lancashire Secretary, Captain Howard. He was in luck. Lancashire had just signed a young leg-spinner from Didsbury Cricket Club on to their staff. He also happened to be training as an accountant and had been taught to score by the Didsbury incumbent. Arthur Wrigley thus became the first BBC scorer and statistician.

His 31-year reign was broken only by wartime service in the RAF and occasional appearances at Midlands Tests by Jack Price. His premature demise from cancer at the age of 53 following emergency surgery on 30 October 1965 changed my life.

left-arm spinner, Hedley Verity, took 14 wickets (see opposite). Such a prodigious feat of bowling inspired the BBC to the realisation that their solitary commentator could do with the services of a scorer – though not yet an expert summariser. Arthur Wrigley was the man called in to keep the record for the next Test Match at Old Trafford.

In the early 1930s, the BBC's relationship with MCC seems to have had its ups and downs. There were periods when reporting from within Lord's was not allowed and to report on a Test Match, Marshall would have to leave the ground and go to a microphone installed in a nearby house. He used to tell the story of rushing to the basement room where this facility awaited him, only to hear, as the red 'on the air' light was about to come on, someone starting to practice piano scales, as he wrote later 'with startling clarity'. His engineer was despatched upstairs to persuade the young pianist to desist while Marshall started his report with the tinkling of piano keys as an accompaniment. He was to be further distracted, as he laboured on, by the arrival of the mother of the musician, demanding to know how long the lesson was to be delayed.

The Howard Marshall recording from 1934 has been frequently aired because of its historical significance, but surely more celebrated is the commentary from the Oval in 1938, when a young man called Len Hutton was approaching a landmark score (see overleaf). Marshall's rich, relaxed voice described the scene, relaying the enormity of Hutton's innings with phrases such as, '… It sounds like the total of the whole side … with the gasometer sinking lower and lower.'

Cricket commentary in England was still confined to short reports and broadcasts, though that record score by Len Hutton, which stood for 56 years, and the building of the huge England score in that timeless Test at the Oval must have provided the nudge that planners sometimes need to be persuaded to disrupt their schedules.

During that same Test series something else new was being tried on the broadcasting front on the other side of the world, in the studios of the Australian

England v Australia Second Test

22–25 July 1934 Lord's, London

ENGLAND FIRST INNINGS

CF Walters	c Bromley b O'Reilly	82
H Sutcliffe	lbw b Chipperfield	20
WR Hammond	c & b Chipperfield	2
EH Hendren	c McCabe b Wall	13
* RES Wyatt	c Oldfield b Chipperfield	33
M Leyland	b Wall	109
† LEG Ames	c Oldfield b McCabe	120
G Geary	c Chipperfield b Wall	9
H Verity	st Oldfield b Grimmett	29
K Farnes	b Wall	1
WE Bowes	not out	10
Extras	(lb 12)	12
Total	(all out, 198.3 overs)	440

Fall of wickets 1-70, 2-78, 3-99, 4-130, 5-182, 6-311, 7-359, 8-409, 9-410

Bowling	O	M	R	W
Wall	49	7	108	4
McCabe	18	3	38	1
Grimmett	53.3	13	102	1
O'Rielly	38	15	70	1
Chipperfield	34	10	91	3
Darling	6	2	19	0

Hedley Verity (centre) has Australia's Stan McCabe caught by Patsy Hedren in the second innings. Verity's final-day haul of 14 wickets earned England their only win against the Aussies at Lord's in the 20th century and convinced the BBC that their cricket commentator could do with the services of a scorer.

AUSTRALIA FIRST INNINGS

* WM Woodfull	b Bowes	22
WA Brown	c Ames b Bowes	105
DG Bradman	c & b Verity	36
SJ McCabe	c Hammond b Verity	34
LS Darling	c Sutcliffe b Verity	0
AG Chipperfield	not out	37
EH Bromley	c Geary b Verity	4
† WAS Oldfield	c Sutcliffe b Verity	23
CV Grimmett	b Bowes	9
WJ O'Reilly	b Verity	4
TW Wall	lbw b Verity	0
Extras	(b 1, lb 9)	10
Total	(all out, 109 overs)	284

Fall of wickets 1-68, 2-141, 3-203, 4-204, 5-205, 6-218, 7-258, 8-273, 9-284

Bowling	O	M	R	W
Farnes	12	3	43	0
Bowes	31	5	98	3
Geary	22	4	56	0
Verity	36	15	61	7
Hammond	4	1	6	0
Leyland	4	1	10	0

SECOND INNINGS FOLLOWING ON

* WM Woodfull	c Hammond b Verity	43
WA Brown	c Walters b Bowes	2
SJ McCabe	c Hendren b Verity	19
DG Bradman	c Ames b Verity	13
LS Darling	b Hammond	10
AG Chipperfield	c Geary b Verity	14
EH Bromley	c & b Verity	1
† WAS Oldfield	lbw b Verity	0
CV Grimmett	c Hammond b Verity	0
WJ O'Reilly	not out	8
TW Wall	c Hendren b Verity	1
Extras	(b 6, nb 1)	7
Total	(all out, 53.3 overs)	118

Fall of wickets 1-10, 2-43, 3-57, 4-94, 5-94, 6-95, 7-95, 8-95, 9-112

Bowling	O	M	R	W
Farnes	4	2	6	0
Bowes	14	4	24	1
Verity	22.3	8	43	8
Hammond	13	0	38	1

England won by an innings and 38 runs

FROM THE COMMENTARY BOX

'Here's Fleetwood-Smith again to Hutton. Hutton hits him – oh, beautiful shot! There's the record! [Cheering from the crowd.]

Well, that was the most lovely stroke. A late cut off Fleetwood-Smith's leg-break, which absolutely flashed to the boundary for four runs to give Hutton the record – beating Bradman's record made at Leeds in 1930 of 334. Beating that record for the highest score ever made by an individual in Test Matches in this country … Not just in this country, but between England and Australia ever and equalling Hammond's record in Test Matches of any kind made at Auckland in 1933.

They're singing … Terrific reception. The whole crowd is standing up and cheering. Thousands of them, all round the ground they're all standing up. Bradman's been rushed across to shake Hutton by the hand. The whole Australian team have congratulated him. And now everybody cheering.

Oh, it really is a wonderful scene. Here in this brilliant sunshine, they won't stop cheering.'

HOWARD MARSHALL, THE OVAL 1938

Len Hutton plays a majestic straight drive on the way to his record score by an individual in Tests of 364. In one of the last timeless Test Matches played, his innings lasted more than 13 hours and won the match for England. However, the series ended level and Australia retained the Ashes.

England v Australia Fifth Test

20–24 August 1938 Kennington Oval, London

Umpires **F Chester and FI Walden**

ENGLAND FIRST INNINGS

L Hutton	c Hassett b O'Reilly	364
WJ Edrich	lbw b O'Reilly	12
M Leyland	run out	187
* WR Hammond	lbw b Fleetwood-Smith	59
E Paynter	lbw b O'Reilly	0
DCS Compton	b Waite	1
J Hardstaff jnr	not out	169
† A Wood	c & b Barnes	53
H Verity	not out	8
Extras	(b 22, lb 19, w 1, nb 8)	50
Total	(7 wks dec, 335.2 overs)	903
Did not bat	K Farnes, WE Bowes	

Fall of wickets 1-29, 2-411, 3-546, 4-547, 5-555, 6-770, 7-876

Bowling	O	M	R	W
Waite	72	16	150	1
McCabe	38	8	85	0
O'Reilly	85	26	178	3
Fleetwood-Smith	87	11	298	1
Barnes	38	3	84	1
Hasset	13	2	52	0
Bradman	2.2	1	6	0

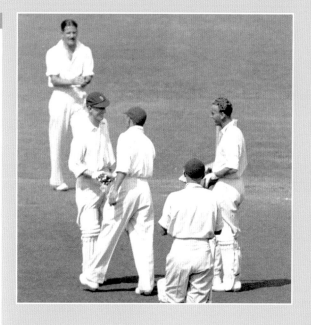

Don Bradman, whose record of 334 scored against England at Leeds in 1930 had been beaten, is the first to congratulate Hutton on his considerable achievement.

AUSTRALIA FIRST INNINGS

WA Brown	c Hammond b Leyland	69
CL Badcock	c Hardstaff b Bowes	0
SJ McCabe	c Edrich b Farnes	14
AL Hassett	c Compton b Edrich	42
SG Barnes	b Bowes	41
† BA Barnett	c Wood b Bowes	2
MG Waite	b Bowes	8
WJ O'Reilly	c Wood b Bowes	0
LO Fleetwood-Smith	not out	16
* DG Bradman	(absent hurt)	-
JHW Fingleton	(absent hurt)	-
Extras	(b 4, lb 2, nb 3)	9
Total	(all out, 52.1 overs)	201

Fall of wickets 1-0, 2-19, 3-70, 4-145, 5-147, 6-160, 7-160, 8-201

Bowling	O	M	R	W
Farnes	13	2	54	1
Bowes	19	3	49	5
Edrich	10	2	55	1
Verity	5	1	15	0
Leyland	3.1	0	11	1
Hammond	2	0	8	0

SECOND INNINGS FOLLOWING ON

WA Brown	c Edrich b Farnes	15
CL Badcock	b Bowes	9
SJ McCabe	c Wood b Farnes	2
AL Hassett	lbw b Bowes	10
SG Barnes	lbw b Verity	33
† BA Barnett	b Farnes	46
MG Waite	c Edrich b Verity	0
WJ O'Reilly	not out	7
LO Fleetwood-Smith	c Leyland b Farnes	0
* DG Bradman	(absent hurt)	-
JHW Fingleton	(absent hurt)	-
Extras	(b 1)	1
Total	(all out, 34.1 overs)	123

Fall of wickets 1-15, 2-18, 3-35, 4-41, 5-115, 6-115, 7-117, 8-123

Bowling	O	M	R	W
Farnes	12.1	1	63	4
Bowes	10	3	25	2
Verity	7	3	25	2
Leyland	5	0	19	0

England won by an innings and 579 runs

Broadcasting Commission (ABC) in Sydney. Rivalry in cricket commentaries had become very competitive in Australia, particularly during the 1932–33 'Bodyline' series. Commercial stations vied with each other to the point that the Australian Cricket Board started to worry about the effects that broadcasting might have on match attendances. Surprisingly, perhaps, French commercial stations had spotted that the interest in the unfolding drama of that historic series was echoed in Britain. Radio Paris led the way with lengthy reports, but Poste Parisien went a bit further, by bringing the former Australian player, Alan Fairfax, over to France. Supplied by cables from Australia, starting at 6 a.m. – as a Test Match day in Australia would be coming to its conclusion – Fairfax mounted a synthetic condensed 'commentary' on the day's play, crammed into two hours.

So, in 1938, unwilling to throw themselves on the mercy of unreliable technology in a direct broadcast line from England, the ABC's Head of Sports Broadcasting, Charles Moses, decided that they would have live commentary, but that it would be done in Sydney on the information of a series of cables sent by their man at the match. But, unlike the French broadcasts, it would be done – as nearly as possible – in 'real time'.

Four men sat round a table in the studio, with a large picture of the ground in England where the match was being played mounted in front of them and a man operating a scoreboard. The cables would arrive with each over cryptically described. An effects tape would provide atmosphere and – if the operator got his timing right – appropriate applause. The great Australian commentator, Alan McGilvray, in at the birth of this, always insisted that they had provided the sound of bat on ball with a pencil on a block of wood, an assertion that suggests an unlikely sounding effect, but Australians were hearing every ball and only about ten minutes late.

In the same year that Howard Marshall had commentated on Verity's match-winning performance at Lord's, a persistent and ambitious young man had persuaded the BBC to use him to do studio-based rugby reports. E.W. Swanton went on to do frequent sports round ups for the Empire Service – the forerunner of the World Service. Though he seems to have put a few backs up on the way, he persuaded de Lotbinière, after a trial cricket commentary on a county match at the Oval, that what they needed was a series of live commentary periods and reports from the England tour of South Africa over the winter of 1938–39.

It was a great breakthrough for cricket broadcasting – and for Swanton himself, not least when he was able to broadcast live commentary to a Boxing Day audience of Tom Goddard's hat-trick in Johannesburg in the First Test. A happy coincidence for both audience and commentator that the schedules accommodated the first broadcast Test hat-trick. Swanton ended up enthusing the South African audience enough with this new art, that he was doing additional commentaries for the SABC outside his BBC times.

As the Second World War began, a noticeable appetite for live radio sports and events commentaries had been engendered. Later in the war years that style of live description was to be taken up by reporters, including Howard Marshall himself on the Normandy beaches. Between the victory in Europe and that over Japan in 1945, a series of matches was played – five 'Victory' Test Matches between England and Australia, which were followed in late August by England v the Dominions at Lord's. Increasing amounts of commentary were broadcast by the BBC in the course of the series, much of it by a name new to the airwaves – Rex Alston. He was thrust into the limelight when Howard Marshall, the master at whose feet he was learning the job, was summoned to London from Old Trafford to start working on coverage of the Victory parades. Marshall was never to commentate on a Test Match again.

The year after that – 1946, the first full year of peacetime – an Indian touring team was due in England. A former Hampshire policeman, who had just become poetry producer in the BBC's Eastern Service, was asked to cover the tour for them. The broadcasts he did early that summer to India brought an enthusiastic response from that remote audience and encouraged his Head of Service to keep him doing it – provided, of course, that he still did his poetry programmes. That was the start in cricket commentary of John Arlott.

Alston and Swanton between them handled such commentary periods as there were in the first two post-war summers of 1946 and 1947, though John Arlott made his debut on domestic BBC radio commentary for the last Test of 1947. De Lotbinière made the appointment, with mixed praise, 'Your voice is vulgar, but you have an interesting mind.' That 'vulgar' and possibly unique Hampshire accent was to adorn radio commentaries for a further 34 years.

The BBC's newly appointed poetry producer John Arlott clutches a copy of his recently published poem 'A Nest of Singing Birds' in 1946. The following year he made his debut on domestic radio covering the Fifth Test against South Africa at the Oval.

In 1948, for the first time, every ball of a Test series was to be broadcast. Not all of it would be broadcast on the BBC, but the ABC had asked for continuous commentary on the great Don Bradman's last tour, leading the team that was to become known as the 'Invincibles', and the BBC was going to provide it.

The ABC sent a representative, Alan McGilvray, to join the BBC team, a practice that has continued ever since. John Arlott was now permanently in the commentary team, alongside Alston and Swanton. An unfortunate incident early in the tour, however, was to foster a lifelong antipathy between Arlott and McGilvray. Arlott, on another county ground, overheard a report to Australia being done, in his own rather confidential and intimate style, by McGilvray. A few minutes later, linked to Alston who was at the same early tour match, Arlott unguardedly said, 'My god, Rex, what have you got there?' Alan McGilvray still had his headphones on, heard the remark and never forgave it.

With much of the Outside Broadcasts department's energies being directed towards the coverage of the Olympic Games in London that year, Rex Alston effectively became the BBC's first cricket producer and over the next 59 years was to have only two successors. He recalled that, as they went on the air on the first day of that 1948 Ashes series, light rain started to fall. The umpires made a few trips to the pavilion gate, but the drizzle kept returning. 'We had no idea what we should do,' said Rex, years later, 'until at last I heard a desperate voice in my headphones, saying, "For God's sake, hand back to the studio!"'

The series ended at the Oval with the drama of the Don's last Test innings and another great moment in the BBC archives as John Arlott took over from Rex Alston to describe the great event (see page 22).

The Australians came to England again in 1953, when England regained the Ashes, and in 1956, when they retained them, but still radio commentary was confined to short periods on the Light Programme (the forerunner of Radio 2) and the Home Service (now known as Radio 4).

The Home Service, in fact played a huge part in the development of cricket commentary, which made it all the more appropriate that it was destined to become the home of *Test Match Special* in 1994. Until the BBC plan 'Broadcasting in the Seventies' was produced, a great deal of its broadcasting was regionalised, with the sort of local news opt-outs that we are now used to on television, but which the birth of Local Radio made unnecessary for sound. And part of that regional broadcasting included cricket commentary.

On weekdays in the summer there would be two or three half-hour periods when each region would carry commentary on two County Championship matches. Obviously the north might have both Yorkshire and Lancashire playing away and so an agreement to share the period would be reached with the regions that were broadcasting their matches. Commentators worked with an engineer, usually a scorer and sometimes a producer, or 'No.2', as they were known, but no summariser. The half-hour would be divided between the two matches selected, but rain at one match could leave the other man with a lot of talking to do. And they learned their craft the hard way.

The World Service was also providing a service in that regard. The opening matches of a tour would always be covered by periods of commentary for them, usually involving the visiting commentator, if there was one, but also being used by the home commentators as an exercise in familiarisation before the Test series began.

In August 1955, at Scarborough, the North of England's senior Outside Broadcasts producer, and a very fine commentator, Robert Hudson, found himself approaching the end of one of these regional commentary periods. His anxiety was growing, though, because Fred Trueman had just taken two Nottinghamshire wickets in as many balls and the new batsman was taking his time to come out to face the hat-trick ball.

The clock was ticking remorselessly towards Hudson's allotted time for handing back to the studio. There could be no flexibility in this. The regional opt-out time was ending and they had to re-join the national Home Service. Cyril Poole was

taking his guard with 45 seconds to go. At last Trueman was unleashed. Poole propped forward and played the ball into the hands of short leg. 'It's a hat-trick! Back to the studio.' A shattered Bob Hudson fell back in his chair and decided then that there must be a better way of covering cricket. His suggestion was that use could be made of the Third Network (later to become more of a unified force as Radio 3) if not all day, then at least for periods shared between itself and the Light Programme.

In those days the BBC thrived on its use of memorandums, with carbon copies on flimsy paper filling shelves of files in every office. Plenty of those flew around the in and out trays, as the then Head of Outside Broadcasts, Charles Max-Muller, took up the cause on behalf of his northern producer. It can be well imagined how much understandable resistance was put up by the classical music lobby to any erosion of its diet. Similarly perhaps, the Light Programme executives may well have been keen on the plan to ease any pressure on them to expand.

Discussions went on through 1956 and it cannot have done any harm that that summer saw some superb bowling against the Australians at Old Trafford, when Jim Laker took 19 wickets in the Test – a feat that provided yet another classic piece of archive commentary from John Arlott (see pages 24–5).

Whether that was the final persuasive act that tipped the balance of the hierarchy in favour of the new 'Special Service' is lost among those dusty files of 'flimsies', but for the First Test against the West Indies in 1957 the BBC undertook to broadcast on radio every ball by means of inviting listeners to switch between that service on the Third Network and the Light Programme. The whole generic name given to it was *Test Match Special*.

Above Fiery Fred Trueman, whose hat-trick for Yorkshire against Nottinghamshire at Scarborough in August 1955 nearly caused Robert Hudson a heart attack as he desperately waited for the third batsman to come to the wicket to receive his fate before handing back to the Home Service.

Rex Alston 'And here's the applause for Bradman as he comes in. Well, it's a wonderful reception. The whole crowd is standing and the England team are joining in and – led by Yardley – three cheers for the Don, as he gets to the wicket.

And now the crowd settle down again … 40 minutes left for play and Bradman is now taking guard. Hollies is going to bowl at him and John Arlott shall describe the first ball. So come on John.'

John Arlott 'Well, I don't think I'm as deadly as you are, Rex. [Alston had just described Barnes' wicket falling.] I don't expect to get a wicket. But it's rather good to be here when Don Bradman comes in to bat in his last Test.

And now here's Hollies to bowl to him from the Vauxhall End. He bowls – and Bradman goes back across his wicket and pushes the ball gently in the direction of the Houses of Parliament, which are out beyond mid-off. It doesn't go that far, it merely goes to Watkins at silly mid-off – no run. Still 117 for 1.

Two slips, a silly mid-off and a forward short leg close to him as Hollies pitches the ball up slowly and … he's bowled!

Bradman bowled Hollies, 0. Bowled Hollies, 0.

And – what do you say under those circumstances?

I wonder if you see the ball very clearly in your last Test in England – on a ground where you've played some of the biggest cricket of your life and where the opposing side has just stood around you and given you three cheers – and the crowd has clapped you all the way to the wicket. I wonder if you really see the ball at all.'

England v Australia Fifth Test

14–18 August 1948 Kennington Oval, London   Umpires **HG Baldwin and D Davies**

ENGLAND FIRST INNINGS

L Hutton	c Tallon b Lindwal	30
JG Dewes	b Miller	1
WJ Edrich	c Hassett b Johnston	3
DCS Compton	c Morris b Lindwall	4
JF Crapp	c Tallon b Miller	0
* NWD Yardley	b Lindwall	7
AJ Watkins	lbw b Johnston	0
† TG Evans	b Lindwall	1
AV Bedser	b Lindwall	0
JA Young	b Lindwall	0
WE Hollies	not out	0
Extras	(b 6)	6
Total	(all out, 42.1 overs)	52

Fall of wickets 1-2, 2-10, 3-17, 4-23, 5-35, 6-42, 7-45, 8-45, 9-47

Bowling	O	M	R	W
Lindwall	16.1	5	20	6
Miller	8	5	5	2
Johnston	16	4	20	2
Loxton	2	1	1	0

SECOND INNINGS

L Hutton	c Tallon b Miller	64
JG Dewes	b Lindwall	10
WJ Edrich	b Lindwall	28
DCS Compton	c Lindwall b Johnston	39
JF Crapp	b Miller	9
* NWD Yardley	c Miller b Johnston	9
AJ Watkins	c Hassett b Ring	2
† TG Evans	b Lindwall	8
AV Bedser	b Johnston	0
JA Young	not out	3
WE Hollies	c Morris b Johnston	0
Extras	(b 9, lb 4, nb 3)	16
Total	(all out, 105.3 overs)	188

Fall of wickets 1-20, 2-64, 3-125, 4-153, 5-164, 6-167, 7-178, 8-181, 9-188

Bowling	O	M	R	W
Lindwall	25	3	50	3
Miller	15	6	22	2
Johnston	27.3	12	40	4
Loxton	10	2	16	0
Ring	28	13	44	1

AUSTRALIA FIRST INNINGS

SG Barnes	c Evans b Hollies	61
AR Morris	run out	196
* DG Bradman	b Hollies	0
AL Hassett	lbw b Young	37
KR Miller	st Evans b Hollies	5
RN Harvey	c Young b Hollies	17
SJE Loxton	c Evans b Edrich	15
RR Lindwall	c Edrich b Young	9
† D Tallon	c Crapp b Hollies	31
DT Ring	c Crapp b Bedser	9
WA Johnston	not out	0
Extras	(b 4, lb 2, nb 3)	9
Total	(all out, 158.2 overs)	389

Fall of wickets 1-117, 2-117, 3-226, 4-243, 5-265, 6-304, 7-332, 8-359, 9-389

Bowling	O	M	R	W
Bedser	31.2	9	61	1
Watkins	4	1	19	0
Young	51	16	118	2
Hollies	56	14	131	5
Compton	2	0	6	0
Edrich	9	1	38	1
Yardley	5	1	7	0

Australia won by an innings and 149 runs

Opposite Donald Bradman arrives at the wicket for his last-ever Test Match appearance in England and is greeted with three cheers by the England players.

Above Bradman looks at his stumps in confusion after being bowled, second ball by a googly from Eric Hollies. He was cheered all the way back to the pavilion by a crowd who knew they were unlikely to see him bat again.

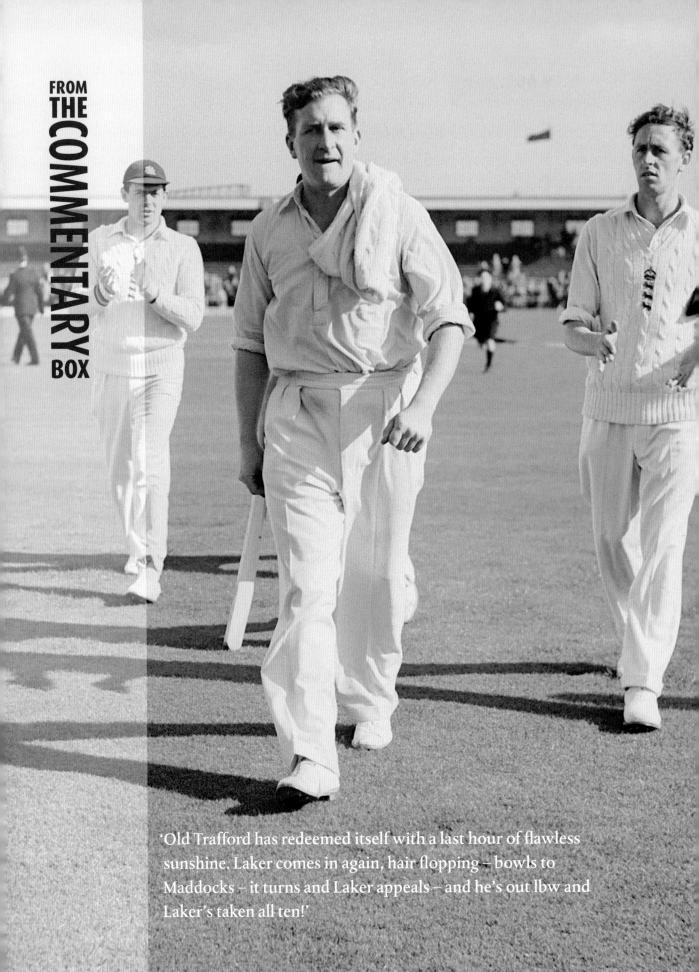

'Old Trafford has redeemed itself with a last hour of flawless sunshine. Laker comes in again, hair flopping – bowls to Maddocks – it turns and Laker appeals – and he's out lbw and Laker's taken all ten!'

England v Australia Fourth Test

26–31 July 1956 Old Trafford, Manchester

Umpires **DE Davies and FS Lee**

ENGLAND FIRST INNINGS

PE Richardson	c Maddocks b Benaud	104
MC Cowdrey	c Maddocks b Lindwall	80
Rev. DS Sheppard	b Archer	113
* PBH May	c Archer b Benaud	43
TE Bailey	b Johnson	20
C Washbrook	lbw b Johnson	6
ASM Oakman	c Archer b Johnson	10
† TG Evans	st Maddocks b Johnson	47
JC Laker	run out	3
GAR Lock	not out	25
JB Statham	c Maddocks b Lindwall	0
Extras	(b 2, lb 5, w 1)	8
Total	(all out, 158.3 overs)	459

Fall of wickets 1-174, 2-195, 3-288, 4-321, 5-327, 6-339, 7-401, 8-417, 9-458

Bowling	O	M	R	W
Lindwall	21.3	6	63	2
Miller	21	6	41	0
Archer	22	6	73	1
Johnson	47	10	151	4
Benaud	47	17	123	2

'The first man to congratulate him is Ian Johnson. And England have won by an innings and 170 and Laker has taken all ten wickets for 53 in the second innings … And there are friends of mine who were not going to come today. They thought it would rain. Well it did look as if it was going to rain. They missed a very great piece of bowling.'

JOHN ARLOTT

Opposite Jim Laker leads the England team off the Old Trafford pitch having taken 19 Australian wickets in the match and all ten in the second innings. England won the series 2-1 and retained the Ashes they had won for the first time in 19 years in 1953.

AUSTRALIA FIRST INNINGS

CC McDonald	c Lock b Laker	32
JW Burke	c Cowdrey b Lock	22
RN Harvey	b Laker	0
ID Craig	lbw b Laker	8
KR Miller	c Oakman b Laker	6
KD Mackay	c Oakman b Laker	0
RG Archer	st Evans b Laker	6
R Benaud	c Statham b Laker	0
RR Lindwall	not out	6
† LV Maddocks	b Laker	4
* IWG Johnson	b Laker	0
Extras		0
Total	(all out, 40.4 overs)	84

Fall of wickets 1-48, 2-48, 3-62, 4-62, 5-62, 6-73, 7-73, 8-78, 9-84

Bowling	O	M	R	W
Statham	6	3	6	0
Bailey	4	3	4	0
Laker	16.4	4	37	9
Lock	14	3	37	1

SECOND INNINGS FOLLOWING ON

CC McDonald	c Oakman b Laker	89
JW Burke	c Lock b Laker	33
RN Harvey	c Cowdrey b Laker	0
ID Craig	lbw b Laker	38
KD Mackay	c Oakman b Laker	0
KR Miller	b Laker	0
RG Archer	c Oakman b Laker	0
R Benaud	b Laker	18
RR Lindwall	c Lock b Laker	8
* IWG Johnson	not out	1
† LV Maddocks	lbw b Laker	2
Extras	(b 12, lb 4)	16
Total	(all out, 150.2 overs)	205

Fall of wickets 1-28, 2-55, 3-114, 4-124, 5-130, 6-130, 7-181, 8-198, 9-203

Bowling	O	M	R	W
Statham	16	10	15	0
Bailey	20	8	31	0
Laker	51.2	23	53	10
Lock	55	30	69	0
Oakman	8	3	21	0

England won by an innings and 170 runs

2

DON'T MISS A BALL

Radio Times for the last week of May 1957 carried the programme title *Test Match Special* for the first time, and with it the slogan, 'Don't miss a ball, we broadcast them all.' It was designed to persuade listeners that by a fancy bit of re-tuning, either by study of the radio schedules, or as directed by the commentary team, they could switch from the Light Programme to the Third Network's Special Service and back again and hear a complete day's play for the first time. That first *TMS* team, chosen to cover the Test series against the visiting West Indies, comprised commentators Rex Alston, John Arlott, E.W. Swanton and Ken Ablack, expert summarisers Gerry Gomez and Bill Bowes and scorer Jack Price.

Rex Alston was the staff commentator who opened the broadcast. By now he had a dedicated cricket producer, Michael Tuke-Hastings, to back him up. The Corporation had charged Tuke-Hastings with the job of steering the new programme out into

Right The cover of *Radio Times* for the week beginning 26 May 1957 features the name *Test Match Special* for the first time. On the inside pages were details of how, with a bit of retuning during the day, the listener could keep in touch with a whole day's play.
Opposite Rex Alston, the first voice ever heard on *Test Match Special*.

deeper waters. Alston had been a schoolmaster at Bedford School, who had first come in to contact with the BBC during the war when he was given the responsibility of billeting some of their personnel on school premises. His light, pleasant baritone voice quickly earned him a place on the air.

As well as his voice Alston had another advantage in the field of sports broadcasting. He had been a very talented sportsman himself, beaten only by the Olympic gold medallist, Harold Abrahams, in the sprint while running for Cambridge against Oxford in 1923, speed that also made him a telling wing-threequarter for Rosslyn Park and Bedford. He then went on to captain Bedfordshire at cricket. In those days, when sports kept to their seasons, it was feasible to do all those things, and later on to commentate on them, too. As well as playing cricket, athletics and rugby, he was also a regular member of the commentary team at Wimbledon, despite confessing little in-depth knowledge of tennis, though Wimbledon was and still is an 'all-hands-to-the-pump' operation.

Alston retired from the BBC in 1961, but continued to commentate on *Test Match Special* for another three years, then doing some county cricket coverage (in which capacity he found a young 'No.2' called Peter Baxter wished upon him for his first outside broadcast at Lord's in 1966). In subsequent years he was also to be seen on leafy county grounds during the summer reporting for the *Daily Telegraph* and for the same newspaper on cold rugby grounds in the winter, wearing an outrageous, long, furry overcoat.

In 1985, at the age of 84, he attended a wonderful Outside Broadcasts department reunion at Lord's. Later that night he was admitted to hospital feeling unwell. By coincidence that same night, an obituary on him for *The Times*, having been updated, somehow got into the wrong tray and was published in the morning's paper. It appeared with his breakfast at his hospital bedside, to the amusement of the nursing staff, whose patient was happily out of danger. Fortunately, Alston knew the author and was able to ring him up to make a couple of minor corrections. It also gave him the opportunity to complete an unusual double, when the announcement of his second marriage appeared in the same paper the year after that of his death.

Alston's voice remained youthful in timbre to the end; his commentary style had a little of his earlier schoolmasterly calling about it, no better exemplified than in his commentary on the end of the West Indies win at Lord's in 1950 (see opposite).

Schoolmasterly he may have sounded, but his commentary was competent, concise and comprehensive.

It was an experienced commentary team that covered the 1957 series and so launched the newly titled *Test Match Special*. In truth, they had commentated on enough Test Matches between them by then that they probably scarcely noticed that they were at the start of something new. John Arlott had now been commentating on domestic radio for ten years and E.W. Swanton had first commentated on a Test Match on the 1938–39 England tour of South Africa.

Swanton was six years Alston's junior, but had been in cricket journalism all his working life, with the notable exception of the war years. As the late Archbishop of Canterbury, Lord Runcie, brilliantly put it from the pulpit at his funeral in 2000, 'Jim was not a man plagued by self-doubt.' But in his next breath, he went on to add the comment of someone who served with him in the Second World War who described him as, 'Arrogant … but the bravest officer I ever knew.' His obituary in *Wisden* states in unqualified terms that he was 'the most influential and most durable cricket writer of the 20th century.'

Despite having been christened Ernest William, he was called Jim by his mother from a very early age. In the newspapers he wrote for – most notably for 30 years as Cricket Correspondent of the *Daily Telegraph* – and in his radio and television billings it would always be 'E.W. Swanton', but to all colleagues and friends it was 'Jim'.

Grand old man that he became in journalism, he had learned the business from the bottom up, making the tea at the Amalgamated Press at the start of his long career. By the end of 1927, he had moved on to

'There are one or two West Indian characters coming out on the field, waving their hats as the West Indies players walk quietly off the field. Yes, there are several West Indian supporters running from the far end and they are going to escort their team off the field. The score is 274.

Goddard running in with his stump, being chased harem scarem by lots of West Indian supporters. Such a sight never been seen before at Lord's.'

REX ALSTON, LORD'S 1950

The West Indies victory in the Second Test at Lord's in 1950, their first ever in England, saw unprecedented scenes at the headquarters of cricket as crowds of their supporters invaded the pitch in celebration. The famous calypsonian, Lord Kitchener (with guitar), led delighted West Indians around the ground singing what some claim was the first version of 'Cricket, Lovely Cricket' in honour of the spin twins Sonny Ramadhin and Alf Valentine who took 18 wickets between them in the match.

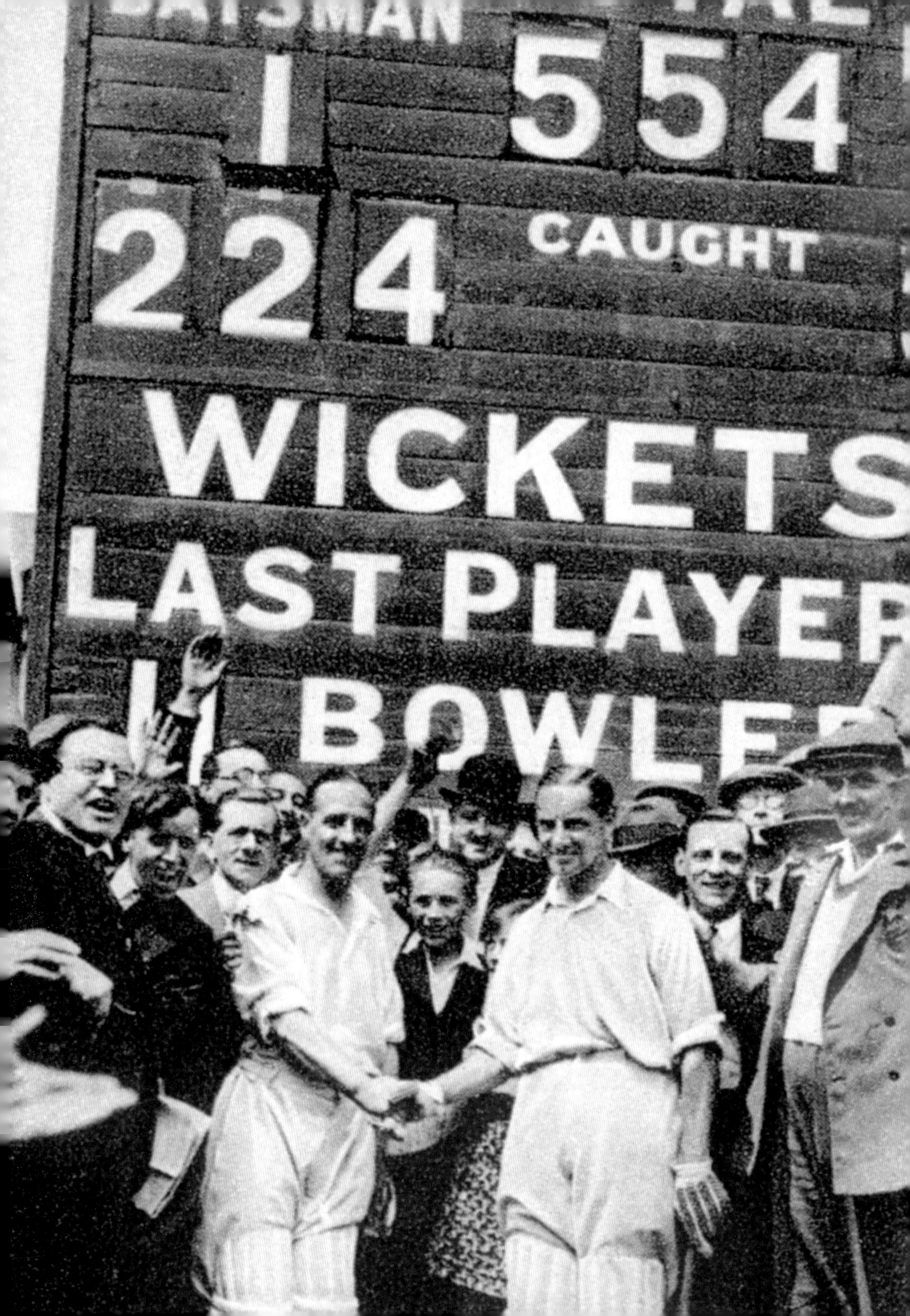

554
224
CAUGHT
WICKETS
LAST PLAYER

the *Evening Standard*, starting as their rugby correspondent and reporting cricket for them the following year. By 1930 he was reporting Test cricket.

Jim would always tell the tale of how he missed the chance to go on the Bodyline tour in 1932–33 for the *Standard*. Having just witnessed at Leyton the celebrated opening stand of 555 for Yorkshire against Essex by Percy Holmes and Herbert Sutcliffe, he found himself too late in the scramble for the one available telephone to phone his copy through. He missed the edition and the sports editor took the unforgiving view that, if he could not get through from Essex, he would have little chance from New South Wales. As a bitter opponent of Douglas Jardine's bodyline tactics in that series, he really believed that his reporting of it might have seen it tempered. In the event, the celebrated telegram from the Australian Board to the MCC, describing the tactic as 'unsportsmanlike', took Lord's completely by surprise. Despite this setback, Jim's career was moving on inexorably, with his first radio broadcasts in 1934 and coverage of his first MCC tour to South Africa in 1938.

On the outbreak of war he joined the Bedfordshire Yeomanry, an artillery regiment, which found itself posted to the Far East. They arrived in Singapore early in 1942 at the same time as the Japanese. It was the start of a harsh incarceration that lasted over three years, but Jim had kept with him one crucial companion since his departure from home. He had his 1939 *Wisden Cricketers' Almanack*.

That small and increasingly battered volume became a prop in mocked up radio features with which he entertained and raised the morale of his fellow prisoners. Throughout his life Jim did manage to provoke some animosity, but years after the war there were veterans of the Bedfordshire Yeomanry who continued to pay the warmest tributes to the way Major Swanton helped them through that nightmare time.

It speaks volumes for his resilience that at the start of the English cricket season that followed his liberation, Jim was again at the microphone for the BBC. For the Second Test of that 1946 series between England and India he was doing the ball-by-ball

commentary with Rex Alston and C.B. Fry. The following season it was all three Tests against South Africa and all five for the visit of Bradman's Invincibles in 1948. Even more significant to Jim's long-term future in 1946, was his appointment as *Daily Telegraph* Cricket Correspondent, a post with which he would be identified for a generation.

Television coverage of Test cricket at that stage was confined to matches in London, but the 1948 Tests at Lord's and the Oval saw E.W. Swanton's name down for both broadcasting services. Eventually his contributions to both radio and television Test Match coverage would become the close-of-play summary. Brian Johnston always delighted in one tale of his televised version at Trent Bridge, when the ground had just installed one of the first electrified scoreboards. Swanton ended with, 'So let me leave you with a reminder of today's remarkable close-of-play score.' He waved his arm at the scoreboard behind him, finding too late that the lights had all been switched off and the thing was blank. Fingers were snapped for a scorecard to be thrust into his hand.

In the *Test Match Special* box, well into the 1970s, Swanton's arrival was the first sign that the end of the day's play was nigh. He made his great presence felt in the box. A stopwatch would be given to him, running on clock time, and a card with the time he had to finish clearly inscribed on it. Woe betide the young producer if he gave him a signal to indicate a minute to go. Jim would always finish bang on time.

His summaries were masterly essays on the day, delivered unscripted to a time that could vary considerably. In those days before the number of overs bowled dictated the length of the day's play, *Test Match Special* came off the air ten minutes after

Percy Holmes (left) and Herbert Sutcliffe celebrate their record opening stand of 555 for Yorkshire against Essex at Leyton in June 1932 (the scoreboard behind was a little slow in recording the final run). According to Jim Swanton, his failure to phone the story through to the *Evening Standard*'s sports desk in time for the late edition resulted in his not being sent to Australia to cover the Bodyline tour later that year.

stumps were drawn. Swanton could have the full ten minutes, or, if a fast bowler had started an over with half a minute to go, he might have five minutes. He controlled the pace of his summary by his use of the scorecard. Every night he started, 'I shall begin by reading the scorecard.' The young producer would have been told in no uncertain terms that he must wrest that scorecard out of the commentator's hands before the last over began and follow it with the bowling figures as soon as they were updated.

In 1987, during the MCC Bicentenary Test at Lord's, it was a delight for the entire *Test Match Special* team when Rex Alston and Jim Swanton rolled the years back and came on to do a spell together.

The fourth commentator for the 1957 visit of the West Indies was a Trinidadian, Ken Ablack. He was working in the Caribbean Section of the BBC World Service in Bush House in London, having played three matches for Northamptonshire over a few years since the war as an orthodox slow left-arm bowler. He had made his debut with the domestic BBC Radio commentary team on the previous West Indies tour of England in 1950. His first Test, indeed, was the famous West Indies victory at Lord's, when 'those two pals of mine, Ramadhin and Valentine,' spun England to defeat. A gentle soul, Ken returned to Trinidad later, where he became a power in the affairs of the Queen's Club, the headquarters of Trinidad and Tobago cricket. Years later, he could be found under the ceiling fans in the members' pavilion there, chewing over the progress of a game with a circle of old friends.

The other West Indian in that first *Test Match Special* team was expert summariser Gerry Gomez. Also from Trinidad, Gomez was once heralded by a Trinidadian placard as 'the greatest cricketer in the world'. In his service to the different facets of the game, he certainly came close to that claim. He played for, captained, managed, selected, commentated on, administered and even umpired the West Indies team. Some of those functions overlapped along the way.

In his teens, his batting for Trinidad got him into the West Indies side just before the Second World War. During the years of conflict when international cricket took rather a back seat, he added medium-

pace bowling to his repertoire. In all he only played 29 Tests between 1939 and 1953, captaining the side in one match, but unfortunate perhaps to be around at the same time as the commanding Jeffrey Stollmeyer. But when the West Indies went to Australia in 1960 for the tour that started with the tied Test at Brisbane, Gomez was manager of that very popular team, captained by Frank Worrell.

By the time the Australians made the return visit to the West Indies, Gomez was a selector. And then in Georgetown, Guyana, he added another string to his bow, when, on the eve of the Third Test, a dispute arose about the umpires. In those days before neutral country umpires, the local umpires' association felt

Opposite (From left to right) Jim Swanton, Brian Johnston and Peter West, three voices of cricket whose abilities in the commentary box were recognised by both BBC Television and Radio.

Below Ken Ablack, a journalist from the BBC World Service Caribbean Section, was first invited to commentate on the West Indies tour to England in 1950.

that both the officials should be Guyanese. They insisted that their man, therefore, should refuse to stand with a Barbadian and so he withdrew. Another Trinidadian was sent for, but, when he arrived, everyone felt that Gomez, who had never before umpired a first-class game though he held the appropriate certificate, was doing such a good job as a stand-in that he should continue.

That experience must have made him ideal material for the presidency of the West Indies Umpires Association, a post which he held for 30 years. He was also on the West Indies Board for many years and President of the Queen's Park Cricket Club. As late as 1990, he was alongside his old friend, Trevor Bailey, working with *Test Match Special* at the Trinidad Test Match – a generous and insightful commentator on the game and a delightful man. It was a sign of his energy that Gerry Gomez died from a heart attack while playing tennis at the age of 76.

The other summariser was something of a contrast – the old Yorkshire fast bowler, Bill Bowes. His appearance as a tall, angular, bespectacled sage, suited him better in old age than when he was in the field for Yorkshire and England but he is best known for one ball in Test cricket, the story of which, having become in later years an accomplished journalist, he told for radio. It was the Second Test on the Bodyline tour, on which Bowes was the third string bowler in the leg-theory plan to curb Don Bradman, who had missed the First Test. After a huge ovation for the Australian champion, Bowes bowled him first ball (see opposite).

In fact that was Bowes' only Test wicket on that 1932–33 tour – his only full overseas tour for England – in a first-class career that brought him 1,638 wickets. Like so many, his career was effectively ended by the Second World War, even though he did play a couple of seasons after it. In later years his regular Headingley Test Match seat was just in front of the *Test Match Special* box, from where he would bestow on the commentary team a genial smile.

So Alston, Arlott, Swanton, Ablack, Gomez and Bowes, with the support of producer, Michael Tuke-Hastings and scorer, Jack Price, made up the first *Test*

Match Special team for the opening Test, and they had been provided with a new commentary box for the occasion. One portent for the future came through from the commentary from that first match. Alston and Swanton both had sore throats and made comment on that fact on the air. Rex Alston later recorded that 'throat lozenges and herbal remedies arrived by the sackful from concerned listeners.' A new trend had started. And what a Test Match they had to get their vocal chords round.

Edgbaston had not hosted a Test Match for 28 years, so it was a huge occasion for Warwickshire – and an important one for England too, who had been bamboozled by the bowling of Ramadhin and Valentine and hammered by the batting of the three Ws seven years earlier on West Indies' last visit. Those five were here again, together with a young man called Gary Sobers, who was already making a name for himself. There was also the great potential of Rohan Kanhai, playing in his first Test, and O.G. 'Collie' Smith.

Peter May led an England side that included some of the great names. There was May himself and Colin Cowdrey in the middle order, fast bowlers Fred Trueman and Brian Statham, spinners Jim Laker and Tony Lock, Trevor Bailey the all-rounder and the inimitable Godfrey Evans behind the stumps. Two of them – Bailey and Trueman, of course – would, in the fullness of time, become regulars in the *Test Match Special* box.

May won the toss and England batted first. They knew the danger to them from the little Trindadian, Sonny Ramadhin, with the baffling mixture of off- and leg-spin that had so confused them in 1950 and he was soon introduced and rattled through the England batting in the afternoon, suggesting that not much had changed in seven years.

Colin Cowdrey used to tell of how Everton Weekes, in the slips, would chuckle at the English batsmen's inability to pick Ramadhin's variations. Trevor Bailey reckoned when the leg-cutter was coming, he could 'scent it' rather than pick it, because it was tossed a fraction higher. But that wasn't the ball that got him that day, as Ken Ablack and Gerry Gomez described:

FROM THE COMMENTARY BOX

TMS summariser Bill Bowes only took one wicket on England's 1932–33 tour to Australia, but what a wicket it was. At Melbourne in the Second Test, Don Bradman, who had missed the First Test through injury, walked to the wicket to thunderous applause. Bowes had to pause in his run up for the noise to subside. He ran in again. Bradman, expecting a bouncer, moved across his stumps to hook, but Bowes pitched the ball up and clean bowled him.

'And there was a dead silence on that Melbourne ground. You could hear the trams rattling over the points a couple of miles away. A stunned silence. The only movement was Jardine, the usually sphinx-like figure that we had. He had his hands above his head and he was doing a sort of Indian war dance in his extreme delight.'

BILL BOWES

The Trinadadian spinner Sonny Ramadhin bowls at Peter May
during the First Test at Edgbaston in 1957, with Colin Cowdrey at
the non-striker's end. Ramadhin took 9 for 228 in the match from
an astonishing 129 overs.

Ken Ablack 'Now Ramadhin again to Bailey. Bailey forward –
and he's bowled!'

Gerry Gomez 'It was an off-spinner – flighted – much slower than
the previous ball, which had hurried through … Frankly, having
played against Bailey quite a few times, I've never seen him more
conclusively bowled than on this occasion. I think that Bailey
will admit that it's one of the better balls that he has received
in his Test career. He was beaten in the flight where he started
moving forward to the pitch of it, but never got there and it hit
the off stump.

Ken Ablack 'Well, what a sudden dramatic change – England
93 for 2 at lunch, now 116 for 5.'

And Ramadhin had four of them – and by tea he had taken three more and England had been dismissed for 186 in four hours. Ramadhin 7 for 49 in 31 overs.

England stayed in reasonable contention until the latter stages of the second day, when 'Collie' Smith and Frank Worrell took it away from them with a sixth-wicket stand of 190, Worrell making 81 and the 24-year-old Jamaican, Smith, in his first Test in England going on to get 161. 'Collie' Smith, who showed such potential of great things to come, was tragically killed in a car crash two years later, an accident which his friend Gary Sobers survived.

Peter May leads Colin Cowdrey off the Edgbaston ground at the end of the fourth day's play. Their 411-run stand, which won England the match, still remains the highest partnership for England for any wicket.

England's second innings started halfway through the third day, facing a deficit of 288. The introduction of Ramadhin reduced them to 65 for 2. Years later, Peter May told *Test Match Special* of coming out to bat with 223 more runs needed just to avoid an innings defeat. He scarcely dared look at the scoreboard.

But May and Brian Close survived the rest of that day and it was Roy Gilchrist who, after the Sunday off, removed Close on Monday morning. Peter May and the new batsman, Colin Cowdrey, were close friends and now they were to find themselves together in one of the most famous partnerships in cricket history.

They began it early on the fourth morning, when England were still 175 runs behind. Ramadhin wheeled away, hour after hour, still mystifying the batsmen regularly, but they had worked out how to play him. With the lbw law as it then was, if the ball pitched outside the off stump they could play deliberately with the pad, with impunity. Rex Alston recalled later that the partnership did not make for easy commentary. 'There are only so many ways of describing exactly the same shot or delivery. Keeping the dialogue fresh was a great challenge.' May and Cowdrey batted through to the end of the fourth day. Trevor Bailey was the next man in and he too found the hours of waiting rather challenging, though for him Ramadhin's frequent appeals was also quite unnerving. With every appeal, he was out of his seat and reaching for his gloves.

May's hundred had taken him over four hours and early on the fifth day there were more milestones to be described (see commentary below).

If we can, after all this time, spare Jack Price the task, the 411 that May and Cowdrey put on remains the highest partnership for England for any wicket and the highest fourth-wicket stand by anyone in Test cricket.

Cowdrey eventually fell – to Smith – for 154, but May was still there with 285 when he declared. He had batted a shade under ten hours and was so tired that he had to ask the umpires how far ahead England were. Poor Trevor Bailey, after sitting with his pads on for the best part of two days, never did get to bat in the innings. His nerves were shot and Godfrey Evans went in instead to crash the ball around until the declaration came at 583 for 4.

A *Test Match Special* stalwart of the future, Fred Trueman, now took the stage, whistling the West Indies openers out quickly. With Laker and Lock reducing them to 72 for 7 when time ran out, there was inevitably some feeling that May had been too cautious in his declaration. But a marker had been put down. Ramadhin never again had quite the same hold over English batsmen and England took the series 3–0.

And so, history had been made at Edgbaston in 1957 – by both cricketers and broadcasters.

'And England must be looking for runs now. Smith bowls short – Cowdrey has placed it gently towards third man – and the extra applause is because the partnership is now worth the monumental figure of 400 … Now, Jack Price, here's a problem for you. What's the highest partnership by a couple of Englishmen in a Test Match in England? Can you work that one out – quietly – while Sobers starts the fresh over with the score 513 for 3.

And now May – 247 – faces Sobers – and May has hit the next one high in the air … it's six! Into the pavilion – just over mid-on. And he's also scored a mere 250 … 253 to be precise.'

REX ALSTON, 1957

England v West Indies First Test

30 May–4 June 1957 Edgbaston, Birmingham

ENGLAND FIRST INNINGS

PE Richardson	c Walcott b Ramadhin	47
DB Close	c Kanhai b Gilchrist	15
DJ Insole	b Ramadhin	20
* PBH May	c Weekes b Ramadhin	30
MC Cowdrey	c Gilchrist b Ramadhin	4
TE Bailey	b Ramadhin	1
GAR Lock	b Ramadhin	0
† TG Evans	b Gilchrist	14
JC Laker	b Ramadhin	7
FS Trueman	not out	29
JB Statham	b Atkinson	13
Extras	(b 3, lb 3)	6
Total	(all out, 79.4 overs)	186

Fall of wickets 1-32, 2-61, 3-104, 4-115, 5-116, 6-118, 7-121, 8-130, 9-150

Bowling	O	M	R	W
Worrell	9	1	27	0
Gilchrist	27	4	74	2
Ramadhin	31	16	49	7
Atkinson	12.4	3	30	1

SECOND INNINGS

PE Richardson	c sub b Ramadhin	34
DB Close	c Weekes b Gilchrist	42
DJ Insole	b Ramadhin	0
* PBH May	not out	285
MC Cowdrey	c sub b Smith	154
† TG Evans	not out	29
Extras	(b 23, lb 16)	39
Total	(4 wks dec, 258 overs)	583
Did not bat	TE Bailey, GAR Lock, JC Laker, FS Trueman, JB Statham	

Fall of wickets 1-63, 2-65, 3-113, 4-524

Bowling	O	M	R	W
Gilchrist	26	2	67	1
Ramadhin	98	35	179	2
Atkinson	72	29	137	0
Sobers	30	4	77	0
Smith	26	4	72	1
Goddard	6	2	12	0

WEST INDIES FIRST INNINGS

BH Pairaudeau	b Trueman	1
† RB Kanhai	lbw b Statham	42
CL Walcott	c Evans b Laker	90
ED Weekes	b Trueman	9
GS Sobers	c Bailey b Statham	53
OG Smith	lbw b Laker	161
FMM Worrell	b Statham	81
* JDC Goddard	c Lock b Laker	24
DS Atkinson	c Statham b Laker	1
S Ramadhin	not out	5
R Gilchrist	run out	0
Extras	(b 1, lb 6)	7
Total	(all out, 191.4 overs)	474

Fall of wickets 1-4, 2-83, 3-120, 4-183, 5-197, 6-387, 7-466, 8-469, 9-474, 10-474

Bowling	O	M	R	W
Statham	39	4	114	3
Trueman	30	4	99	2
Bailey	34	11	80	0
Laker	54	17	119	4
Lock	34.4	15	55	0

SECOND INNINGS 296 RUNS TO WIN

BH Pairaudeau	b Trueman	7
† RB Kanhai	c Close b Trueman	1
GS Sobers	c Cowdrey b Lock	14
ED Weekes	c Trueman b Lock	33
FMM Worrell	c May b Lock	0
CL Walcott	c Lock b Laker	1
OG Smith	lbw b Laker	5
* JDC Goddard	not out	0
DS Atkinson	not out	4
Extras	(b 7)	7
Total	(7 wks, 60 overs)	72
Did not bat	S Ramadhin, R Gilchrist, FS Trueman, JB Statham	

Fall of wickets 1-1, 2-9, 3-25, 4-27, 5-43, 6-66, 7-68

Bowling	O	M	R	W
Statham	2	0	6	0
Trueman	5	3	7	2
Laker	24	20	13	2
Lock	27	19	31	3
Close	2	1	8	0

Match drawn

A familiar pose? Being next man in, a padded-up Trevor Bailey had to wait for the best part of two days for the May/Cowdrey partnership to be broken. In the end, he was too nervous to bat and Godfrey Evans went in instead.

3

JOHN ARLOTT AND BRIAN JOHNSTON

by Christopher Martin-Jenkins

Brown and Blair, Morecambe and Wise, Rice and Lloyd-Webber, Gilbert and Sullivan, Statham and Trueman, Laker and Lock: the secret of many a great partnership might be summed up by the French phrase *vive la différence*. John Arlott and Brian Johnston, the poet and the jester, the twin pillars of *Test Match Special* for more than 20 years, were superbly compatible as professionals but in style, personality and outlook as different as any number of the successful partnerships of history, cricketing or otherwise.

A mix of voices and personalities has always been part of the attraction of *TMS* and the two most famous and fondly remembered commentators proved it. In voice and character alike they were poles apart; but as a professional act (although in both cases they were natural broadcasters who never

Right John Arlott (left) and Brian Johnston are the two commentators most closely associated with *Test Match Special*. One serious, one light-hearted; one who seemed to take life seriously and one who definitely did not; one who was concerned with the high arts and one who had the common touch. But they were inextricably linked by their professionalism, their natural flair for broadcasting and their deep love of cricket.

Opposite Clive Lloyd, whose century during the 1975 World Cup Final at Lord's inspired some of John Arlott's finest commentary.

needed to act) they were as complementary as cornflakes and milk. They were linked by their talent, their love of cricket, the freedom offered them by the burgeoning BBC Outside Broadcasts department in the years after the Second World War and the affection and admiration in which they were held by grateful listeners.

They were separated by much more. Where Arlott was often sombre and serious, Johnston was skittish and comical; where Arlott paced himself like an Oriental spinner, Johnston rushed in like an Aussie fast bowler; where Arlott treasured words

like the poet he was and mulled them over as if he were testing the nose of a vintage Château Lafitte, Johnston used them with gay abandon, without art or pretension. One was a student of the game who became a professor; the other an eternal schoolboy who believed that every day's cricket might, at its dawn, become the greatest and most exciting he had ever witnessed. One was sometimes maudlin, heavy as a brooding cloud, the other invariably light as a soufflé. One carried and dwelt upon the burdens of life; the other cast them aside as quickly as he could.

Both were original, completely true to themselves. If Arlott was more troubled by self-doubt and insecurity, deep down he knew that he was a man worthy of his calling. Johnston never doubted it: he could not believe his good fortune at finding a medium that suited him so well. If Arlott's performances as a cricket commentator were less consistent than Johnston's, he was capable of truly virtuoso performances of inspired description, especially when there was an influential audience – for example, when the BBC's managing director, Ian Trethowan, came into the box at Lord's during the World Cup Final in 1975 and Clive Lloyd was batting

majestically. Both, however, in their contrasting way were consummate broadcasting professionals. To listen to them was a delight and to work with them an extraordinary privilege. I did so from 1972 until, in Arlott's case, he retired to a quieter, contemplative life on Alderney in 1980, and in Johnston's until he had a fatal heart attack while still working hard at the age of 81 in 1993.

It was not possible to be their colleague for so long without becoming immensely fond of them both. I knew Brian longer and better; often during Lord's Test matches staying with him and Pauline, his pretty, forceful, sometimes impetuous but always staunchly supportive wife, in the house at Boundary Road in St John's Wood that succeeded the family home a few hundred yards away, at Hamilton Terrace, one of the most elegant streets in London. He was wonderful company, as funny in private conversation as he was on his feet after dinner on a public occasion. He loved to pun, and gossip, not least, of course, about people in cricket. All his huge fund of stories became familiar in time but it was his flair for entertainment, both in private and in public, that made them genuinely funny every time. Barry

Brian and I both suffered uncontrollable giggles on another occasion during a meaningless World Cup match between England and Canada to which practically no one can have been listening. On that occasion there was simply a long silence: it seemed to us interminable and in the studio in London the engineers thought the line must have gone down.

It did not matter what age you were with Brian. As welcoming and open in life as he was on the air, he simply loved company although on the rare occasions when he allowed himself a holiday he was no less happy relaxing in a deck-chair with a book. Pauline has been a professional photographer and one of her most memorable images of her husband was taken in just such a pose on the Greek island of Lefkas, with a floppy sunhat on his head, the prominent nose and ears in profile and the sea lapping at the frame of the chair.

As a young and impecunious married man I found dining with John, as I sometimes did at hotels during Test Matches, at once stimulating and somewhat daunting. Not because one knew one was out of one's depth as far as knowledge and experience were concerned but because John, the gourmet and wine expert, would choose what he fancied and say to the head waiter, 'split the bill between all of us if you will'. It was worth it for the conversation, which might range anywhere, always with the great man directing it. Hotels were one thing, however, an invitation to lunch at his wonderfully spacious house in Alresford – Hampshire, of course – was quite something else. You could forget plans to do anything else for the rest of the day, especially if you were as weak minded as I was. When his second wife, Valerie, was alive, a woman as intelligent and bibulous as himself, they were as hospitable as each other and I cringe still at my state of inebriation when I left their company at about five o'clock one late Autumn afternoon – having 'stayed for a spot of lunch'. I had already been to the loo several times but the first thing I did after turning my car in the direction of Sussex was to find the nearest hedge in a country lane for further relief. I continued on the rural route and drove very slowly.

Johnston, Brian's eldest son, recalls in his excellent biography of his father how, sometimes, his reaction to something that had amused him on television – a bad piece of acting, perhaps or the way that someone had said something – would start Brian giggling and soon have the whole family overcome by tears of laughter too, sometimes without even knowing what had started it. The famous 'leg over' incident with Jonathan Agnew, a classic example of why live broadcasting is so often more interesting or amusing than recorded, was a case in point. What created the uncontrollable mirth, of course, was the very professionalism of them both: the desperate attempt to keep going. Aggers soon became speechless but the old trooper did his best to carry on.

At least on that occasion people could hear the giggles and, of course, they were utterly infectious.

Hilarious though it was, Brian Johnston and Jonathan Agnew (left, at the back) rarely worked together in the commentary box after the 'leg over' incident in 1991.

Brian Johnston 'Meanwhile Botham had been joined by Lewis, and Botham in the end out in a most extraordinary way.'

Jonathan Agnew '… Tragic thing about it … he knew exactly what was going to happen and he tried to step over the stumps and just flicked a bail with his right leg …'

Brian Johnston 'To be honest he tried to do the splits over it and unfortunately the inner part of his thigh must have just removed the bails.'

Jonathan Agnew 'Yes, he just didn't quite get his leg over.'

Brian Johnston 'Anyhow … he did very well indeed, batting 131 minutes and hit three 4s, and then we had Lewis playing extremely well for his 47 not out …'

Jonathan Agnew (laughs)

Brian Johnston '… Aggers do stop it … and he was joined by DeFreitas who was in for 40 minutes, a useful little partnership there, they put on 35 in 40 minutes and then he was caught by Dujon off Walsh. Lawrence, always entertaining, batted for 35, 35 … 35 minutes, hit a 4 … over the wicketkeeper's … Aggers for goodness sake stop it …' (laughs uncontrollably)

Jonathan Agnew 'Yes … Lawrence …' (laughs uncontrollably)

Ian Botham in the act of failing to 'get his leg over' at the Oval in the Fifth Test against the West Indies in 1991.

I learned the lesson and thanked my stars but no doubt John would have been appalled had he realised how much of the delicious claret served that day had been consumed by his young guest. By then he was wearing a black tie every day – as he did for the rest of his life when a tie was necessary dress – as penance for the decision to give his beloved eldest son, James, a sports car which, tragically he drove beneath a lorry having fallen asleep at the wheel after a new year's party. No one who loses a child can ever be the same and John could not, even for a day, forget the loss.

Brian had known tragedy too. He was only ten and in his second year at prep school in Eastbourne when his father, Lt. Col. Charles Johnston, 44, father of four and chairman of the family coffee business, was drowned in rough sea off Bude in Cornwall, the traditional venue for Johnston family holidays. In the space of three months, indeed, Brian lost his father and his shattered grandfather, Reginald, who had been Governor of the Bank of England. As a consequence both the home where he had been brought up and much of the Johnston family's financial security were lost too. In his biography, Barry Johnston surmises that Brian's reaction was to put a brave face on things and be cheerful. Very soon he had gained at school the reputation for being a joker that would never leave him.

The truth, I think, is that he was one of those rare human beings who simply have a God-given gift for sharing their pleasure in life. How misguided was the retort of his subsequent housemaster at Eton, A.C. Huson, 'You won't get anywhere in life because you talk too much'. But there was a much more

perceptive verdict from the same source in a report later in his school career, when he had become captain of games, 'He has been, if anything, more conscientious. I cannot recall one single instance of his not being present to encourage, and instruct, any one of his teams, when it was even remotely possible for him to be there. It is a great gift this of Bri's, being able to keep up his enthusiasms … he has a very great power over his fellow creatures.'

These gifts were wasted to a large extent in his brief period in the coffee business before the war but as a Guards officer who gained a Military Cross for his 'dynamic personality, coupled with his untiring determination and cheerfulness under fire' they were very much to the fore and they came across throughout his BBC career.

Born two years later, in 1914, John Arlott had a very different upbringing. Having left Queen Mary's Grammar School at his hometown of Basingstoke after a dispute with his headmaster, he worked for a time at the local town planning office and then as a diet clerk, calculating food allocations, at a mental hospital. In 1934 he joined the police force in Southampton and remained with them for the next 11 years, starting on the beat. When the war came he worked for Special Branch, screening aliens. His first marriage, in 1940, was to Dawn, a cheery looking hospital nurse who bore him two sons, James and Timothy. John himself was a good-looking fellow in his youth, solidly built and naturally strong. He kept his hair, and a pair of prominent eyebrows that added to his aura of wisdom, into old age.

David Rayvern Allen, Arlott's assiduous and exemplary biographer, has recorded how Arlott's voracious reading led to poetry and the realization that 'it said more to me as a human being than anything else did'. Encouraged by John Betjeman and Andrew Young, he began to write his own poems, many of which have found their deserved way into anthologies, not least – but by no means only – cricketing ones. His lines on Jack Hobbs, the master, were themselves masterful. His own gravestone on Alderney contains lines from his poem to Andrew Young that neatly encapsulate his

Opposite Brian Johnston joined the BBC in January 1946. He first worked for the Outside Broadcasts department using his unique broadcasting style, for both radio and TV, to present several magazine-style reports and coverage of royal occasions and cricket. He did not join *Test Match Special* until 1970, but when he did so he claimed 'it was the start of some of the happiest years of my life'.
Overleaf A classic *TMS* line-up at Lord's in 1980: (left to right) Christopher Martin-Jenkins (standing), Brian Johnston, Tony Lewis, Trevor Bailey, Bill Frindall, John Arlott and Fred Trueman.

own sharp eye for the human drama of cricket, so evident in his commentaries:

So clear you see these timeless things
That, like a bird, the vision sings.

Arlott wore his deep literary knowledge lightly, in fact, during his commentaries – and in his cricket writing for the *Guardian* too – but he was familiar with and to many of his contemporary writers, poets, and artists –Betjeman, Edmund Blunden, Cyril Connolly, T.S. Eliot, Osbert Lancaster, John Piper and Vita Sackville-West among them. He became a collector not just of books – or, subsequently of wine – but also of aquatint engravings (he was an expert on these too) and of other objects as diverse as Sunderland glass and herbs from the Himalayas. It was his poetry that led him to Geoffrey Grigson, a BBC West of England producer, who gave him his first chance to broadcast. He was told that he had 'a vulgar voice but

Opposite John Arlott first came to the BBC's attention as a poet and, after appearing on various programmes, was appointed literary programme producer in the summer of 1945.

Above John Arlott's big break in cricket came when he was selected by the Far Eastern Service to follow the Indian touring team, who arrived in 1946 as the first tourists since the war, around the country and send nightly reports on their matches back to India.

an interesting mind'. It was true, yet the voice became one of the most imitated there has ever been outside politics. Towards the end of the war he began to feature on various talk radio programmes until, in the summer of 1945, he was appointed literary programme producer in the BBC's Overseas Service, a position formerly occupied by no less a literary talent than George Orwell. Rather like Brian Johnston, but in quite a different way, the war proved to be a watershed in his life, but perhaps there was hardly anyone of a similar age for whom that was not so.

Arlott remained on the BBC staff until 1953, for the last two years as an instructor in the staff training unit, but he operated as a freelancer for the broadcasting, cricket commentating and writing that increasingly occupied his time. Although for the rest of his life he was busy and in demand – even in retirement on Alderney – he never quite lost the feeling of insecurity common to most people who work only for themselves and their families.

His first opportunity to commentate on cricket (as opposed to contributing talks on the subject) came when the Indians toured in 1946. No one could fail to notice his flair for words or the distinctive slow pace with which they were used and the deliberate, deep voice, always glibly described as a Hampshire burr but actually quite unique. From 1947, when he commentated again on the South Africa tour and on county cricket, he became an established part of the BBC commentary team.

It missed the point, I believe, that Arlott's was so different from the more BBC accents around him, notably those of Jim Swanton and Rex Alston. It was talent, his unhurried, measured style of delivery and his breadth of general knowledge, not the Hampshire accent, that made him so famous so quickly and for so long. He had played just enough cricket to be able to interpret what was going on with insight and he knew enough of the players to be able to add an extra ingredient to his natural – indeed police trained – eye for detail. He superimposed knowledge of the history of the game and of the character of those he watched playing it for a grateful unseen audience. He loved the players and they loved him to the extent of making him President of the Cricketers Association. His innate liberalism – and actual support for a Liberal Party for whom he stood as candidate for Epping in both the 1955 and 1959 General Elections – gave him an awareness of public affairs and a knowledge about the procedure of institutions and committees. He was, therefore, especially useful to the Association when debates raged over the two great issues of his later years as a journalist and commentator, namely cricketing relations with South Africa and the schism in world cricket over television coverage of the game in Australia which led to Kerry Packer's two-year programme of international matches featuring players whose services he had bought for salaries vastly greater than those they had previously been earning.

If Arlott was broadly neutral in the battle between Packer and the Establishment, he was emphatically opposed to the South African government and its pernicious apartheid policy. He had seen and abhorred it at first hand on the England tour of 1948–49. If his commentary role did not allow him to express much personal comment on that subject, other than when it was raining, his better-paid role as Cricket Correspondent of the *Guardian* – only one correspondent removed from Neville Cardus – enabled him to enlighten readers of a like mind.

He kept up a prodigious work rate in and out of the cricket season. He produced numerous character sketches for various publications and his books included a wonderfully astute study of the great Yorkshire and England fast bowler F.S. Trueman, with whom he worked happily in the *TMS* box for his last seven years: *Fred: Portrait of a Fast Bowler*. Later he also wrote for the *Guardian* on wine which had the added advantage, no doubt, of adding some free bottles to the major collection he had in the cellars of the Old Sun in Alresford only some of which was shipped across to Alderney, although there was never a danger of his falling short of supplies there.

Policeman he may have been but I never heard him say that he never drank on duty, unlike our BBC Correspondent today, Jonathan Agnew, who quite rightly spotted the signs of a little too much levity, leading to a lack of professionalism, on the part of some. Arlott, however, could take it and I never saw the extremely large glass of red that he liked to have late in the morning affect his performance, with one notable exception, or near exception, in his final year, when he had announced his retirement in advance and was feted at every ground he attended. In the Lord's Test of that 1980 summer he gave his usual immaculate description of the play in the last 20 minutes before lunch – if, perhaps, a little more ponderous in pace and tone than he had been in his prime. The moment, however, that he said his last words, 'And for his summary of the morning's play it will be Fred Trueman,' he slumped forward on the desk in front of him and went instantly to sleep. This was a matter first of concern, then of amusement to the rest of us in the box, but Fred, eyes fastened on the players coming off the field in front of him, was blissfully unaware until some two minutes later he completed his not uncritical comments on the England fast bowling with the words, 'That's my opinion, anyway. I don't know what you think, John?' He turned to see the heavy form slumped unconscious across the desk beside him and with wonderful presence of mind – despite a look of some horror on his face – he added, 'Well, John is nodding his head vigorously, and with that, back to t'studio.'

Some weeks later, at the Test at Lord's to celebrate the centenary of Australia's first official Test in England, John, famously, refused to make any

MY FIRST TEST MATCH

Bill Frindall

From our initial encounter a few weeks earlier when he had greeted me with 'I hear you like driving. Well, I like drinking. We're going to get on well!' John Arlott had greatly eased the birth of my career as BBC Radio's scorer. It was appropriate that his memorable Basingstoke burr should describe the first ball that I scored for *TMS*: 'Jones, fast left-arm, over the wicket to bowl the first match (ball!) of the first Test of this series to Hunte. He moves in, bowls to him. Short. Hunte gets over it and cracks it square away for four, wide of cover's left hand, just fine of square. Four runs off the first ball!'

That cavalier stroke from one of the greatest West Indian openers launched my *TMS* career on Thursday 2 June 1966 at 11.30 on a sunny morning at Old Trafford. I remember thinking as I entered those runs on one of my three scoring sheets that Test matches were not supposed to start with boundaries. Somehow Conrad Hunte's brutal square-cut relaxed my nervous tension. Years later I recounted that ball to its bowler Jeff Jones (who didn't laugh) and Simon Jones, his son, (who did).

The previous afternoon I had collected John Arlott from Waterloo and driven to Manchester. He fell asleep and woke just as we reached the city's outskirts. Recognising where he was, he sank back into his seat with a heavy sigh. 'Hell's Teeth, Frindalius! Manchester! It's the only city in the world where they teach lifeboat

England v West Indies First Test

2–4 June 1966 Old Trafford, Manchester

Umpires **JS Buller and CS Elliott**

WEST INDIES FIRST INNINGS

CC Hunte	c Smith b Higgs	135
EDAS McMorris	c Russell b Higgs	11
RB Kanhai	b Higgs	0
BF Butcher	c Parks b Titmus	44
SM Nurse	b Titmus	49
* GS Sobers	c Cowdrey b Titmus	161
DAJ Holford	c Smith b Allen	32
† DW Allan	lbw b Titmus	1
CC Griffith	lbw b Titmus	30
WW Hall	b Allen	1
LR Gibbs	not out	1
Extras	(b 8, lb 10, nb 1)	19
Total	(all out; 153.1 overs)	484

Fall of wickets 1-38, 2-42, 3-116, 4-215, 5-283, 6-410, 7-411, 8-471, 9-482

Bowling	O	M	R	W
IJ Jones	28	6	100	0
DJ Brown	28	4	84	0
K Higgs	31	5	94	3
DA Allen	31.1	8	104	2
FJ Titmus	35	10	83	5

ENGLAND FIRST INNINGS

C Milburn	run out	0
WE Russell	c Sobers b Gibbs	26
KF Barrington	c & b Griffith	5
MC Cowdrey	c & b Gibbs	12
* MJK Smith	c Butcher b Gibbs	5
† JM Parks	c Nurse b Holford	43
FJ Titmus	b Holford	15
DA Allen	c Sobers b Gibbs	37
DJ Brown	b Gibbs	14
K Higgs	c Sobers b Holford	1
IJ Jones	not out	0
Extras	(b 1, lb 4, nb 4)	9
Total	(all out; 74.1 overs)	167

Fall of wickets 1-11, 2-24, 3-42, 4-48, 5-65, 6-85, 7-143, 8-153, 9-163

Bowling	O	M	R	W
WW Hall	14	6	43	0
CC Griffith	10	3	28	1
GS Sobers	7	1	16	0
LR Gibbs	28.1	13	37	5
DAJ Holford	15	4	34	3

SECOND INNINGS FOLLOWING ON

C Milburn	b Gibbs	94
WE Russell	b Griffith	20
KF Barrington	c Nurse b Holford	30
MC Cowdrey	c Butcher b Sobers	69
* MJK Smith	b Gibbs	6
† JM Parks	c & b Sobers	11
FJ Titmus	c Butcher b Sobers	12
DA Allen	c Allan b Gibbs	1
DJ Brown	c Sobers b Gibbs	10
K Higgs	st Allan b Gibbs	5
IJ Jones	not out	0
Extras	(b 11, lb 1, nb 7)	19
Total	(all out; 108 overs)	277

Fall of wickets 1-53, 2-142, 3-166, 4-184, 5-203, 6-217, 7-218, 8-268, 9-276

Bowling	O	M	R	W
WW Hall	5	0	28	0
CC Griffith	6	1	25	1
GS Sobers	42	11	87	3
LR Gibbs	41	16	69	5
DAJ Holford	14	2	49	1

West Indies won by an innings and 40 runs

drill on the buses!' Next morning we breakfasted together before visiting Gibbs's Bookshop nearby. There he dramatically extended my meagre library by arranging for me to purchase, at a generous discount, a complete set of *Scores and Biographies*. Making me a present of two other vital volumes, he even asked how I wanted to be introduced on the air. No one helped me more with sage advice and encouragement during those early weeks of my initial season. After the first session of my debut at Worcester, he awarded me a great vote of confidence by saying, 'You'll do. You've got a scorer's mind. You can focus on the play and obliterate everything happening in this box'. Perhaps my RAF service in a NATO war room had provided the perfect training.

The most vital contribution that John made to my career was to inspire me with confidence. He had a caring mentality. No one entering the cricket broadcasting circuit could have received more consideration. He was extremely thoughtful, supportive and encouraging, quick to praise on the air and to give thanks for my help at the end of each broadcast. 'Are you enjoying it?' he would ask frequently. It took me a season before I could truthfully answer in the affirmative.

Our cramped Old Trafford eyrie was sited just left of the Stretford End sightscreen and gave an excellent view of play almost in line with the pitch. Access was via a spiral staircase. Halfway up at throat level was a horizontal metal pole painted in red and white stripes to remind you to duck. John Arlott's fellow commentators for that match were Robert Hudson and Roy Lawrence. Former England captains Freddie Brown and Norman Yardley were our summarisers, with E.W. 'Jim' Swanton providing close-of-play summaries. They all made me feel welcome although they must have greatly missed my long-serving predecessor, Arthur Wrigley, who had died suddenly the previous October.

Taught to score at the age of ten by a desperate young teacher landed with two classes on a rained-off games afternoon, I had scored my first club match a few days later when the appointed scorer failed to appear. When Wrigley's demise coincided with the end of my seven cricket seasons with the RAF, I had written to the Head of Outside Broadcasts (Sound), Charles Max-Muller, and been rewarded with an interview the following week. Years later I asked Johnners if anyone else had applied. 'Well, yes, Bearders, but we weren't going to tell you. There was just one. A New Zealander with poor handwriting living in Auckland – but it was a very close thing!'

My debut match lasted just three days. West Indies made 484, Hunte savagely scoring 135 and Gary Sobers a majestic 161. Off-spinners Fred Titmus (5 for 83) and David Allen (2 for 104 in his final Test) confirmed that the pitch was turning. England were 163 for 8 at the end of the second day. Poor Colin Milburn, also making his debut, was run out for a duck when Eric Russell sent him back. On Saturday England added just four more runs, spinners Lance Gibbs and David Holford sharing eight wickets. England followed on and were dismissed for 277 at 5.45 p.m. Milburn scored 94 off 136 balls before being castled by Gibbs trying to complete his hundred with a six.

I had not proved a good mascot for my country. It was England's first three-day defeat since 1938. It also marked the end of Mike Smith's 25-match reign as captain. First Colin Cowdrey and then Brian Close would lead the side in the remaining four Tests. Had they managed to take the match into the fourth day England would have scraped a draw. Manchester's normal wet weather returned on Monday and no cricket would have been possible on the fifth day either. My baptism was eased by Sobers, mixing his orthodox and unorthodox left-arm spin, and Gibbs bowling 24 overs an hour, the latter taking 10 for 106 in the match. That hectic over rate allowed no time for the commentators to ask me statistical questions.

The BBC had engaged me for only a three-match trial period. When I arrived at Lord's for the Second Test 12 days later, I had no idea how my Manchester contribution had been rated. Then, at lunch on the first day, producer Michael Tuke-Hastings told me that the job was mine if I wanted it. So, after just ten sessions, I was confirmed as the BBC's radio scorer and statistician. After more than four decades no one has telephoned to say the job is no longer mine, so I just keep turning up.

Opposite The fearsome sight of Charlie Griffith coming in to bowl was a factor in the West Indies 3-1 series victory in England in 1963.

dramatic farewell and simply handed over to the next commentator as the final act of his career as a Test commentator. He was not unaware, however, that it was a moment of national importance and when the public address announcer, Alan Curtis, said at the end of an over from Dennis Lillee that John Arlott had just finished his last stint as a Test commentator the great man himself was making his way out of the box at the top of the pavilion. The players turned towards him and joined a standing crowd in a generous ovation.

It was a moving tribute and one that Brian would certainly have received too had he chosen his moment to go. It was his natural friendliness, after all, and the atmosphere of gaiety and fun that he brought to his radio commentaries when television were unwise enough to say that they no longer wanted him, in 1970, that expanded the range and, definitely, the popularity of *TMS*. Robert Hudson, the wise Head of BBC Radio Outside Broadcasts at the time, snapped him up by simply creating space for four commentators instead of three at each match. He told Barry Johnston years later, 'His arrival had a huge impact. From being a worthy but slightly dull programme, it became one to listen to. Brian took chances and no one else had the courage to do what he did. He was a breath of fresh air.'

The remarkable thing was that by then he was 58, only two years away from his official retirement with the BBC. Already he had been working for them for 26 years, the result of his yearning to be an entertainer – originally, he hoped, on the stage – and a chance meeting with two OB stalwarts, Wynford Vaughan-Thomas and Stewart MacPherson, when they were reporting on the allied advance towards the end of the war. Invited for a voice test by his fellow Etonian, Seymour de Lotbinière, the respected Head of Outside Broadcasts, Brian impressed him when, instead of going to Piccadilly Circus to produce a five minute written report on what he had seen, he recorded one instead by going into a record shop and using the 'record your own message' service. His second test was to interview passers-by, in Oxford Street, under the supervision of Wynford

Vaughan-Thomas. The result, by Vaughan-Thomas's reckoning, was 'gloriously uninhibited'.

He soon made his mark as a pioneer in a pioneering department of the Corporation. His love of musicals and the music hall gave him the pleasant job of sifting plays and comedy material for broadcasts, then introducing and linking excerpts from West End shows. It brought him into contact with comedians he revered such as Arthur Askey and Bud Flanagan, whose 'Underneath the Arches' Brian later performed with the great man and with anyone else who would sing with him in years ahead. He carried in his head a tremendous stock of material from those days, especially of the music hall double-act variety. Examples:

'Excuse me, do you know you've got a banana in your ear?'
'I'm sorry?'
'I said do you know you've got a banana in your ear?'
'I'm sorry. I can't hear a word you're saying; I've got a banana in my ear.'

Or:

'Where are you going with those plums?'
'I'm taking them to His Majesty the King'.
'Why on earth are you taking them to the King?'
'Well, it says in "God Save the King", Send him Victorias!'

He was as likely to come out with something like this on the air at appropriate moments as he was in private. He had already made his mark on listeners by the time that he was invited to revive a feature called 'Let's Go Somewhere', started by John Snagge before the war, as part of the Saturday night Home Service programme *In Town Tonight*. Starting with a visit to

the Chamber of Horrors at Madame Tussauds after dark, he made a tremendous success of an enormous variety of features, from serving in a fish and chip shop or broadcasting from the driver's cab in a tube train, to quite dangerous stunts such as being shot 60 feet in the air up a vertical tunnel by a pilot's ejector seat (microphone attached), riding bareback on a circus horse or feigning a robbery and being attacked on a padded arm by a police Alsatian.

It was his old friend Ian Orr-Ewing who, as Head of Outside Broadcasts in the BBC's fledgling television service, first recruited him for cricket commentary. Working with Jim Swanton, Robert Hudson and, a little later, Peter West, on home Tests, he, and from 1964 Richie Benaud, paved the way for the former Test cricketers who now have almost a monopoly as television commentators. As ever Brian was sunny of voice and mien, a pleasure to listen to and charming company whenever his face appeared at intervals in the match. Gradually too, he

began reporting on tours overseas, both for radio and television and in 1963, to his great pride, he was appointed the BBC's first Cricket Correspondent.

Such was his energy that in 1993, still loving his work and claiming that his five children and, by now, several grandchildren, needed his financial support, he undertook a series of one-man autobiographical shows at provincial theatres (32 in all, over nine months) that must have been both mentally and physically demanding. Invariably 'An Evening with Johnners' played to full houses, and always to delighted ones. He loved cricket, he loved life and he himself was greatly loved both by everyone he knew and a

John Arlott surveys the scene at Lord's on the final day of the Centenary Test against Australia in 1980, his last day after 34 years as a commentator. After a final, discreet handover, 'And after Trevor Bailey it will be Christopher Martin-Jenkins', and a moment's silence, the entire ground and both teams gave him a standing ovation.

MY FIRST TEST MATCH

Peter Baxter

1966 was quite a year – certainly for me. I had joined the BBC the previous September in the radio Outside Broadcasts department, where my duties involved arranging OBs for anyone who needed them, whether from our own department or beyond. The producers also used our office, staffed by hopeful young lads, as a source of manpower when someone was needed to go out as a 'No.2', as the broadcaster's backup was known.

Thus in June I went on my first OB. It was a County Championship match on a Saturday at Lord's – Middlesex against Yorkshire. Our box then was in the back of the Warner Stand and in it gathered Rex Alston, a scorer and me, with an engineer in a small room immediately

behind. Rex did give me one scare when he took his time coming back from the gents and the studio were wanting to hand over to him for another period of commentary, but happily he arrived in time to prevent my broadcasting debut.

It was, of course, the summer of England's football World Cup – and I was there. My job for the tournament was to look after all the overseas radio broadcasters and their various demands. Quite apart from being an amazing experience in itself, that was an invaluable grounding in the trade of outside broadcasting.

The cricket producer of the time, Michael Tuke-Hastings, had long since grown weary of going to Test

England v West Indies Fifth Test

18–22 August 1966 Kennington Oval, London   Umpires **JS Buller and CS Elliott**

WEST INDIES FIRST INNINGS

CC Hunte	b Higgs	1
EDAS McMorris	b Snow	14
RB Kanhai	c Graveney b Illingworth	104
BF Butcher	c Illingworth b Close	12
SM Nurse	c Graveney b D'Oliveira	0
* GS Sobers	c Graveney b Barber	81
DAJ Holford	c D'Oliveira b Illingworth	5
† JL Hendriks	b Barber	0
CC Griffith	c Higgs b Barber	4
WW Hall	not out	30
LR Gibbs	c Murray b Snow	12
Extras	(b 1, lb 3, nb 1)	5
Total	(all out, 97.5 overs)	268

Fall of wickets   1-1, 2-56, 3-73, 4-74, 5-196, 6-218, 7-218, 8-223, 9-223

Bowling	O	M	R	W
Snow	20.5	1	66	2
Higgs	17	4	52	1
D'Oliveira	21	7	35	1
Close	9	2	21	1
Barber	15	3	49	3
Illingworth	15	7	40	2

SECOND INNINGS

CC Hunte	c Murray b Snow	7
EDAS McMorris	c Murray b Snow	1
RB Kanhai	b D'Oliveira	15
BF Butcher	c Barber b Illingworth	60
SM Nurse	c Edrich b Barber	70
DAJ Holford	run out	7
* GS Sobers	c Close b Snow	0
† JL Hendriks	b Higgs	0
CC Griffith	not out	29
WW Hall	c D'Oliveira b Illingworth	17
LR Gibbs	c & b Barber	3
Extras	(b 1, lb 14, nb 1)	16
Total	(all out, 85.1 overs)	225

Fall of wickets   1-5, 2-12, 3-50, 4-107, 5-137, 6-137, 7-142, 8-168, 9-204

Bowling	O	M	R	W
Snow	13	5	40	3
Higgs	15	6	18	1
D'Oliveira	17	4	44	1
Close	3	1	7	0
Barber	22.1	2	78	2
Illingworth	15	9	22	2

ENGLAND FIRST INNINGS

G Boycott	b Hall	4
RW Barber	c Nurse b Sobers	36
JH Edrich	c Hendriks b Sobers	35
TW Graveney	run out	165
DL Amiss	lbw b Hall	17
BL D'Oliveira	b Hall	4
* DB Close	run out	4
R Illingworth	c Hendriks b Griffith	3
† JT Murray	lbw b Sobers	112
K Higgs	c & b Holford	63
JA Snow	not out	59
Extras	(b 8, lb 14, nb 3)	25
Total	(all out, 199.5 overs)	527

Fall of wickets   1-6, 2-72, 3-85, 4-126, 5-130, 6-150, 7-166, 8-383, 9-399

Bowling	O	M	R	W
Hall	31	8	85	3
Griffith	32	7	78	1
Sobers	54	23	104	3
Holford	25.5	1	79	1
Gibbs	44	16	115	0
Hunte	13	2	41	0

England won by an innings and 34 runs

Tom Graveney calls for a single off the bowling of Lance Gibbs. He failed to make it and was run out for 165. His partner, John Murray, also scored a century as England won by an innings against a West Indies side that had already won the series .

Matches himself and maintained that he was better placed in the studio, where he could listen properly and supervise the archiving as the game went on. He would therefore need a 'No.2' at the ground. This was a favoured task, usually undertaken by another producer. For the Oval Test of 1966 against the West Indies, however, he asked one P. Baxter.

So, on 18 August, a nervous 19-year-old stepped for the first time into the *Test Match Special* commentary box. Robert Hudson was the only one of the radio commentators I knew, as he was on the staff of the department. Brian Johnston, who I had also met in the corridors of Broadcasting House, was in the television box next door. The others who crammed into the small wooden hut on the flat roof beside the pavilion were new to me – household names though they were.

John Arlott gave me a gruff greeting, no doubt wondering suspiciously who the young pup might be. He did not enjoy a happy relationship with Tuke-Hastings, so he probably feared a plot in my arrival. Norman Yardley and Roy Lawrence were kindly and welcoming and, though Freddie Brown was formidable, I had been to school with his son, which gave us a small piece of common ground. Importantly, I had met the engineers who inhabited a brick-built shed across the flat roof behind the box. And while they probably wondered what the world was coming to, they were my lifeline.

My station was the bench at the back of the commentary box, where I absorbed the instructions from the studio, unable to respond except by telephone and gradually working out which instructions – such as, 'Tell Arlott he's talking rubbish' – not to pass on.

It was a memorable Test Match on the field, too. Brian Close had replaced Colin Cowdrey as captain with England three-nil down coming to the final Test. At the heart of England's belated comeback was a big century from Tom Graveney and then the way the tail wagged around a hundred from their wicketkeeper, John Murray. The 128

that Ken Higgs and John Snow put on for the last wicket took England to a first-innings lead of 259 and captured the attention of a nation. On the Monday I can still remember the shock of the dismissal of Sobers first ball, caught at short leg by Close – helmetless in those days – off Snow. That was the moment we knew for certain that the victory was England's and it came inside four days, by an innings and 34 runs.

Over the next few years there were more such missions to Lord's and the Oval in particular – and other outside broadcasting adventures, too. On Christmas Day 1972 England won a Test Match in Delhi. The BBC had not sent a reporter on the tour, feeling that the communications would not be good enough, and on that day trying to find out what had happened was quite difficult. Sitting in the office I resolved – and probably rather precociously said – that if I were ever lucky enough to be cricket producer, I would make sure that such a lack of coverage never happened. The following March I was appointed cricket producer by the then Head of Outside Broadcasts, Robert Hudson, in succession to Michael Tuke-Hastings who was keen to concentrate on producing his quiz programmes.

My first match in that job was the first-ever one-day international at Swansea. The man in charge of outside broadcasts in Wales was the legendary Alun Williams. As it was such a great moment for Wales, it was decided that he would do the commentary alongside the football commentator, Peter Jones, whose roots were also Welsh, and a youngster from the sports room called Christopher Martin-Jenkins. Trevor Bailey and Peter Walker were the summarisers. We were sent letters in Welsh by Alun to welcome us (fortunately translated) and we started with our studio presenter, one Nigel Starmer-Smith, handing over to 'Alan Williams.' There was a pause at our end. Then, 'It's 'Al – in', to rhyme with sin and gin – and since we've got our first Test Match in Wales, I think you ought to get it right. Good morning'. It was a great start to my cricket production career.

huge array of listeners whom he never met. The cakes sent to him in the commentary box to keep him – and us – going were but one symbol of that affection.

Brian's death in London on 5 January 1994, a few weeks after a severe heart attack that had affected his brain but, even then, not his spirit, was the signal for widespread expressions of affection and tribute. These culminated in a service of thanksgiving in Westminster Abbey on 16 May 1994 which was oversubscribed and at which addresses were given by the prime minister, John Major, and Sir Colin Cowdrey.

The witty verses of Richard Stilgoe, himself a great entertainer, had everyone smiling at the service as Johnners would have wished, and they brilliantly caught the mood:

Above left Brian Johnston describes the scene as he cuts Dorothy Harbin in half for listeners to BBC's *In Town Tonight* in 1949. Watching him closely is husband Robert Harbin (left).
Above right With thoughts only for his listeners, he then undergoes the ordeal himself while maintaining his commentary.
Left Although he 'retired' from the BBC in 1972, Brian Johnston was still a key member of the *Test Match Special* team until shortly before his death in 1994 aged 81.

The Cherubim and Seraphim are starting to despair of him,
They've never known a shade so entertaining.
He chats to total strangers, calls the Angel Gabriel 'Aingers',
And talks for even longer if it's raining.

When St. Peter's done the honours he will pass you on to Johnners,
Who will cry 'Good morning, welcome to the wake.
You're batting Number Seven for the Heaven fourth eleven,
And while you're waiting, have some angel cake.'

Thus passed the jester, only a little more than two years after the poet. Who was the greater commentator? Well, it does not matter. It was a matter of personal taste and both were towering figures in their genre. Arlott was the consummate wordsmith, Johnston the great natural entertainer and both gave great pleasure to a large, disparate but faithful band of listeners for many years. What Michael Parkinson said of Johnston was true of them both, 'Like most of his generation who had been through the war, he had an enlightened perspective on life.' For the best part of a quarter of a century they were the life and soul of *Test Match Special*.

The jester and the poet – the life and soul of *Test Match Special* for more than 20 years.

MY FIRST TEST MATCH

Bryan Waddle

'Best job in the world,' Don Mosey told me as he presented me with a copy of his appropriately named book. Don had become a good friend of my predecessors Alan Richards and Iain Gallaway through his trips down under and how he loved his visits to our part of the world. Knowing Don made my first trip to England in 1990 a lot easier as I nervously fronted up at Trent Bridge for the opening match of New Zealand's three-Test series. I hadn't seen Don in long trousers. Shorts and knee high socks was his uniform in New Zealand.

TMS had always been the model for our commentary style, the relaxed, entertaining approach was superior to the monologue that existed in New Zealand, where each ball was described and the summariser talked between overs. I knew what was required and even before encountering Don in Nottingham I'd been warmly welcomed a few weeks earlier at Lord's by Brian Johnston. It was our first meeting but he greeted me like a long lost friend, adding the traditional 'ers' to my name.

'You must be Wadders' he proclaimed as I stood alone in the commentary box at Lord's breathing in the history and tradition I'd dreamed of for much of my cricketing life. The warmth of my welcome only eased the nerves a little, I was keen to impress and do a professional job. I played a straight bat and managed to make it to lunch with a minimum of fuss on a grey and murky day.

England v New Zealand First Test

7–12 June 1990 Trent Bridge, Nottingham   Umpires **HD Bird and JH Hampshire**

NEW ZEALAND FIRST INNINGS

TJ Franklin	b Malcolm	33
* JG Wright	c Stewart b Small	8
AH Jones	c Stewart b Malcolm	39
MD Crowe	b DeFreitas	59
MJ Greatbatch	b Hemmings	1
MW Priest	c Russell b DeFreitas	26
MC Snedden	c Gooch b DeFreitas	0
JG Bracewell	c Gooch b Small	28
RJ Hadlee	b DeFreitas	0
† IDS Smith	not out	2
DK Morrison	lbw b DeFreitas	0
Extras	(b 1, lb 10, w 1)	12
Total	(all out, 89 overs)	208

Fall of wickets 1-16, 2-75, 3-110, 4-121, 5-170, 6-174, 7-191, 8-191, 9-203

Bowling	O	M	R	W
Small	29	9	49	2
Malcolm	19	7	48	2
Hemmings	19	6	47	1
DeFreitas	22	6	53	5

SECOND INNINGS

TJ Franklin	not out	22
* JG Wright	c Russell b Small	1
AH Jones	c Russell b DeFreitas	13
DK Morrison	not out	0
Extras		0
Total	(2 wks, 17 overs)	36

Did not bat MD Crowe, MJ Greatbatch, MW Priest, MC Snedden, JG Bracewell, RJ Hadlee, † IDS Smith

Fall of wickets 1-8, 2-36

Bowling	O	M	R	W
Small	6	2	14	1
Malcolm	7	2	22	0
Hemmings	2	2	0	0
DeFreitas	2	2	0	1

Match drawn

ENGLAND FIRST INNINGS

* GA Gooch	lbw b Hadlee	0
MA Atherton	c Snedden b Priest	151
AJ Stewart	c Smith b Hadlee	27
AJ Lamb	lbw b Hadlee	0
RA Smith	c Smith b Bracewell	55
NH Fairbrother	c Franklin b Snedden	19
† RC Russell	c Snedden b Morrison	28
PAJ DeFreitas	lbw b Bracewell	14
GC Small	c Crowe b Hadlee	26
EE Hemmings	not out	13
DE Malcolm	not out	4
Extras	(b 2, lb 3, nb 3)	8
Total	(9 wks dec, 138 overs)	345

Fall of wickets 1-0, 2-43, 3-45, 4-141, 5-168, 6-260, 7-302, 8-306, 9-340

Bowling	O	M	R	W
Hadlee	33	6	89	4
Morrison	22	3	96	1
Snedden	36	17	54	1
Bracewell	35	8	75	2
Priest	12	4	26	1

After lunch came my first trial. I'm not sure who, perhaps CMJ or Fred, probably Fred as I sat down, I was presented with a *TMS* tie and told that to keep it I needed to tie it round my neck while commentating. Was it a set-up or normal rules? I fell for it and without the required mirror I got most of the 'unders', 'overs' and 'throughs' to pass muster.

'Further,' said Backers, 'you must wear it on the first day of every Test series you cover.' I proudly wore it for a couple of years till touring India where nobody wears a tie.

It's true that during my early *TMS* experience I was like a boy in a candy shop, wide eyed and where do I begin type of thing. There I was sitting alongside many of my idols in the game. As a young boy I'd been Fred Trueman in backyard Tests, and sitting alongside him was a revealing experience in more ways than one. Fred had a style of his own and the strong Yorkshire accent combined with years of smoking that huge pipe made him as distinctive as any commentator.

After Trent Bridge we went to the Second Test at Lord's, another overcast first day which was interrupted mid-afternoon by rain. 'There won't be any more play today' said Fred, 'why don't we go down to the Bollinger tent at the nursery end, I've got a few mates there.' No second invitation was needed, I followed, to drown in the wisdom of the great man. Drown, I almost did but, sadly after three bottles of Bollinger, the skies cleared, play resumed and I trudged back to the commentary box a little uncoordinated in my stride to round out the day. But a 'few' at lunch hour was nothing new to some of the *TMS* team I was told later.

Fred had many mates and he didn't mind telling you. A long lunch at Lord's with Brian Statham wasn't the recipe for one afternoon session. An hour before tea Fred joined me for some expert comments, but mid-spell I gave the score as the ideal in-point for his assessment but there was nothing, just silence. As I turned, Peter Baxter nudged Fred, who awoke startled, mumbled then stood up as Trevor Bailey took his place. I didn't realize till then that I was a cure for insomnia.

'Nothing like forty winks during the day to freshen you up' said Fred afterwards.

Many of the experts were memorable characters in their own right as well as being outstanding players.

Working with the likes of 'Bumble', Foxy Fowler, and 'Skidder' Marks often provided moments of near uncontrollable laughter, which threatened the professionalism for which we all prided ourselves. But being human and natural is what makes *TMS* such a great product. My memories are more of the summarisers as they are the ones I have had the exchanges with, but the warm, friendly personalities of Aggers, CMJ, 'my dear old thing' Blowers and the many others I worked with have been easily identifiable in maintaining the lasting quality of the programme.

And holding it altogether there's always been Peter Baxter. I doubt many people realise the importance of a good producer, just to have one in New Zealand would suit me, but Backers in my experience has maintained a fatherly, perhaps headmasterly control over what seems at times seemingly uncontrollable. He's shared the humour with often unheard asides from his seat at the back of the box, shuffled paper to remind commentators of the shipping forecast and, of course, the stern glare when the standard lurched towards the unacceptable.

My one regret is never having the privilege of working with John Arlott as Alan Richards had done. For as long as I can remember John Arlott and the ABC's Alan McGilvray were the role models for the modern commentator. I spent many hours recording their commentary, listening to it and assessing what made them so good. They provided what was almost a blueprint for the successful commentator, knowledge, understanding, timing, humour and the instant recall of facts so much a part of the game of cricket.

Among my many recordings of John Arlott is one that still brings a smile when I recall it. The Lord's Test of 1978, the sound effects microphone captured the distinct tones of a spectator, which prompted Arlott to react mid-commentary as Ian Botham was bowling to Geoff Howarth. 'We've got a beauty of a loudmouth over in the Mound Stand now, talking pure alcohol,' there was a slight pause as the piercing voice spills forth again, 'Hear that?' he said, 'worse than the Sydney Hill but fewer in number, 95 for 2.'

A simple point made with telling effect.

Opposite Richard Hadlee appeals successfully having trapped England opening batsman and captain Graham Gooch with the first ball of the innings. Gooch looks suitably fed up.

4

THE COMMENTATORS

At least as much as any radio programme, *Test Match Special* depends on its voices. The memories of well-loved radio broadcasters inevitably fade with each generation and names such as Rex Alston, John Arlott and Brian Johnston – all remembered elsewhere in this book – will already mean little to a new era of radio listeners. But, for the record, these are the commentators – the ball-by-ball men – who have brought *Test Match Special* to the air for home Tests since the programme was first broadcast in 1957.

Robert Hudson (b. 1920) ▶
First radio Test 1956

He may never have been the greatest household name, but Bob Hudson was quite possibly the most complete commentator of all. Surely no one ever went on the air better prepared. It may be that his seven years in the Army before he joined the BBC gave him ideal preparation for a career as producer, administrator

Meticulous in his research and detailed in his delivery, BBC stalwart Robert Hudson was a first-class commentator during the late 1950s and early 1960s.

and broadcaster. And as a broadcaster his specialities were cricket, rugby and state occasions.

Bob first commentated on a Test Match for television at Lord's in 1949 and for radio in 1956, but his appearances were all too infrequent because of his 'day job' as the North of England Outside Broadcasts producer. However, for years after he retired he was amused that his commentary on a Richard Sharpe try was replayed regularly to mark the last time England had beaten Wales at rugby in Cardiff. It was a record he was happy enough to erase, when the jinx was eventually broken.

On the big state events, royal weddings, Trooping the Colour, the Cenotaph Service of Remembrance and the like, he was unsurpassed. He would be armed with pages of notes – most of the material arranged onto cards, sometimes even with a few appropriate phrases already written out in cramped handwriting (indecipherable by anybody else), against the chance that they might be needed. He would have made up a chart to show who was who among the throng round the Cenotaph or the great congregations in Westminster Abbey, but always there was the knowledge that not every note had to be used. When they all were was the moment that the commentator was in trouble.

His role in the birth of *Test Match Special* has already been recorded. Having given up sports commentary – though he was encouraged to continue with the major events – he became Head of Outside Broadcasts, working hard to merge the conflicting departments of Sports News and Outside Broadcasts in the early 1970s. In 1973, as Head of Sport and Outside Broadcasts, as the expanded department was now known, he made two long-lasting appointments for which the recipients owe him a great deal. Christopher Martin-Jenkins became the second Cricket Correspondent of the BBC and Peter Baxter its third radio cricket producer.

For all that his deliberately self-effacing manner made him largely anonymous with the public, Robert Hudson's style on the air was warm and inclusive. Gaffes were rare, but the one he most recounted happened at Lord's, when the teams in a Test Match were being presented to the Queen. 'This,' he declared, with all the attendant gravitas, 'is a moment they will always forget.'

The voice remained young sounding and, after his early retirement from the staff, he was frequently to be heard on Sunday afternoons, commentating on Sunday League cricket for BBC Radio London. For many years, too, he continued with those commentaries on state events – always an object lesson in organised commentary.

Peter West (1920–2003) ▶
First *TMS* Test 1958

It comes as a surprise to many that the man who was the face of television cricket coverage for so many years also did commentary for *Test Match Special* – but only for two Tests in 1958. Like so many broadcasters, radio commentary had been his start and in the 1970s he returned to radio as an exceptionally good rugby commentator, forming an excellent team with

Peter West: only covered two matches for *Test Match Special*, in 1958, but his name is synonymous with BBC cricket coverage through his work on television.

two former Scottish internationals, Chris Rea and Ian Robertson.

Peter's entry to the world of sports journalism came when he helped C.B. Fry out by telephoning his copy to his newspaper from a county match at Taunton in 1947. The great man was impressed by the youngster's delivery enough to put forward his name to the BBC and on that slender audition he was interviewed by Seymour de Lotbinière, the Head of Outside Broadcasts, and then given a trial commentary at Lord's. The real thing came later that summer when Warwickshire played the touring South Africans.

The translation from journalist and radio broadcaster on county cricket to television Test Match commentator came in 1952 and the following year he ventured into non-sporting television with the chairmanship of panel games. Throughout his considerable time covering rugby, Peter West would resent jibes about *Come Dancing*, the BBC television programme he presented for 15 years, but the choice of him to do that job and to be the front man for the television cricket coverage for so long was a tribute to his unflappable, reassuring style. Bluff and matter-of-fact in his delivery, viewers and listeners always felt safe in his hands.

Alan Gibson (1923–1997)
First *TMS* Test 1962

There was a mischievous irreverence about Alan Gibson, which could make him infuriating to his producers, but it was also at the heart of his genius as a writer and broadcaster. Those who may think they have never heard any of his commentary may just remember hearing the finale of an epic Test Match at Lord's in 1963:

'There are two balls to go. England, needing 234 to win, are 228 for 9, with Cowdrey, his left forearm in plaster, coming out to join Allen.'

It fell to Gibson to describe that finish, as David Allen kept the last two balls from Wes Hall out, to draw the Test and save the injured Colin Cowdrey from having to face the bowling.

An academic, who joined the staff of the BBC in Bristol, Alan made his first appearance on *Test Match Special* in 1962. He was the son of a Baptist minister and after an early childhood in Yorkshire, his family moved to a house overlooking the County Ground at Taunton, the very venue where, some 15 years earlier, Frank Gillingham had done the first cricket outside broadcast. His schooling at Taunton brought him to the real heart of his cricket and the West Country became his cricketing, writing and broadcasting parish. He had a great enjoyment of words and a voice that could deliver them with the sort of authority that saw him employed often by the BBC Natural History Unit in Bristol, to provide voiceovers for their films.

A man with a gleam in his eye, Gibson's sense of mischief was never far away. Once asked to delay a full read of the scorecard for a minute as the World Service was about to join the commentary and he would only have to read it again, he said, 'My producer has asked me not to read the scorecard, dear listener, but I don't think you should be deprived, so I shall read it anyway.'

When writing for *The Times* his readers were often treated to more information on his journey – usually involving a change of trains at Didcot – than on the match. The cricket might be given comparatively short shrift – as in a piece which told that Sussex had collapsed during the afternoon session. 'I did not see much of that, because I met an old friend behind the pavilion. John Snagge and I agreed that the BBC is not what it was.'

◄ Peter Cranmer (1914–1994)
First *TMS* Test 1965

Despite having captained Warwickshire before and after the Second World War, Peter Cranmer achieved more fame for his rugby exploits. He played 16 times for England as a centre-threequarter in the days when there were fewer opportunities for caps. Most celebrated of those must have been the 1936 win over the All Blacks at Twickenham. He used to tell how

the team had gathered the afternoon before for a bit of a run about, with the forwards practising their scrummaging against the backs.

When he retired from playing cricket, he was a regular on the half-hour regional county commentaries, where he had a charming, relaxed style, but notoriously poor timekeeping. That comfortable manner led to a couple of Test Match commentaries, in 1965 and 1968.

Neil Durden-Smith (b. 1933)
First *TMS* Test 1969

After a career in the Royal Navy, 'Durders' was taken on by the BBC to work on the organisation of the coverage of the 1966 football World Cup. But cricket was his first love. He had played for the Combined Services as a middle-order batsman and was at one stage not far from a career in county cricket. Subsequently he became a stalwart of the Lord's Taverners, on and off the field, serving as chairman in the early 1980s. He and his wife, the broadcaster, Judith Chalmers, have remained very active for the charity.

As an accomplished hockey player, his CV included television commentary on that sport, as well as radio commentary on a variety of events and appearances on quiz shows, but he suffered frustration at the difficulty of commanding a regular place in the *TMS* team.

He did at least give Brian Johnston great pleasure when he announced once, 'During this over I'll run round the field for you'. From the back of the box came loud comments about finding him his running shoes. And he achieved a certain notoriety in the Outside Broadcasts department, when, covering a county match at Grace Road, he was late on the air after an interval. His broadcast excuse was, 'I was having tea with the Bishop of Leicester.' That

Peter Cranmer: a superb sportsman, his relaxed almost conversational commentary style earned him two Test Match commentaries in the mid-1960s.

prompted Alan Gibson, doing the next county report on the programme, to start, 'No Episcopal visitations here.'

◄ Christopher Martin-Jenkins
(b. 1945)
First *TMS* Test 1973

Having been a fine schoolboy cricketer, captained the Crusaders at Cambridge University for two years and been good enough to play for Surrey second XI, Christopher was taken on as assistant editor at *The Cricketer* magazine at the instigation of E.W. Swanton. Two years later, in 1970, he joined the BBC Radio Sports News department. The hard-bitten editor of those days, Angus Mackay, greeted him with the news that, 'We shall call you Chris Jenkins.' But Christopher, who was not happy with this decision, stuck to his guns to preserve his full name (which takes up two lines in *Radio Times*), and to his great credit the abbreviation that has accompanied him throughout his career is 'CMJ'.

Not particularly happy doing the Football League Division Three and Four round up on *Sports Report* CMJ's big break came when Robert Hudson, then Head of Outside Broadcasts, spotted his commentary talent and gave him two of the first-ever one-day internationals in England in 1972, before making him Cricket Correspondent at the end of the following summer in succession to Brian Johnston and in time for England's winter tour of the West Indies. At the time radio reports on sporting events were beginning to become shorter and sharper and CMJ proved himself the master of the one-minute report, which is slightly ironic in the light of his subsequent reputation for poor timekeeping.

Christopher had two spells as BBC Cricket Correspondent; the first from 1973 to 1980, after which he returned to *The Cricketer* as editor. In his second incarnation, he combined the two jobs from 1985 to 1991, when he gave up both roles to become Cricket Correspondent of the *Daily Telegraph*, moving to *The Times* in 1999.

His concise, accurate style of commentary has altered very little over 35 years of broadcasting on the game. The style scarcely reflects the habitual panic that precedes him to the microphone. He usually so busy that at the time he should be setting off to an appointment – or a spell of commentary from his seat in the press box – he always seems to have a couple more things to do.

We do have a bit of fun at Christopher's expense, by laughing at his foibles. His life often seems to recreate that of Basil Fawlty, moving from one catastrophe to the next. But over the years he has provided us and the listeners with a few laughs.

CMJ's DOINGS

- He has invented his own particular collection of swearwords, in order not to give offence. Hence 'Fotheringay Thomas!' and 'Fishcakes and buttercup pie!' which accompany each latest crisis in his life.
- In Jamaica in 2000, he was trying to make contact with his office on his mobile phone. After much frustrated button punching, his travelling companion pointed out that he was using the TV remote control from the hotel.
- On the same tour, he was happily bringing his newspaper cuttings book up to date, accompanied by sweet sounds from his Walkman, when all went quiet. He found he had cut through the earphone cable.
- Later, in Barbados, he drove through Bridgetown oblivious to the fact that he was scattering his golf clubs over the island from the back of his Mini Moke.
- On an earlier West Indies tour he took with him to the frequently rain-soaked country of Guyana, a new pair of galoshes and, with not a little smugness, put them on to cross a corner of the saturated outfield. He stepped out of the pavilion gate into 18 inches of standing water – to the huge amusement of all onlookers.

Christopher Martin-Jenkins: late as ever, he's pictured trying to take a shortcut to the commentary box in Napier, New Zealand in 1992.

- On one occasion it took a little while – and a nasty taste in the mouth – for the realisation to dawn that the layer of cream on top of the Danish pastry he had in his golf bag was in fact sun-cream.
- During one of *TMS*'s frequent periods of uncertainty about its future, the newly appointed Managing Director of BBC Radio, Liz Forgan, was brought up to the Lord's commentary box. She was introduced to all present, but CMJ somehow missed the name. After standing with her for a bit, he said, 'My family thought you were awfully good in *Blackadder*'. A puzzled Miss Forgan moved away, while CMJ checked, 'That was Miriam Margoyles, wasn't it?'
- In 2006, en route to a one-day international at the Oval he rang in. 'I may be a little late. I went to Lord's.'
- On hearing about CMJ's abortive trip to Lord's, a listener emailed in to say that he or she had recently seen CMJ trip over the pavilion steps at Canterbury, fall flat on his face and continue as if nothing untoward had happened.
- When England won the final Test in Bombay in 2006, an end-of-series *TMS* dinner was planned. CMJ recommended a place with the unlikely name – for Bombay – of 'the Copper Chimney'. Setting off inevitably after everyone else was at the restaurant, he found a taxi driver who knew only of another 'Copper Chimney' half an hour's drive away. After a series of heart-rending text messages, he turned up as the bill was being paid.
- At the start of the 2006 season, there was a meeting of the commentators in Broadcasting House to explain some of the possibilities of new technology. As the meeting went on, Christopher suddenly exclaimed that his car was on a meter which now needed feeding and the chairman called a secretary to ask her to do that. When she later set off for home, Christopher became convinced that she had his car keys. Many anxious phone calls later he found them in his pocket.

Above The rain sodden ground in Guyana, moments before CMJ stepped into 18 inches of water to the amusement of everyone.

Opposite Henry Blofeld: became so popular with the supporters on the Hill at the Sydney Cricket Ground in the 1980s that they started a Blow-Fly fan club.

Henry Blofeld (b. 1939) ▶
First *TMS* Test 1974

Those who saw Henry as a schoolboy wicketkeeper/batsman are unequivocal in their insistence that he was going to play for England. His achievements were mounting, but in 1957 came the event that altered that course. Cycling to the cricket nets at Eton, as captain of the XI, he was hit by an excursion bus and for a while his life hung in the balance. Things were never quite the same on the field after that, but it says a lot for his talent that, though he had lost some of the old flair, he was still able to gain a Blue at Cambridge.

In 1962, through the good offices of *The Times* Cricket Correspondent, John Woodcock, he was rescued from a career in the city with the chance of some cricket reporting. *The Times* led on to the *Guardian* and the *Observer* and the following year he managed to put together enough of a portfolio of newspaper commissions to get himself on the winter tour of India. The story is often told of how close he came to playing in the Second Test in Bombay, where injury and illness had reduced M.J.K. Smith's side to barely eleven upright players.

Gradually expanding journalistic experience and contact with the big names in the business led to a radio commentary audition in 1969, which was considered enough of a success for his name to be

added to the list of available commentators for county cricket. But the call never seemed to come. Blowers' first serious commentary was to come from West Indian commercial stations on New Zealand's tour of the Caribbean in 1972.

Rumours of this must have filtered through to Broadcasting House, because during the following summer, he was asked to cover some Saturday afternoon county cricket and that led to an invitation to commentate on two of the one-day internationals against Australia at the end of the season. His elevation to Test Match commentary followed at the beginning of 1974.

Fifteen years later, with enormous apologies to all, Blowers was lured to television. The differential in the fees on offer from radio and from Sky was simply too great to ignore. It had an immediately amusing consequence in our commentary box, when Brian Johnston felt that the letters of enquiry as to Henry's whereabouts deserved an answer. So, not wishing to give too much of a plug to a rival organisation, Johnners said on the air, 'I'm afraid Blowers has gone to a place in the Sky,' which he felt was suitably cryptic. The following day the black-edged envelopes started to arrive, containing cards sympathetic to the grief we were obviously bearing so bravely.

Blowers' sojourn 'in the Sky' was fairly short-lived, thanks to changing television contracts, though it was followed by periods of work with television companies in New Zealand, the West Indies and India, where his habit of commenting on the ladies' earrings in the crowd seemed to earn as much attention as anything he said about the cricket.

Following Brian Johnston's death early in 1994, *Test Match Special* inevitably had a huge gap to fill. Brian was, of course, irreplaceable and suggestions of such a replacement had to be rebuffed. It was an historic summer, too, with the return of South Africa on a tour to England for the first time for 29 years. The occasion required something a bit different. The occasion was ripe for the return of Blofeld.

It is extremely unusual for a commentator to receive no criticism at all, but for the two Tests of that series on which Henry commentated, there was nothing but pleasure expressed at his return.

When he started out as a radio commentator, he concentrated very much on the 22 yards in the middle. It was suggested to him – rashly it sometimes seems now – that he could afford to raise his eyes to take in the whole scene. It has led to some extraordinary flights of fancy.

BLOWERS' SAYINGS

- Pigeons round the world have been described as 'thoughtful', 'soporific' and one in 2005 was even 'benevolent'.
- Buses have been a particular favourite and have produced a plethora of timetables, sent in by listeners. He was particularly delighted by the London Transport decision to start running the 'bendy bus' past the Oval.
- The Lord's media centre affords an excellent view of aircraft on their final approach to Heathrow and an alarming number of these are described as 'medium-paced aeroplanes'.
- He once talked – from the safe distance of the commentary box 150 yards away – of a butterfly 'walking' across the pitch.
- Favourite similes pulled from the locker include 'He hit that like a kicking horse' and 'He set off after that like a lamplighter'.
- He incurred the wrath of Lancashire County Cricket Club on one occasion by deploring their hotel within the ground, the Trafford Lodge. 'No room to swing a cat', he observed, prompting a suggestion to be made in committee that he should be barred from the ground.
- The experienced expert summarisers in the team have come to know that when Blowers responds vaguely to some detailed critique of the situation with, 'You're absolutely right', he hasn't been listening to a word they've just said.
- But the expression for which he is best known must be, 'My dear old thing', born originally from the affliction that strikes us all – the inability to remember anyone's name.

MY FIRST TEST MATCH

Henry Blofeld

I shall never forget the nerves that were fluttering about in my tummy as I drove up from London to Old Trafford for the First Test against India in June 1974 – my first for *Test Match Special*. Without the help of motorways, the journey seemed to go on forever. In those days the *TMS* team stayed in the Swan Hotel at Bucklow Hill, a couple of miles south of Altrincham. As I drove into the rather austere, modern red brick quadrangle of motel-like bedrooms tacked onto the back of an old pub, I saw John Arlott talking to Trevor Bailey.

I suddenly realised that even if I was the lesser among equals, I was there on equal terms with them as a member of the team although it didn't help my nerves.

Dinner that evening was a jolly affair along the sort of charred-mixed-grill-lines with Brian Johnston endlessly pulling Arlott's leg who, in turn, was busy keeping the wine waiter on his toes. But I'm afraid I was little more than a hyper-anxious spectator. The others couldn't have been more friendly and told me before they went to bed they were sure it would go well for me the next day.

My main problem was not with the actual cricket for I felt I could cope with that. I was terrified about the periods when rain or bad light stopped play and there was no cricket. As listeners will know we then plough on talking about anything and everything. There is a fair amount of laughter and lots of reminiscences. I didn't see

England v India First Test

6–11 June 1974 Old Trafford, Manchester

Umpires **HD Bird and DJ Constant**

ENGLAND FIRST INNINGS

G Boycott	lbw b Abid Ali	10
DL Amiss	c Madan Lal	
	b Chandrasekhar	56
JH Edrich	b Abid Ali	7
* MH Denness	b Bedi	26
KWR Fletcher	not out	123
DL Underwood	c Solkar b Bedi	7
AW Greig	c Engineer b Madan Lal	53
† APE Knott	lbw b Madan Lal	0
CM Old	c Engineer b Chandrasekhar	12
RGD Willis	lbw b Abid Ali	24
Extras	(b 1, lb 7, w 1, nb 1)	10
Total	(9 wks dec; 143.3 overs)	328
Did not bat	M Hendrick	

Fall of wickets 1-18, 2-28, 3-90, 4-104, 5-127, 6-231, 7-231, 8-265

Bowling	O	M	R	W
S Abid Ali	30.3	6	79	3
ED Solkar	13	4	33	0
S Madan Lal	31	11	56	2
S Venkataraghavan	5	1	8	0
BS Bedi	43	14	87	2
BS Chandrasekhar	21	4	55	2

SECOND INNINGS

G Boycott	c Engineer b Solkar	6
DL Amiss	c Gavaskar b Bedi	47
DL Underwood	c Engineer b Abid Ali	9
JH Edrich	not out	100
* MH Denness	not out	45
Extras	(b 4, lb 2)	6
Total	(3 wks dec; 70 overs)	213
Did not bat	KWR Fletcher, AW Greig, † APE Knott, CM Old, RGD Willis, M Hendrick	

Fall of wickets 1-13, 2-30, 3-104

Bowling	O	M	R	W
S Abid Ali	11	2	31	1
ED Solkar	7	0	24	1
BS Chandrasekhar	11	2	38	0
BS Bedi	20	2	58	1
S Venkataraghavan	9	1	17	0
S Madan Lal	12	2	39	0

INDIA FIRST INNINGS

SM Gavaskar	run out	101
ED Solkar	c Willis b Hendrick	7
S Venkataraghavan	b Willis	3
* AL Wadekar	c Hendrick b Old	6
GR Viswanath	b Underwood	40
BP Patel	c Knott b Willis	5
† FM Engineer	b Willis	0
S Madan Lal	b Hendrick	2
S Abid Ali	c Knott b Hendrick	71
BS Bedi	b Willis	0
BS Chandrasekhar	not out	0
Extras	(b 3, lb 3, nb 5)	11
Total	(all out; 84 overs)	246

Fall of wickets 1-22, 2-25, 3-32, 4-105, 5-129, 6-135, 7-143, 8-228, 9-228

Bowling	O	M	R	W
RGD Willis	24	3	64	4
CM Old	16	0	46	1
M Hendrick	20	4	57	3
DL Underwood	19	7	50	1
AW Greig	5	1	18	0

SECOND INNINGS 296 TO WIN

SM Gavaskar	c Hendrick b Old	58
ED Solkar	c Hendrick b Underwood	19
* AL Wadekar	c Knott b Greig	14
GR Viswanath	c Knott b Old	50
BP Patel	c Knott b Old	3
† FM Engineer	c Knott b Hendrick	12
S Madan Lal	hit wicket b Willis	7
S Abid Ali	c Boycott b Greig	4
S Venkataraghavan	not out	5
BS Bedi	b Old	0
BS Chandrasekhar	st Knott b Greig	0
Extras	(b 1, lb 2, nb 7)	10
Total	(all out; 85.1 overs)	182

Fall of wickets 1-32, 2-68, 3-103, 4-111, 5-139, 6-157, 7-165, 8-180, 9-180

Bowling	O	M	R	W
RGD Willis	12	5	33	1
M Hendrick	17	1	39	1
DL Underwood	15	4	45	1
CM Old	16	7	20	4
AW Greig	25.1	8	35	3

England won by 113 runs

how I could have anything to add to the general sense of wellbeing when it came my turn to be at the microphone in those situations.

Brian and John, with the help of Fred Trueman and Trevor Bailey, did it so easily. The chatter and the laughter just flowed along. My fears were underlined by the weather forecast, which was diabolical – for all five days as far as I can remember. The next morning the clouds were pretty leaden although it was still dry, and I didn't enjoy the drive to Old Trafford. The commentary box then was a miniscule wooden hut perched precariously in the scoreboard at the Stretford End of the ground. The climb up to it would have alarmed the most doughty mountaineer and once inside it was small enough to induce claustrophobia. I have an idea that the architect who designed it had once been to Calcutta where he had visited the famous Black Hole and rather admired it.

Play began on time and somehow I stumbled through my first 20-minute spell and felt a little better although I couldn't take my eyes off those black clouds. It rained at intervals, but I was extremely lucky on that first day that it was dry when my turn came to commentate and the hold-ups did not go on for that long. To my intense relief, therefore, I got away with it and never had to contribute to any of the prattling-on spells. But there were still four days to go and dinner that night was not a much less nerve-wracking affair than it had been the night before although I do remember John Arlott soliloquising with considerable humour about some cricketing adventure

The weather the next day was perfectly ghastly. Somehow I managed to survive unscathed until lunchtime. Afterwards there was no escape. It came down like stair rods. Brian presided with his usual aplomb over the first 20 minutes of post-prandial chatter. I was next on and at about 2.29 I tiptoed into the box hoping that no one would notice me. Of course Brian did and two minutes later I found myself sitting in his place in front of the microphone.

By then I had thought of a few things to say and I set off at a great rate. I gabbled away I thought fluently and entertainingly for no less than 7 minutes and 45 seconds and I was decidedly pleased with myself. Then, I ran out of steam and turned to my right where certainly one and maybe two colleagues should have been sitting. To my heart-stopping dismay I saw that there was no one there at all. There was just a piece of paper almost in front of me and in Brian's scrawled handwriting it said, 'Keep going until 6.30 and don't forget to hand back to the studio'.

Total panic set in and what had been fluent, eloquent and interesting now became a stuttering, incoherent nonsense. I could think of nothing to say and no words with which to say it. They left me to stew in my own juice for a couple of minutes before they came tumbling back into the box. Brian should have been a schoolmaster. What he was saying to me was, 'Don't forget, you're playing a team game'. He had done it with great humour and I was the only person left with egg all over his face. The thought of it all still gives me nightmares.

I have one other commentating memory of this match when I was able to see the genius of John Arlott at close quarters for the first time. Because of the weather there were not many spectators at the ground on this particular day. There was a brief let up in the rain and the players were coming back down the pavilion steps onto the ground. John was describing the scene and the few small groups of spectators huddled together against the rain. In that inimitable Hampshire burr he said, 'And there's a small knot of spectators on the middle balcony of the pavilion, the one with the portly iron railing'. The railing, which was not high, went straight down for a foot or two before bulging out in the shape of many middle-aged and elderly stomachs. It was Arlott's genius that he was able to pluck out of thin air the perfect adjective to descibe it. That word told the whole story. If any of the rest of us had thought of it, it would have been in the middle of the following night. Oh yes, and England (the word 'we' was most definitely not allowed) beat a poor Indian side by 113 runs.

Don Mosey (1925–1999) ▶
First *TMS* Test 1974

When Don was Outside Broadcasts producer for the North of England, he would often refer to himself as 'the Cock of the North'. No London-based producer would dare to venture onto 'his patch' without first clearing it with him. But he ran the radio outside broadcasting in his region with meticulous efficiency. Brian Johnston, working on a quiz show in the north of England, once saw Don looking very much in character at a reception in the Mayor's Parlour and promptly christened him 'the Alderman'. The name stuck.

He had come to the BBC from a career in newspapers, most notably the *Daily Mail*'s northern edition, for which for a time he had been their man following the Yorkshire cricket team. That had been the pinnacle and he was unforgiving to those who, unlike him, had not gone through the old apprenticeships of their trade – in his case court reporting and the rest of a junior provincial newspaperman's lot. He could also be intolerant of those who he felt had been born to privilege. The words 'public schoolboy' would be spat out with particular venom.

It was a lucky photographer who managed to get a shot of him smiling and yet he was capable of being the biggest giggler in the commentary box. Once Brian Johnston's infectious laughter – this time over the inconsequential revelation that the Israeli tenth-wicket record was held by Solly Katz and Beni Wadwaker, a fact that he was totally unaware of, or indeed that that was the cause of the Johnstonian mirth – reduced Mosey to shoulder-heaving inability to speak at the microphone.

It became something of a joke in the commentary box that, through some accident of the rota, whenever he sat down at the microphone it seemed to coincide with a drinks interval, or a particularly soporific

Don Mosey (right) had a deep knowledge of cricket based on his own experience playing the game and his friendship with Yorkshire players Brian Close, Ray Illingworth and Fred Trueman.

passage of play which might see perhaps one leg bye scored in the whole of his 20-minute spell. This had its genesis in his first ever *TMS* commentary, when his arrival was neatly timed for a bomb scare at Headingley. He looked out of the window to see stands emptying for the police search.

For his last year on the staff he was appointed Cricket Correspondent – a job that he felt should have been his a great deal earlier. He had already done several cricket tours for BBC Radio, including New Zealand, India, Pakistan and the West Indies, but never – to his bitter disgust – Australia.

In the latter stages of his time on *TMS* he proved himself an expert at the resurrected ten-minute summaries of the day's play. These he carried out with only a few notes, but they enabled him to give full vent to his command and enjoyment of the English language.

Tony Lewis (b. 1938) ▼
First *TMS* Test 1977

It is a rarity to have someone on the programme who has done both the expert summariser's job and the ball-by-ball commentary. Tony Lewis did both with great facility and then moved on to television to step into Peter West's shoes as the main 'front man' of the commentary.

A double Blue at Cambridge for cricket and rugby, Tony led Glamorgan to the County Championship in 1969 and then, in the absence of the incumbent captain Ray Illingworth, captained the England tour of India and Pakistan in 1972–73. This meant that he played his first Test as captain, but it was a successful debut as England won in Delhi on Christmas Day with the captain 70 not out at the end. The rest of the tour did not quite live up to that bright beginning and troublesome knee problems shortened his career. But the statistic of having played nine Test Matches, the first eight as captain, is unlikely to be matched in the future.

Tony moved easily from playing into journalism and broadcasting. Starting in the expert's chair, the

need for extra commentators for the 1979 World Cup gave him the opportunity to try the other discipline. His style was spare: short, incisive sentences, cutting to the heart of the matter. Later he was to try the close-of-play summaries in the not inconsiderable footsteps of E.W. Swanton – and to make a good fist of those, too.

Also on his lengthy CV can be found time as Cricket Correspondent of the *Sunday Telegraph*, Chairman of Glamorgan CCC, President of MCC and Chairman of the Welsh Tourist Board.

Jonathan Agnew (b. 1960) ▼
First *TMS* Test 1991

Towards the end of the 1990 season, Christopher Martin-Jenkins let it be known that he was about to depart the BBC for the *Daily Telegraph*. We had a winter to find a new correspondent. A number of names went into the hat. Aggers had just retired from his playing career with Leicestershire to join the ultimately ill-fated *Today* newspaper as their Cricket Correspondent and as such was sent to Australia to cover the winter tour.

'No,' he said, when approached about the BBC job. 'I've got much too good a deal with *Today*.' But within a couple of weeks the paper had betrayed him by publishing an article which he did not write – he was away helping with net practice – and giving it his by-line. 'Put my name in the hat,' he declared and the following April he became the fourth man to be BBC Cricket Correspondent.

By that time he was already no stranger to *Test Match Special*, having been recruited to – and in part been the inspiration for one of the then teatime features, 'County Talk' – for which a trio of country players: Aggers, Vic Marks and Graeme Fowler – were issued with a basic broadcasting kit. At the close of play on the evening before a Test Match, they each had to find the radio box on whatever ground they were playing at, plug in and make the machine work. This was less likely to test Jonathan than the other two, as he had spent several close seasons working on Radio

Leicester with a minimum of technical backup, and somehow he usually made it work.

Aggers might easily have played more than the three Tests he did, being ignored by the selectors at times when he was having his most purple patches as a fast bowler in county cricket. Memorably, after he had joined the BBC, and almost two years after retiring from first-class cricket, a long injury list at Leicestershire saw him invited back to play in a NatWest Trophy semi-final at Grace Road against Essex – a match on which he was originally meant to be commentating. He had to think long and hard about agreeing to play, but it was a successful enough venture in that he got through his 12 overs economically, also taking a wicket, and Leicestershire got into the final. With continuing injury problems, the approach for him to be on standby for the final was made, but the prospect of potentially making a fool of himself in front of a full house at Lord's was enough for him to decide not to tempt fate a second time.

His first appearances on *Test Match Special* were as summariser to get him used to the *TMS* atmosphere. Though the BBC's Cricket Correspondent stayed in the expert's chair for a while, his abilities as a natural broadcaster were soon recognised and he quickly became one of the mainstays of the team.

Simon Mann (b. 1963)
First *TMS* Test 1996

A regular and accomplished club cricketer, Simon, like CMJ before him, came to *Test Match Special* from the Radio sports room. Having been sent to report on a couple of England 'A' tours, he commentated on the two Tests in Zimbabwe on England's tour of 1996–97.

Opposite Tony Lewis: known in the commentary box as 'ARL', Tony Lewis covered his first Test Match for radio in 1979 then left to take over from Peter West as BBC Television's main cricket presenter in 1986.

Overleaf Trying to reach a wider audience, Aggers enlists the help of the England captain, Michael Atherton, in launching the new radio hats at Edgbaston in 1996.

MY FIRST TEST MATCH

Simon Mann

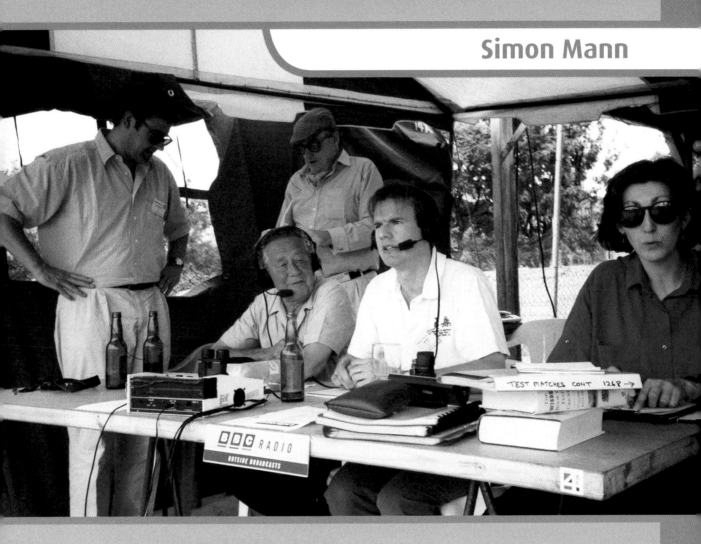

A drawn Test might not seem the most exciting way to begin a *Test Match Special* career, but it was a draw like no other in the history of the game. The match, in December 1996, was also notable for an row involving the England coach, and an incident in the commentary box that has taken Henry Blofeld a long time to live down.

It was hard to escape the impression that the tour was viewed as a grudging exercise in fixture fulfilment by England. Zimbabwe had been given Test status in 1992, a move opposed by the English authorities primarily because Zimbabwe were not considered strong enough to join the elite. It was small fry in the media as well. Jonathan Agnew was excused so he could spend Christmas

with his family and many of the senior correspondents from the national newspapers did not travel either, including Christopher Martin-Jenkins. It allowed me my chance. Zimbabwe, though, had a point to prove and three days before the First Test, they beat England by two wickets in the first one-day international of a series they went on to win three-nil.

Our broadcasting location at the picturesque Queens Club in Bulawayo was less than glamorous. It was a tent at

Simon Mann (centre) making his debut in good company as (left to right) Chris Cowdrey, Trevor Bailey, Henry Blofeld and scorer Jo King stand by to help him out.

Zimbabwe v England First Test

18-22 December 1996 Queens Sports Club, Bulawayo   Umpires **RS Dunne (New Zealand) and ID Robinson**

ZIMBABWE FIRST INNINGS

GW Flower	c Hussain b Silverwood	43
SV Carlisle	c Crawley b Gough	0
* ADR Campbell	c Silverwood b Croft	84
DL Houghton	c Stewart b Croft	34
† A Flower	c Stewart b Tufnell	112
AC Waller	c Crawley b Croft	15
GJ Whittall	c Atherton b Silverwood	7
PA Strang	c Tufnell b Silverwood	38
HH Streak	b Mullally	19
BC Strang	not out	4
HK Olonga	c Knight b Tufnell	0
Extras	(lb 4, w 3, nb 13)	20
Total	(all out; 137.5 overs)	376

Fall of wickets 1-3, 2-130, 3-136, 4-206, 5-235, 6-252, 7-331, 8-372, 9-376

Bowling	O	M	R	W
AD Mullally	23	4	69	1
D Gough	26	4	87	1
CEW Silverwood	18	5	63	3
RDB Croft	44	15	77	3
PCR Tufnell	26.5	4	76	2

SECOND INNINGS

GW Flower	lbw b Gough	0
SV Carlisle	c Atherton b Mullally	4
* ADR Campbell	b Croft	29
DL Houghton	c Croft b Tufnell	37
† A Flower	c Crawley b Tufnell	14
AC Waller	c Knight b Gough	50
BC Strang	c Mullally b Tufnell	3
GJ Whittall	c Croft b Tufnell	56
PA Strang	c Crawley b Croft	19
HH Streak	not out	8
HK Olonga	c Stewart b Silverwood	0
Extras	(b 4, lb 6, w 2, nb 2)	14
Total	(all out; 101 overs)	234

Fall of wickets 1-6, 2-6, 3-57, 4-82, 5-103, 6-111, 7-178, 8-209, 9-233

Bowling	O	M	R	W
D Gough	12	2	44	2
AD Mullally	18	5	49	1
RDB Croft	33	9	62	2
CEW Silverwood	7	3	8	1
PCR Tufnell	31	12	61	4

ENGLAND FIRST INNINGS

NV Knight	lbw b Olonga	56
* MA Atherton	lbw b PA Strang	16
† AJ Stewart	lbw b PA Strang	48
N Hussain	c BC Strang b Streak	113
GP Thorpe	c Campbell b PA Strang	13
JP Crawley	c A Flower b PA Strang	112
RDB Croft	lbw b Olonga	7
D Gough	c GW Flower b Olonga	2
CEW Silverwood	c Houghton b PA Strang	0
AD Mullally	c Waller b Streak	4
PCR Tufnell	not out	2
Extras	(b 4, lb 4, w 1, nb 24)	33
Total	(all out; 151.4 overs)	406

Fall of wickets 1-48, 2-92, 3-160, 4-180, 5-328, 6-340, 7-344, 8-353, 9-378

Bowling	O	M	R	W
HH Streak	36	8	86	2
BC Strang	17	5	54	0
PA Strang	58.4	14	123	5
HK Olonga	23	2	90	3
GJ Whittall	10	2	25	0
GW Flower	7	3	20	0

SECOND INNINGS 205 RUNS TO WIN

NV Knight	run out	96
* MA Atherton	b Olonga	4
† AJ Stewart	c Campbell b PA Strang	73
N Hussain	c Carlisle b PA Strang	0
JP Crawley	c Carlisle b Whittall	7
GP Thorpe	c Campbell b Streak	2
D Gough	not out	3
Extras	(b 2, lb 13, w 3, nb 1)	19
Total	(6 wks; 37 overs)	204
Did not bat	RDB Croft, CEW Silverwood, AD Mullally, PCR Tufnell	

Fall of wickets 1-17, 2-154, 3-156, 4-178, 5-182, 6-204

Bowling	O	M	R	W
HH Streak	11	0	64	1
HK Olonga	2	0	16	1
PA Strang	14	0	63	2
GW Flower	8	0	36	0
GJ Whittall	2	0	10	1

Match drawn (scores level)

wide long on with, bizarrely, a huge elephant's head made of fibreglass for company to our right. The technology that allows us to broadcast in perfect sound quality from anywhere in the world these days was not available to us so we were on a 'four-wire' circuit, basically a glorified telephone line. Heath Streak out on the field, Heath Robinson in the 'box.'

I was nervous and hoping for a low-key start to my first commentary spell, but I should have known better. Henry could not restrain himself. Like a circus ringmaster, he gave me the big build-up 'And now, after a word from Trevor Bailey, for the very first time on *Test Match Special*, it will be none other than Simon Mann.' I forget my first words, indeed anything I said. I cannot remember who was batting or bowling. But I can certainly recall my relief when my first 20 minutes were up.

When you commentate on *TMS*, you are conscious of the programme's heritage and the celebrated commentators that have gone before. It can be unnerving. You are aware of being judged against them. There is nothing wrong with that, but life moves on. There is no point trying to imitate them. You have to develop your own style of commentary and hope your employers and the listeners will like it.

The match itself, played on a good pitch, was hard fought, but there was little that was memorable about it until the dramatic and controversial final day. Zimbabwe began it on 107 for 5, a lead of 77. England appeared well placed, but Zimbabwe's lower order resisted until well into the afternoon. England needed 205 from 37 overs to win.

It was a one-day target without one-day rules and that is where the problem lay. Zimbabwe's bowlers did not have to bowl where the batsmen could hit the ball. So they didn't. Eventually England required 13 from the final over. After Nick Knight had deposited Streak over square leg for six, the target was down to five runs off three balls. The next delivery was unreachable, but not called wide. Five off two became three off one with nine fielders on the boundary. Knight was run out going for the third. The match was drawn with the scores level for the first time in Test history.

The umpires were Steve Dunne of New Zealand and Ian Robinson of Zimbabwe. At a social occasion before the series, Robinson was heard to say, 'I believe I'm one of the best three umpires in the world and not necessarily number three'. The England party would not have had him in their top hundred. They were angry that Robinson, in particular, failed to punish Zimbabwe's tactics by calling wides.

There was controversy in the commentary tent as well. Henry took the view that he had been flown out as the senior commentator and he was determined to be at the microphone when the drama reached its climax. But the climax was a long time coming. Every ball was vital and so Zimbabwe's captain, Alistair Campbell, increasingly aided by the team's player-coach, Dave Houghton, took things slowly. Very slowly indeed.

As it turned out, Henry would have had time to give up the microphone, allow Peter Baxter and me to return for a further 20 minutes each, and still be in position for the game's finale. Henry is teased about this even now and the shout of 'Bulawayo' at the back of the box is the signal for any commentator who has become so wrapped up in the game that he has gone over his allotted time.

I was not aware of Henry's broadcasting marathon at the time because, believing that I had done my final commentary, I left the tent to enjoy the finish elsewhere. By chance, I spent the closing overs in the vicinity of a simmering David Lloyd, the England coach. David had left the dressing room to pace the outfield. He was feeling the pressure and, on a hot afternoon, his frustration spilled over at the end of the match. He clashed with a senior local official in the dressing room area and then fired off to the press. 'We murdered 'em and they know it,' he said. 'We flippin' hammered them. One more ball and we'd have walked it.' It is fair to say those comments stirred up opinion both in Zimbabwe and back home.

But a fraught day had an amusing and uplifting conclusion. The hotel bar in the evening was heaving with players, journalists and some raucous members of the Barmy Army. On seeing the Zimbabwe players, the Army taunted them playfully with choruses of 'you bowl wides and you know you do' to the tune of 'Go West.' The situation had the potential to become embarrassing.

Campbell though handled matters brilliantly. Buoyed by his team's narrow escape and a couple of drinks, he stood up, spread his arms wide and belted out, 'We bowl wides and we know we do.' Everyone laughed, including the England players. They were hurt by failing to win, but did not resent Zimbabwe's tactics. As one England player told me after the game, they would have done the same.

After that he took the plunge of going freelance, while still regularly appearing on Radio Five's sports desk. It enabled him to do other things – newspaper writing and television commentary among them.

Someone – probably trying to provoke him – gave him the nickname 'Grumpy', to which he only occasionally lives up. 'Apprehensive' might have been a more apt name when he was billeted at Langar Hall, the wonderful hotel the *TMS* team always stay at for Trent Bridge Tests, in a chalet in the garden. This is a very comfortable chalet on the edge of the croquet lawn – but also on the edge of the graveyard. The prospect of being alongside the long-departed villagers of Langar did not appeal at all and another volunteer for the hut had to be found. He was more stoical in Chittagong, when spending his 40th birthday in the gloomy Hotel Harbour View – a misnomer on both counts.

He is a very good travelling companion on a tour, tackling any adversities with the appropriate amount of good humour and remaining thoroughly professional in all aspects of the commentary, reporting and interviewing requirements.

Jon Champion (b. 1965)
First *TMS* Test 1997

Jon came to the Radio Sports department at the BBC by the well-trodden route of BBC Local Radio – in his case Radio York and then Radio Leeds, and in his time has covered a great deal of soccer, including three World Cups and also three Olympic Games. But, as a keen club cricketer, he has a special place in his heart for cricket.

Sadly for *Test Match Special*, just as he got his career off to a good start, John was spirited away to ITV as a soccer commentator. During the two Tests on which he worked he had time to reveal an impressive amount of homework and a polished commentary style. It would have been good to have heard more as he relaxed into the job.

Mark Saggers: a real all-rounder, Mark Saggers's voice has become a familiar one to listeners of *TMS* and *Radio Five Live* in recent years.

Arlo White (b. 1973)
First *TMS* Test 2005

By the time he made his *TMS* debut in Multan in Pakistan in November 2005, Arlo had already commentated on a Test series there for Five Live Sports Extra and the BBC Asian Network when they covered the 2004 series between Pakistan and India.

Having already gained broadcasting experience from a stint on Australian commercial radio, Arlo emerged, blinking into the daylight, after two years doing the sports news on Radio Five Live's breakfast programme. Sent out to South Africa as part of a large team for that network's coverage of the 1993 Cricket World Cup, he quickly found himself with the unenviable problems of trying to navigate to a small township ground for a warm-up game and once there attempting to make broadcast contact with London. It was a baptism of fire, but a useful grounding for presenting a day of programmes for Radio Five Live from Soweto.

Mark Saggers (b. 1959) ▶
First *TMS* Test 2006

Mark is surely unique – at least for *TMS* – in that he joined the commentary team having once been the production assistant on the programme. A very accomplished schoolboy cricketer and then minor county wicketkeeper/batsman, he had joined the BBC looking for any career in sports broadcasting. His potential was apparent, even doing the humdrum minutiae of programme administration in the late 1980s.

Radio Cambridgeshire offered him a chance to present and from there came an opening in Sky Sports News. He eventually returned to BBC Radio to present evening and weekend sports programmes on Radio Five Live, round whose schedules his time on *Test Match Special* has to be arranged. After several one day internationals, we managed at last to give him his first Test Match commentary in 2006 at Headingley.

5

THE SUMMARISERS

The 'expert comments man' or summariser was a luxurious addition to radio commentary that came in the early 1950s, some time after Howard Marshall had been allowed the services of a scorer. At the start their major role was to give the commentator a breather between overs, but as fashions in broadcasting changed the style of interaction between the two became more conversational with comments sought and given at any time during play. Usually the expert is selected from candidates with experience of playing Test cricket. Without doubt the finest experts to have appeared on the programme are Fred Trueman and Trevor Bailey and they are remembered in Chapter 7, but this chapter remembers the others who have occupied the summariser's chair for home Tests over the last half-century.

Norman Yardley (1915-1989)
First radio Test 1956

Norman gave a reassuring feeling of friendliness, competence and calm, which probably helped Cambridge University, Yorkshire and England each in turn to make him captain. He was one of those cricketers whose career was interrupted by the Second World War, in which he was wounded while serving in the Army in the Western Desert.

A good enough batsman to pass a thousand runs in a season eight times, he was also a useful seam bowler who claimed Bradman's wicket in three successive Test innings in Australia in 1946–47. He became an England selector while still playing first-class cricket in the 1950s.

He was a regular on radio cricket coverage for nearly 20 years, with an avuncular, sympathetic style that included all and made all criticism charitable. Throughout that time he was a delightful companion in the box.

Ernest Eytle (1918-1968) ▶
First radio Test 1952

Born in British Guiana, Ernest Eytle came to England in 1937 to practise law at the Bar. He was a good enough cricketer though to play for Learie Constantine's XI and the British Empire XI during the Second World War. Having made his first appearance on radio cricket commentary in 1952 at Lord's, he had to wait five years for his second chance during West Indies visit in 1957.

Freddie Brown (1910–1991)
First *TMS* Test 1957

Brown and Yardley were the Bailey and Trueman of *TMS* in their day. Though both were former captains of Cambridge University and went on to be amateur captains and later selectors of England, theirs was a contrast in personalities and styles – Brown larger than life; Yardley quiet and gently mannered.

The story is often told how Brown's leadership on the 1950–51 tour of Australia earned the barrow boy's cry, 'Cauliflowers with hearts as big as Freddie Brown's'. Australia won the first four Tests of that series, but even Australians, it seemed, were happy to see Brown's Trojan efforts rewarded with an eight-wicket win in the final match in Melbourne – a victory to which he contributed six wickets.

His spirit as much as anything else made Len Hutton ask him to play in the 1953 Test Match at Lord's, by which time he was a selector. He came out to bat after the epic Watson/Bailey stand to ensure the draw, which ultimately made the Ashes victory possible.

In the commentary box he was a hearty, tweed-suited presence, bluff and eternally cheerful, giving his opinions as if he was just talking to one person by the fireside.

Richie Benaud (b. 1930) ▼
First *TMS* Test 1960

Another broadcaster thought of as being only a television commentator, Richie made his BBC debut on *Test Match Special* while still playing at the top level. Indeed he was back the following year as captain of Australia to retain the Ashes. It is typical of his meticulous nature that he went on a BBC course in 1956 to learn the art and the basics of broadcasting.

He did four of the five Tests in 1960, but when he returned to a BBC microphone in 1964, it was as a

Ernest Eytle: lawyer, cricketer and pioneer expert summariser, Eytle went on to become an eminent journalist in the Caribbean and to write a famous biography of one of the West Indies finest cricketers: *Frank Worrell: The Career of a Great Cricketer* in 1963.

in British broadcasting, though Australian television audiences still heard his voice and *News of the World* readers still received his opinion.

Ron Roberts (1927–1965)
First *TMS* Test 1964

Ron Roberts was a journalist who organised and managed cricket tours to many non-Test playing countries, several of them under the banner of the International Cavaliers. He worked on three Tests in the summer of 1964 and died the following year at the tragically young age of 38.

Ted Dexter (b. 1935) ▼
First *TMS* Test 1967

Another broadcaster remembered for his time on BBC Television where he started in 1968, Ted Dexter appeared on the programme for one Test the previous year. He was actually back in the England

television commentator. There he worked happily with his great friend, Brian Johnston, until Brian's departure to radio. When the Packer revolution hit cricket in 1977 the two friends found themselves on opposite sides, but valued their friendship so much that they agreed that it would be an utterly taboo subject between them.

Richie had a hand in another revolution, too, when Channel 4 were given the nod over the BBC by the England and Wales Cricket Board for the television rights in 1999. By then he was the senior commentator, helping to pass on his expertise to a new generation. The change from Channel 4 to Sky for the 2006 season spelled the end of his great career

Above Richie Benaud: attended a BBC course on the art of broadcasting in 1956 while still playing at the top level as captain of Australia.

Right Ted Dexter: another TV cricket man who actually began his broadcasting on the radio for *Test Match Special* in 1967, three years before he retired from first-class cricket.

Opposite Mike Gatting: pictured with his favourite people, the *TMS* 'tea ladies', at Trent Bridge in 2002.

side by the end of 1968 for his last two Test Matches and did not retire from first-class cricket until 1970.

It was from the radio commentary box at Lord's in 1963 that John Arlott said of him as he faced Wes Hall, 'There is about Dexter, when he chooses to face fast bowling with determination, a sort of air of command that lifts him above ordinary players. He seems to find time to play the fastest of bowling and still retain dignity – something near majesty – as he does it.'

Many who saw him bat would recognise that.

Mike Gatting (b. 1957) ▲
First *TMS* Test 1981

Mike was to wait 23 years after his *TMS* debut before he returned to the box in England, but on the 1981–82 tour of India, when he failed to make the side for the First Test in Bombay, he first took part in the *Test Match Special* commentary. That Test was memorable for being the only one of the six that produced a positive result, with India winning by 138 runs. 'Gatt's' debut was memorable for the arrival above his head in the less-than-pristine commentary box of a rather unsavoury looking spider, followed shortly by the collapse of the summariser's chair. That is not necessarily the reason it took 23 years to entice him back.

Way back then, as a bustling young all-rounder, through to the present day, as an exceptionally successful and popular President of the Lord's Taverners, Mike has always been approachable and keen to do anything for the game of cricket and those around it.

He takes all the many jokes about his love of food in remarkably good part. 'If Shane Warne's first ball in Tests in England had only been a pork pie, Gatt would have eaten it, instead of being bowled by it,' they say. Onlookers in Calcutta at the Test Match there on the 1984–85 tour observed the captain, David Gower, laughing heartily as he talked to his bowler, Chris Cowdrey. We found out later that the exchange had been,

'Cow, do you want Gatt a yard wider?'

'If he was a yard wider, he'd burst!'

His participation in that 1984–85 tour had been very much on the insistence of David Gower, who had wanted him as his vice captain, against the preference of the selectors. He repaid that faith with his first Test hundred, albeit in a losing cause, in Bombay and then his double-hundred in Madras which helped to secure the series.

It seems astonishing that as England captain he only pulled off two Test wins. But what wins they were – both in Australia on the 1986–87 tour to retain the Ashes against all expectation. The pitfalls of Shakoor Rana, Rothley Court and a subsequent South African adventure lay not too far ahead, but it was a glorious moment in Melbourne, when Gladstone Small held the catch that kept the urn in England.

Colin Milburn (1941–1990) ▶
First *TMS* Test 1983

The tragedy of Colin Milburn's cricket career was its abrupt end when he lost the sight of one eye and damaged the other in a car crash in 1969. His Test career just seemed to be burgeoning, after he had been called from Western Australia, where he was wintering, to join the England team in Pakistan. As soon as he arrived he made a brilliant Test hundred and must surely have been a fixture in the team for the summer ahead.

He remained a jovial, rotund figure, which earned him the nickname, 'Ollie', after Oliver Hardy. Part of his touring experience was to form a duet with

Above Colin Milburn: a fine player and a popular broadcaster with a big personality and an appetite for life to go with it. His fine singing voice was often heard on tour accompanied by pianist, Brian Johnston.

Opposite Robin Jackman: boards a plane in Guyana in 1981. His inclusion in the England team caused the Second Test in Georgetown to be cancelled because of his South African connections.

Brian Johnston. With Brian at the piano, they would sing 'Me and My Shadow'.

After the car accident, Ollie did try to play more first-class cricket for Northamptonshire, but his vision simply was not good enough. When he started on *Test Match Special*, he was working as a holiday camp entertainer, but his employers were always very good about releasing him for a few Tests every summer.

His Geordie accent gave him something different on the commentary team where he was universally popular, though he did blot his copybook memorably during one Headingley Test. During a lengthy Saturday rain break, he fell foul of the extravagant hospitality of Ian Botham and Allan Lamb, who were both out of action with injuries. The jollity continued through the Sunday rest day and so, on the Monday morning, when he was due to feature from the ground on the *Today* programme on Radio 4, he had instead to be phoned at his hotel. He might have got away with it, but when Garry Richardson started the interview with, 'What's the weather like there this morning, Colin?' The response was, 'I don't know, Garry, I'll just get up and draw the curtains to have a look.'

England were playing a Test Match in Jamaica early in 1990, when the news came that he had

collapsed and died in a pub car park. There was no one in cricket who did not feel the world was a poorer place.

Ray Illingworth (b. 1932)
First *TMS* Test 1984

Raymond got into broadcasting the year after he retired from his remarkable career in first-class cricket. The off-spinning, all-rounder had left a championship-winning Yorkshire side to take the captaincy of Leicestershire (where he had the services of the young J. Agnew at his disposal) and in his time there he kept them always in contention for silverware, starting with the Benson and Hedges Cup in 1972. Having never captained his native county, in his first season at Leicester – 1969 – he was also appointed captain of England.

He returned to Yorkshire, after ten years at Leicester, as manager and reacted to three years of frustration by taking over the captaincy at last at the age of 50. The job of England coach also came to him a great deal later than he would have wanted. He took them to South Africa and the World Cup in 1995–96, but by then seemed to have little common ground with his captain, Mike Atherton.

His time with BBC Radio and Television – he alternated between the two – occupied the ten years between playing and managing. He was always one to speak his mind without fear or favour, which made him very much his own man as an expert summariser.

Robin Jackman (b. 1945) ▲
First *TMS* Test 1985

Christened 'the Shoreditch Sparrow' by Alan Gibson in *The Times*, Robin was certainly chirpy and celebrated for one of the loudest appeals in first-class cricket. His legacy in cricket history will always be 'the Jackman affair' when his arrival as a replacement on the 1981 tour of the West Indies caused a Caribbean

MY FIRST TEST MATCH

Mike Selvey

Mike Selvey (centre) makes his *TMS* debut at the 'trestle table' commentary box in Bombay in the company of Michael Carey (second left), Tony Lewis (second right) Ashish Ray (right).

Under the circumstances it was a surprise that the match took place at all. The tour had begun with a brace of tragedies. The team had barely arrived in India at the end of October 1984 when they awoke to hear that the Indian Prime Minister Indira Gandhi had been assassinated. After an uneasy time in New Delhi, the team found respite in Sri Lanka for the period of official mourning in India.

What affected the team on a more personal level, however, was the shooting dead, less than four weeks later on the eve of the First Test, of the British deputy High Commissioner, Percy Norris on the way to work in Bombay. Only the previous evening he had entertained the team at his home and they had got on famously. Understandably, with no established reason for the shooting and no claimant, the players, feeling vulnerable might well have asked to return home, and but for the advice of the Foreign and Commonwealth Office that, on the basis of an uneducated guess, there was no connection between the second assassination and a potential threat to themselves would have done so. Even so there was an element who felt they were railroaded by management into agreeing to stay and play.

India v England First Test

28 November–3 December 1984 Wankhede Stadium, Bombay   Umpires B Ganguli and S Kishen

ENGLAND FIRST INNINGS

G Fowler	c & b Sivaramakrishnan	28
RT Robinson	c Kirmani b Sivaramakrishnan	22
MW Gatting	c & b Sivaramakrishnan	15
* DI Gower	b Kapil Dev	13
AJ Lamb	c Shastri b Kapil Dev	9
CS Cowdrey	c Kirmani b Yadav	13
RM Ellison	b Sivaramakrishnan	1
† PR Downton	not out	37
PH Edmonds	c Gaekwad b Shastri	48
PI Pocock	c Kirmani b Sivaramakrishnan	8
NG Cowans	c Shastri b Sivaramakrishnan	0
Extras	(b 1)	1
Total	(all out, 96.2 overs)	195

Fall of wickets 1-46, 2-51, 3-78, 4-78, 5-93, 6-94, 7-114, 8-175, 9-193

Bowling	O	M	R	W
Kapil Dev	22	8	44	2
Sharma	11	4	28	0
Shastri	17	8	23	1
Amarnath	3	2	1	0
Sivaramakrishnan	31.2	10	64	6
Yadav	12	2	34	1

SECOND INNINGS

G Fowler	lbw b Sivaramakrishnan	55
RT Robinson	lbw b Kapil Dev	1
MW Gatting	c Patil b Sivaramakrishnan	136
* DI Gower	c Vengsarkar b Shastri	2
AJ Lamb	st Kirmani b Sivaramakrishnan	1
CS Cowdrey	c Vengsarkar b Yadav	14
† PR Downton	lbw b Sivaramakrishnan	62
RM Ellison	c Vengsarkar b Yadav	0
PH Edmonds	c Kapil Dev b Sivaramakrishnan	8
PI Pocock	not out	22
NG Cowans	c Vengsarkar b Sivaramakrishnan	0
Extras	(b 4, lb 8, nb 4)	16
Total	(all out, 135 overs)	317

Fall of wickets 1-3, 2-138, 3-145, 4-152, 5-199, 6-222, 7-228, 8-255, 9-317

Bowling	O	M	R	W
Kapil Dev	21	8	34	1
Sharma	9	2	39	0
Shastri	29	8	50	1
Sivaramakrishnan	46	10	117	6
Yadav	29	9	64	2
Gaekwad	1	0	1	0

INDIA FIRST INNINGS

* SM Gavaskar	c Downton b Cowans	27
AD Gaekwad	run out	24
DB Vengsarkar	c Lamb b Cowans	34
M Amarnath	c Cowdrey b Pocock	49
SM Patil	c Gower b Edmonds	20
RJ Shastri	c Lamb b Pocock	142
N Kapil Dev	b Cowdrey	42
† SMH Kirmani	c Lamb b Pocock	102
C Sharma	not out	5
NS Yadav	not out	7
Extras	(b 4, lb 2, nb 7)	13
Total	(8 wks dec, 137 overs)	465
Did not bat	L Sivaramakrishnan	

Fall of wickets 1-47, 2-59, 3-116, 4-156, 5-156, 6-218, 7-453, 8-453

Bowling	O	M	R	W
Ellison	18	3	85	0
Cowans	28	6	109	2
Edmonds	33	6	82	1
Pocock	46	10	133	3
Cowdrey	5	0	30	1
Gatting	7	0	20	0

SECOND INNINGS 48 RUNS TO WIN

* SM Gavaskar	c Gower b Cowans	5
AD Gaekwad	st Downton b Edmonds	1
DB Vengsarkar	not out	21
M Amarnath	not out	22
Extras	(b 2)	2
Total	(2 wks, 15.1 overs)	51
Did not bat	SM Patil, RJ Shastri, N Kapil Dev, † SMH Kirmani, C Sharma, NS Yadav, L Sivaramakrishnan	

Fall of wickets 1-5, 2-7

Bowling	O	M	R	W
Edmonds	8	3	21	1
Cowans	5	2	18	1
Pocock	2.1	0	10	0

India won by 8 wickets

I arrived in Bombay on the morning of the Norris assassination. My playing career had finished that previous summer, my personal life was in limbo and I sought some sanctuary in the game that had enveloped me since early childhood (and which still does). On the basis of a NatWest quarter-final at Taunton, on which I was invited to summarise, Peter Baxter agreed to use me at the first two Tests of the winter, in Bombay and Delhi, where Vic was first to appear on the *TMS* scene while I was confined to the khazi.

The players were nervous before the match. At practice they had joked about the potential for danger, but there was an edge, their sense of security not heightened by one English photographer approaching a senior figure in the promised 'ring of steel' protecting them, stating that he was from the IRA and would like to go to the dressing room, and being escorted there. It was, then, small wonder that England were to lose the opening encounter comfortably by eight wickets.

Broadcasting from the subcontinent was homespun, the links some way from the era of satellite, requiring communication between various transmission stations. The producer's blood pressure rose and fell as a connection was lost here, a wire inadvertently pulled out there, and all the while a crush of people leaning over to watch him at work. For the First Test, we broadcast from a trestle table that had been set up on the terraces of the Wankhede Stadium, the featureless concrete arena that had succeeded the lovely old Brabourne just down the road as a Test venue following a spat between the CCI, India's MCC, who owned it, and the Board of Control. The noise levels, we were to discover as the match moved to its climax, were on the verge of intolerable. The sound of a thunderflash exploding right next to an effects microphone is not readily forgotten.

England were undone by a combination of their own unease, some engagingly erratic umpiring from the enormous figure of the umpire Swaroop Kishen, whose bulk caused bowlers to run wide of the crease, inept batting in the first innings, and some mesmeric leg-spin from the 18-year-old debutant Laxman Sivaramakrishnan. He was a young man so blessed that far from being named after one god, he took on the mantle of three. I was struck by his apparent vulnerability, a slight fellow with limbs like twiglets, and the dark skin and flashing eyes of southern India. His 6 for 64 in the first innings, sent England reeling to 195 all out, with India, themselves in trouble at 156 for 5 at one stage, reaching 465 for 8 declared thanks to centuries from Ravi Shastri and the wicketkeeper Syed Kirmani.

England's response second time around was altogether more accomplished, and characterised by the batting of Mike Gatting who after 53 unsuccessful cracks at it, reached his maiden Test century. I had known Gatting since he first joined Middlesex as a young, slimmer boy with a coalscuttle haircut, and so it was a pleasure to be on air as he approached the milestone. It was not made easy for him by the Indian captain Sunil Gavaskar, who, aware of the occasion, made him wait an eternity on 99 while he set the field, reset it, and then moved everyone back to precisely where they had been in the first place. Undaunted, he advanced down the pitch (to Shiva? I can't quite remember but sentiment demands that it was) and managed to find enough weight in a mistimed attempt at a lofted drive to clear mid-on and give him the run he needed. That Gatting should make a century in such a manner, in such conditions against bowling of this calibre, not just from Shivaramakrishnan, who followed his first-innings haul with 6 for 117 second time around (including Gatting for 136) was typical in that he had been regarded as one of the best readers and players of spin in England. His footwork, fearless on a wearing, albeit slow track, was faultless. Three matches later, in the cauldron at Chepauk in Madras, he went further, making 207 and adding 241 for the second wicket with Graeme Fowler, who made 201. Both, of course, were to become skilled and popular summarisers.

During the match, Peter Baxter was able to supplement his broadcasting team with the occasional player appearance, most notably Allan Lamb, who, on his first stint, was in the process of putting headphones on when an England wicket fell. He used the 'f' word, which went undetected as he had yet to pick up his lip mic. 'Lamby', I whispered, 'you cannot say that on air'. He picked up his mic. 'Shit, did I say that?'

journalist to question his South African connections at a time when that country was still a pariah under the apartheid regime.

Jackman had a South African wife and spent his English winters playing there for Western Province. Some Caribbean countries took a harder line than others over the presence of South African stamps in a passport and Guyana, where the 'affair' blew up, was one of them. The Guyana Test Match was cancelled and the governments of the other countries held talks in Barbados to decide whether the tour could continue. It did and Jackman found himself playing his first Test in Barbados – even taking a wicket in his first over.

He started to express an interest in broadcasting while still playing for Surrey, even auditioning as a ball-by-ball commentator. When he retired from first-class cricket, though, he went to live in Cape Town, so the work he did as a summariser had to be fitted in when he came over to England. However, in South Africa he started a very successful career as a television commentator, retaining the same cheerful irreverence that characterised his playing career.

Jack Bannister (b. 1930) ▶
First *TMS* Test 1985

A fast medium bowler for Warwickshire for 20 years, Jack retired from the game at the end of the 1969 season and went into journalism for the *Birmingham Post* and Mail, drawing on a rich experience of county cricket and many a yarn about its characters.

He provided the original 'leg over' remark – years before Aggers joined the BBC – when he was helping out by joining in an ABC commentary on a one-day international in Australia. As he later said, 'like a

Above Jack Bannister (left) and Peter Baxter are reduced to covering the start of the Lahore Test in 1987 on the telephone, while the broadcasting lines are connected.

Overleaf Vic Marks: who was advised on his unexpected *TMS* debut in India in 1984 to, 'sit down and have a conversation, and shut up when the bowler's running up to bowl'.

rabbit in the headlights', he followed a comment on David Gower's lack of footwork from his summariser, 'Gower would have done better to get his leg over', by saying, 'Wouldn't we all?'

He also participated brilliantly in an elaborate wind-up of Aggers, when he and Fred Trueman were being interviewed by Jonathan, as he believed, live on BBC television. A rambling answer from Trueman was capped by Jack saying only, 'Well, I agree with Fred,' as Aggers floundered.

Jack was another who alternated between television and radio and then later helped to set up the Talk Sport commentary that secured a few overseas contracts in 1999, displacing *Test Match Special* from five England tours.

Mike Selvey (b. 1948)
First *TMS* Test 1984

'Selve' was a consistently useful fast-medium bowler for Middlesex, who found himself – as a result of a string of injuries to other candidates – propelled into the England team at Old Trafford in 1976. He had a sensational start – a wicket in his first over and by halfway through his fourth over he had figures of 3 for 6. He finished that Test Match with six West Indian wickets, but a century in each innings for Gordon Greenidge and the usual devastating fast bowling meant that he finished on the losing side.

After 11 seasons at Middlesex, he accepted an invitation to captain Glamorgan, which he did for a couple of years, before retiring to take up journalism. Speculatively, he went to India for the start of the 1984–85 England tour, writing pieces for the *Guardian* and making his *Test Match Special* debut in the less than salubrious commentary position in Bombay.

He was still there for the Second Test in Delhi, but on the final morning of what became a great England victory, he found himself caught short in the way travellers in those parts of the world often do and beat a hasty retreat.

Vic Marks (b. 1955) ▲
First *TMS* Test 1984

Plucked from the England dressing room in Delhi, with Mike Selvey detained in the smallest room, Victor's celebrated chuckle quickly endeared him to listeners and he and Selve (though they did not work together on that tour) became the Fred and Trevor of the start of the 21st century. Victor's book, *Marks Out of Eleven*, reflects the great spirit that existed within the team and between players and press on that tour. It is no coincidence that the founding members of TMS's 'County Talk' all came from that team.

Vic Marks

I have always held Michael Selvey in the highest esteem. He can smite a golf ball 250 yards – actually several of us can but his ball usually stays on the fairway; he understands how my laptop works and on 17 December 1984 he had the good grace to succumb to Delhi belly.

England were engaged in a Test Match against India, the second of the series; I was engaged on twelfth man duties, my usual function on overseas expeditions. Already it had been a tumultuous tour. Six hours after our arrival in India Mrs Gandhi had been assassinated. Amid the public unrest we all assumed that we would be flying straight back home. Instead, after a week imprisoned in a luxury hotel in Delhi, we took refuge in Sri Lanka for ten days.

A couple of weeks later on the eve of the First Test in Bombay the British deputy High Commissioner, Percy Norris, was assassinated. This time we were sure we were going home. Whereupon David Gower, toured the rooms with his henchman, Mike Gatting, to announce that we were going nowhere except to the Wankhede Stadium for some practise. 'What? Target practise?' enquired Graeme Fowler. Unsurprisingly England lost that Test by eight wickets. The fear was that from now onwards the pitches

Having just started his *TMS* career Vic Marks (left) felt the need to celebrate by appearing with Chris Cowdrey as the two wise men at the England team's Christmas party in Calcutta, 1984.

India v England Second Test

12–17 December 1984 Feroz Shah Kotla, Delhi

Umpires **DN Dotiwalla and PD Reporter**

INDIA FIRST INNINGS

* SM Gavaskar	c Downton b Ellison	1
AD Gaekwad	b Pocock	28
DB Vengsarkar	st Downton b Edmonds	24
M Amarnath	c Gower b Pocock	42
SM Patil	c Pocock b Edmonds	30
RJ Shastri	c Fowler b Pocock	2
N Kapil Dev	c Downton b Ellison	60
† SMH Kirmani	c Gatting b Ellison	27
M Prabhakar	c Downton b Ellison	25
NS Yadav	not out	28
L Sivaramakrishnan	run out	25
Extras	(b 1, lb 12, nb 2)	15
Total	(all out, 125.2 overs)	307

Fall of wickets 1-3, 2-56, 3-68, 4-129, 5-131, 6-140, 7-208 8-235, 9-258

Bowling	O	M	R	W
Cowans	20	5	70	0
Ellison	26	6	66	4
Edmonds	44.2	16	83	2
Pocock	33	8	70	3
Gatting	2	0	5	0

SECOND INNINGS

* SM Gavaskar	b Pocock	65
M Prabhakar	c Downton b Cowans	5
DB Vengsarkar	b Cowans	1
M Amarnath	b Edmonds	64
SM Patil	c Lamb b Edmonds	41
RJ Shastri	not out	25
N Kapil Dev	c Lamb b Pocock	7
AD Gaekwad	c Downton b Edmonds	0
† SMH Kirmani	b Pocock	6
NS Yadav	c Lamb b Edmonds	1
L Sivaramakrishnan	c & b Pocock	0
Extras	(b 6, lb 10, w 1, nb 3)	20
Total	(all out, 103.4 overs)	235

Fall of wickets 1-12, 2-15, 3-136, 4-172, 5-207, 6-214, 7-216, 8-225, 9-234

Bowling	O	M	R	W
Cowans	13	2	43	2
Ellison	7	1	20	0
Edmonds	44	24	60	4
Pocock	38.4	9	93	4
Gatting	1	0	3	0

ENGLAND FIRST INNINGS

G Fowler	c Gaekwad b Prabhakar	5
RT Robinson	c Gavaskar b Kapil Dev	160
MW Gatting	b Yadav	26
AJ Lamb	c Vengsarkar b Yadav	52
* DI Gower	lbw b Sivaramakrishnan	5
CS Cowdrey	c Gavaskar b Sivaramakrishnan	38
† PR Downton	c Kapil Dev b Sivaramakrishnan	74
PH Edmonds	c Shastri b Sivaramakrishnan	26
RM Ellison	b Sivaramakrishnan	10
PI Pocock	b Sivaramakrishnan	0
NG Cowans	not out	0
Extras	(b 6, lb 13, nb 3)	22
Total	(all out, 169.1 overs)	418

Fall of wickets 1-15, 2-60, 3-170, 4-181, 5-237, 6-343 7-398, 8-411, 9-415

Bowling	O	M	R	W
Kapil Dev	32	5	87	1
Prabhakar	21	3	68	1
Sivaramakrishnan	49.1	17	99	6
Yadav	36	6	95	2
Shastri	29	4	44	0
Amarnath	2	0	6	0

SECOND INNINGS 125 RUNS TO WIN

G Fowler	c Vengsarkar b Sivaramakrishnan	29
RT Robinson	run out	18
MW Gatting	not out	30
AJ Lamb	not out	37
Extras	(b 4, lb 7, nb 2)	13
Total	(2 wks, 23.4 overs)	127
Did not bat	* DI Gower, CS Cowdrey, † PR Downton, PH Edmonds, RM Ellison, PI Pocock, NG Cowans	

Fall of wickets 1-41, 2-68

Bowling	O	M	R	W
Kapil Dev	6	0	20	0
Prabhakar	3	0	18	0
Sivaramakrishnan	8	0	41	1
Yadav	2	0	7	0
Shastri	4	0	20	0
Gavaskar	0.4	0	10	0

England won by 8 wickets

would become flatter and that four turgid draws would follow, as had been the case on England's previous tour under Keith Fletcher in 1981–82.

The day before the Second Test in Delhi John Thicknesse of the *Evening Standard*, sought the opinion of Sunil Gavaskar, the Indian captain. 'Have you seen the Taj Mahal?' asked Sunil mysteriously. 'Yes', replied Thicknesse. 'Well, if you want to go again, book up on the fourth or fifth day of the Test match'.

In fact the pitch declined to deteriorate as expected. At lunch on the fifth day India led by 95 with 6 wickets remaining. There was an air of resignation in the English dressing room, soon to be replaced by one of astonishment. Our captain was the charming, laid-back, unruffled David Gower, who now proceeded to harangue his men at full volume in unadulterated Anglo-Saxon. Who taught him all those words? The message, suitably diluted for public consumption, was 'Do you want to win this Test or not?'

Well, England wanted to win it more than India wanted to save it. In a wanton display of batsmanship after lunch Kapil Dev holed out to long-off and with India losing six wickets for 28 runs, England required a mere 125 runs for victory in 32 overs. It was about this time that the familiar loping gait of the *TMS* producer, Peter Baxter, could be spotted at the back of the pavilion in Delhi. Not for the first time in India Baxter had a problem.

Subsequently I've seen Baxter's serene, phlegmatic nature tested to the full on the subcontinent as he tries to find that line to London. I can picture a commentary box in Calcutta, filled with delightful ladies, who were on hand to provide technical aid to the BBC. Unfortunately none of them spoke a word of English and Baxter's face acquired the hue of a beetroot as he bellowed hopelessly, 'London. Get me London'.

Then a more tranquil moment when Baxter pointed to a solitary, frayed, seemingly random piece of wire, which looked as if it could snap at any time as it meandered around the commentary box. 'See that wire: that's our connection to London', he explained.

None of us really knows how he does it. I'm not sure he does. But out of his Mary Poppins bag, he can produce the right screwdriver, the ubiquitous roll of black sticky tape and – in dire emergencies – the bottle opener, and somehow we get through.

But on this particular occasion Baxter was not preoccupied by a technical problem. He lacked manpower. England were on the verge of an epic victory in Delhi and he had no summariser. The urbane Abbas Ali Baig, once of Somerset and India, had casually announced at the start of the match that he had to attend a wedding at some point during the game. What the producer may not have recognised immediately was that an Indian wedding can last a couple of days. There was no chance of Baig being around for the end of the Test. But he had Selvey up his sleeve, until Selvey succumbed. Anyone who has been afflicted by stomach cramps in Delhi or anywhere else in India knows that this is no time for heroics. A hasty retreat to the hotel is the only option.

So Baxter pops his head into the dressing room. In those days that was possible; the England dressing room did not yet resemble Fort Knox. On that tour, with no Ian Botham to excite the tabloids, players and press (about a dozen stalwarts) drank in the same bars and travelled in the same buses. I was stationed there alongside assistant manager, Norman Gifford, who had just filled his pipe in anticipation of the climax of the match (that would not happen today either). 'I need a summariser now', said Baxter. 'Anyone will do'. I volunteered. So I sat alongside Michael Carey and Tony Lewis, while Mike Gatting and Allan Lamb knocked off the runs. I remember being struck by how excited this pair and Baxter were about England's imminent victory. I don't suppose they had witnessed many like it.

Moreover on that tour there was an unusually close bond between players and press. There were times when we felt tossed in the deep end together. Twenty years on, I can still recall the Christmas party (press and players together) and the musical parodies of Carey and Baxter: 'I'm Dreaming of Sivaramakrishnan' and 'Old Man Robbo', a tribute to Tim Robinson, who had been prolific in the series:

He's not like Gower, he's not like Gatting.
For some strange reason he keeps on batting.
Dat old man Robbo he just keeps batting along.

So does *TMS*, though how it will survive on future tours of India without Baxter's Mary Poppins bag is a mystery.

Captain of Oxford University in 1976, Vic had made his Somerset debut the previous year as an off-spinning, all-rounder. During the final Test of 2006, a helpful listener and regular correspondent checked and endorsed his belief that Vic was 'the most plundered bowler' of the 1980s – conceding more runs in that decade than any other bowler. But, as a charitable colleague pointed out, he had to have been a decent bowler to be kept on long enough to go for all those runs.

In his last three Test innings – in Pakistan in 1984 – he scored 83, 74 and 55 and for 17 years he had the best one-day international bowling figures for England – taking 5 for 20 against New Zealand in Wellington also in 1984.

His retirement from playing the game was settled between spells as a *TMS* summariser on a NatWest semi-final in 1989 at Southampton, where he received the offer to become the Cricket Correspondent of the *Observer*. On his first tour in that role that winter, he distinguished himself at a Graham Gooch press conference in Jamaica by answering a question put by the correspondent of the *Evening Standard* with, 'Oh, well, that's obvious …'

'Maybe, Victor', said that very senior journalist, 'But I'd much rather the captain told me so.'

With just the right touch of expertise, self-effacing humour and lightness of touch, Victor is surely the classic voice of *Test Match Special*.

David Lloyd (b. 1947) ▶
First *TMS* Test 1990

Before 'Bumble' had his first go as a summariser on *TMS*, it had been mentioned by a number of people that he was such a good after-dinner speaker that he would surely make a great broadcaster. We started him on the Refuge Cup in 1989, the short-lived end of season knockout competition for the top four teams in the Sunday League, and in his first match at Old Trafford, he found himself in the potentially awkward position of being at the microphone when his son, Graham, took the field. He coped with it with his usual humour, 'I'm sure I left him still in bed this morning.'

The next season he joined *Test Match Special* proper, quickly enjoying and adding to the fun of the box. Early on in his time a 'View from the Boundary' interview was picked with an eye on our then network hosts, Radio 3. The conductor, James Judd, was on his way to an engagement with the Halle Orchestra, when he joined us at Edgbaston.

Brian Johnston always got a little worried about interviewing someone of whom he knew very little and so on this occasion Bumble decided to help. On BBC headed paper he wrote a few notes, which purported to come from a senior music producer, telling Brian that James Judd was sponsored by Weetabix to be the principal conductor of the Reykjavík Symphony Orchestra, that he was a keen supporter of Aldershot Football Club and that he kept ferrets, which gave him the nickname in music circles of, 'Ratty'.

David Lloyd: became a first-class umpire shortly after his retirement from playing in 1985, he then joined *TMS* in 1990. A six-year stint in the box ended when he was appointed England coach. He is now a fixture on Sky television.

The note was put through the photocopier, so that it looked like an incoming fax and – slightly to our surprise – the normally difficult to fool Brian lapped it up. Happily, Mr Judd enjoyed the joke, too, and a week or two later we all received CDs of Elgar's First Symphony, signed 'Ratty Judd'.

After Brian's death, the duty of the 'View from the Boundary' interviewing was passed around the box and Bumble's first allocation was the Scottish goalkeeper, Andy Goram, who also played cricket for his country and had had a youth trial for Lancashire. David was up very early to do his homework and was noticeably tense as the interval approached. The problem was, however, that Andy Goram never showed up and, despite many enquiries, we never found out what happened to him.

David Lloyd's nickname 'Bumble' came in his early days at Lancashire at a time when the comedian, Michael Bentine, had a television show which included some extraordinary puppet characters, 'the Bumblies'. Someone in the dressing room felt there was a distinct resemblance in the new recruit. Others agreed and the name stuck.

Bumble has always been passionate about his cricket: as captain of Lancashire, in which capacity he took the county to three successive Gillette Cup finals, or as coach of either county or country. A tense finish can get him very wound up when he is involved with the team such as when he became England's coach in 1996. It led to the infamous 'we murdered 'em' comment in Zimbabwe. England had just ended a Test Match in Bulawayo with the scores level, but England not yet all out – so, a draw, rather than a tie. The England coach, keen to state his team's near triumph in what had been a tremendous run-chase, told a press conference and then a radio interview that, 'I was here and I know that we've murdered 'em.'

His time as England coach ended with the rather lacklustre performance by the team in the World Cup in England in 1999, when they failed – almost carelessly – to reach the second phase of the tournament. A quiet preparatory word had been muttered in his ear months before that about a possible return to radio and *Test Match Special*, but the offer that came from Sky television represented lucrative full-time security.

He remains a welcome visitor to the radio box, perhaps his heart's home, and he still arrives frequently bearing spoof messages signed by people with dubious names.

Mike Hendrick (b. 1948)
First *TMS* Test 1993

The good common sense that made Mike such a reliable seam bowler for Derbyshire and England – for whom he played 30 Tests – was brought to his time on the air, which only came to an end in 1995 when he moved to Ireland to take over as coach of the Ireland cricket team.

During his time at Derbyshire he used to stage a comedy double act with Geoff Miller. They played two old yokels expressing their opinions on the game in hand. That great sense of humour stood him in good stead in the commentary box from where he performed admirably during his two-year stint.

Graham Gooch (b. 1953) ▼
First *TMS* Test 1994

Graham had not finished his Test career when he expressed an interest in coming to Jamaica to act as the *TMS* summariser for the First Test of the 1994 England tour of the West Indies. To have the captain of the England side that had won at Sabina Park on the previous tour gave the BBC team a great edge.

As England captain he was always careful not to fall into the trap of saying too much, having seen all too well how the unguarded word can get you into trouble in the press. Happily, as a summariser he has a bit more to say and it is a huge asset to have one of the great players of his generation in the box, giving the benefit of the experience of 118 Tests. That experience is also passed on to those he coaches at Essex, the county whose interests he proudly wears on his sleeve.

Graeme Fowler (b. 1957)
First *TMS* Test 1995

'Foxy' Fowler makes up the last of the trio that first appeared on the programme as part of the 'County Talk' feature. As a player and a broadcaster he has always been just that little bit different. He has that cheerfully relaxed Lancastrian humour about him, coming, like David Lloyd, originally from Accrington.

Also like Bumble, he was a left-handed opening batsman, though his flamboyance at the crease was more evident. He was one of those for whom a swing

Above Graham Gooch (right) makes his debut in the commentary box with Christopher Martin-Jenkins and scorer Keith Booth in the West Indies in 1994.

Opposite Chris Cowdrey: son of the great Colin Cowdrey, Chris nearly got his father arrested by taking the wicket of Kapil Dev in his first over in Test cricket causing dad, listening on the car radio back home, to turn the wrong way up a one-way street in his excitement.

and a miss was more of a cause for amusement than self-recrimination and he was likely to put that behind him and drill the next ball for four.

He is another who has made a great name for himself as an after-dinner speaker and appears, too, on Sky television. But his day job is as coach of the Durham University Cricket Centre of Excellence, an idea that he pioneered, and he also coaches the British Universities team. There are several young players who have come to the forefront or are on the verge of doing so, who owe a lot to him.

Foxy's greatest moment on the field was the double-century he scored at Madras in 1985, to help England to go one-up in the series. A *Daily Mail* cartoon of the time had a man shovelling snow from his front path, angrily also shovelling away a radio, which is saying, 'And another four for Fowler, pluckily toiling away in this fierce Madras heat.'

It was Graeme's first connection, perhaps, with *Test Match Special*.

Chris Cowdrey (b. 1957) ▶
First *TMS* Test 1995

If Chris has felt the burden of following such a famous father as Colin Cowdrey, he has worn it lightly. There is the tale of the late Lord Cowdrey listening on his car radio as his son was given his first bowl in Test cricket in Bombay at the end of 1984. In his excitement, he turned the wrong way into a one-way street and was stopped by a policeman. As he was explaining the reason for this aberration, Chris took his first Test wicket. The policeman joined in the celebration by letting Cowdrey senior off.

In fact, Chris was a very different sort of player than his father and was particularly effective as a one-day all-rounder in a successful Kent side. His captaincy of that side led to him being made captain of England in the chaos that followed the sacking of Mike Gatting in 1988. It was originally a two-match appointment, but the first hint of an injury led the selectors to change their minds after just one Test.

That experience fuelled some excellent and very amusing anecdotes in the relaxed style that made Chris an entertaining summariser on *Test Match Special*. It was a disappointment, therefore, when he left us for Talk Sport when they were surprisingly awarded the broadcasting rights for the 1999–2000 England tour of South Africa. For him though, the move satisfied his desire to move from the summariser's chair into ball-by-ball commentary.

Geoff Boycott (b. 1940) ▼
First *TMS* Test 1995

His habit and indeed love of being outspoken has made Geoffrey an often controversial figure, but one always sought out for his views on cricket matters. It is the product of 108 Test Matches in a playing career that also courted its fair share of controversy. In the middle – as now in the commentary box – he liked to do things his way.

Though he did not take part in *Test Match Special* in England until 2006, his first appearances as a

summariser were in 1995 in South Africa. There he was the unaccustomed victim of an Agnew leg-pull. Aggers worked out that, as we were sharing commentary with SABC, there were periods when they were taking their commentary in Afrikaans from the next-door box. One of these spells each day coincided with Radio 4 being away for *Yesterday in Parliament*. So, for 25 minutes, we were not broadcasting live to anyone, just recording the commentary for archive highlights. 'Of course, you were a very stodgy player, Geoffrey,' said Jonathan. Boycott looked a little surprised as Aggers described the next ball. Then, 'I mean really boring.'

Geoff tried to change the subject, but Aggers persisted, slipping in between commentary on each delivery, 'God, you were boring!' It was some time – an uncomfortable time for one member of the team – before Radio 4 listeners were welcomed back. 'Good to have you back at the Wanderers. We have

just been talking to ourselves for the last half-hour or so.' The penny dropped for Geoff and the celebrated lop-sided grin reappeared.

Angus Fraser (b. 1965)
First *TMS* Test 2001

The somewhat weary look that Angus carried as a bowler for Middlesex and – in 46 Tests – for England is echoed these days in the press box as a deadline for the *Independent* newspaper approaches. It belies a great sense of humour, keen spirit and a passionate love of the traditional form of the game. That love has been recognised by the ICC to the extent of putting him on their cricket committee – a position

that sees him generally ribbed in the commentary box over any innovation in the running of the game, which his colleagues always claim is the product of another few days on the beach in Dubai.

Gus's world-weary look may have been caused by some of the slings and arrows of fortune. For instance, when he took a magnificent 5 for 28 in Jamaica, to set up the win in the First Test of the 1990 series, Allan Lamb's century stole the headlines. And in Barbados four years later a first-innings 8 for 75 failed to win him the Man of the Match award, which went to Alec Stewart for his century in each innings. Such whims of fate are greeted with the wryest of smiles.

... and in support

From the start of *Test Match Special* in 1957 until 1973 the cricket producer was Michael Tuke-Hastings. For much of that time he was also producing the quiz programmes, *Treble Chance*, *Sporting Chance* and *Forces Chance*. A large, fair-haired man, he had a certain presence, which probably was the cause of an attendant mishearing him one day and announcing his arrival at a reception as, 'Michael, Duke of Hastings'. He wore the title well.

Until the early 1980s outside broadcasts outside London – such as Test Matches at Trent Bridge, Edgbaston or Headingley – were always in the hands of a regional producer. Don Mosey was in charge of BBC North until he became a commentator in 1973, while in the Midlands the producer for many years was Richard Maddock.

A charming man, Dick had been a television announcer and his voice became familiar to *TMS* listeners as he was frequently called to do the studio presentation when a Test Match was away from his region. His retirement from the BBC at the start of the 1980s largely ended the regional producer's role on the programme.

Almost ever-present in the commentary box since the start of cricket coverage has been the scorer. Jack Price and Arthur Wrigley were in at the start, but since the mid-1960s it has been Bill Frindall who has supplied the dots and the records. Brian Johnston recognised what a wonder he was and, shrewdly noticing a beard, made the leap of christening Bill the 'Bearded Wonder' – inevitably shortened to 'Bearders'. He has chronicled his arrival in the commentary box elsewhere in this book.

For a short spell, Bill combined his *TMS* job with that of Cricket Correspondent of the *Mail on Sunday*. That meant that he could not score for us on the Saturday of a Test Match and he used to hand over the precious scoresheets to a stand-in. For the two London grounds it would be Peter Byrne, a familiar figure in the Lord's press box. In the Midlands the job was done by Ian Croxall, whose beautiful copperplate

writing was already celebrated by all those who had had his assistance at county matches. And in the North, Malcolm Ashton was the man. He was to go on to a more permanent position with television, which led to him becoming the England scorer on tour and then the analyst.

Finally, and to many of us most importantly, we come to the production assistants, whose role (and indeed job title) has increased steadily over the years. Inevitably there used to be quite a turnover, but somehow over the last 20 years, we have enjoyed the support of three remarkably able young women. Kate Hempsall eventually left to pursue a career in public relations starting with Surrey County Cricket Club. Her successor, Louise Jones, was a wonderful 'gatekeeper' for the programme and outstandingly efficient. That brings us to Shilpa Patel. She is simply the best 'fixer' imaginable. The arranging of the guests for 'A View from the Boundary' has gradually become almost exclusively her preserve. She can produce almost any dignitary in the commentary box for an interview and, among all the other administrative tasks that keep the programme going in an increasingly bureaucratic world, she charms hotel reservations staff into giving us favourable rates wherever we go. Commentators who vacillate over their bookings, though, soon find out that her tongue can have a sharp edge to it. Suffice to say that we are now utterly dependent on her.

MY FIRST TEST MATCH

Angus Fraser

My earliest memories of *Test Match Special* are from the winter of 1978–79, when Alastair, my brother, and I used to play floodlit Subbuteo cricket on our bedroom floor whilst listening to commentary of England's successful defence of the Ashes. In our pyjamas and dressing gowns, and with plastic Subbuteo floodlights acting as illumination, we would play our own mini Test Matches during the Christmas holidays whilst the voices of Christopher Martin-Jenkins and Alan McGilvray described the action from Melbourne and Sydney.

During this period coverage of England tours was limited, with visits to Australia being the only matches that were consistently covered. But the crackled

commentary of what was taking place had a profound effect on Alastair and me, in that it strengthened our desire to one day be out there playing on that stage.

By 1982–83 we had grown out of Subbuteo, preferring instead to lie in bed listening to the coverage. Yet I can still remember Henry Blofeld's description of the dismissal of Jeff Thomson – caught by Geoff Miller at slip via Chris Tavare, off Ian Botham's bowling – a wicket that took England to a dramatic three-run victory over Australia in Melbourne.

As a professional cricketer with Middlesex, *TMS* gave me enormous pleasure too. When I wasn't playing for England my radio would be set on 198 long wave whenever there was a Test or other international match

India v England First Test

3–6 December 2001 Punjab CA Stadium, Mohali, Chandigarh Umpires **SA Bucknor (WI) and S Venkataraghavan**

ENGLAND FIRST INNINGS

MA Butcher	c Laxman b Yohannan	4
ME Trescothick	b Yohannan	66
* N Hussain	c Laxman b Kumble	85
GP Thorpe	c Laxman b Siddiqui	23
MR Ramprakash	c Das b Harbhajan Singh	17
A Flintoff	c Kumble b Harbhajan Singh	18
C White	c Dravid b Kumble	5
† JS Foster	lbw b Harbhajan Singh	0
J Ormond	not out	3
RKJ Dawson	c Laxman b Harbhajan Singh	5
MJ Hoggard	c sub b Harbhajan Singh	0
Extras	(lb 7, nb 5)	12
Total	(all out, 76.3 overs)	238

Fall of wickets 1-4, 2-129, 3-172, 4-200, 5-224, 6-227, 7-229, 8-229, 9-238

Bowling	O	M	R	W
Yohannan	18	3	75	2
Siddiqui	11	2	32	1
Bangar	5	2	17	0
Kumble	19	6	52	2
Tendulkar	4	3	4	0
Harbhajan Singh	19.3	4	51	5

SECOND INNINGS

MA Butcher	c sub b Yohannan	18
ME Trescothick	c Siddiqui b Yohannan	46
* N Hussain	b Kumble	12
GP Thorpe	c & b Kumble	62
MR Ramprakash	lbw b Kumble	28
A Flintoff	c Ganguly b Kumble	4
C White	c Dasgupta b Harbhajan Singh	22
† JS Foster	lbw b Harbhajan Singh	5
J Ormond	b Kumble	0
RKJ Dawson	b Kumble	11
MJ Hoggard	not out	0
Extras	(b 10, lb 13, w 1, nb 3)	27
Total	(all out, 77.4 overs)	235

Fall of wickets 1-68, 2-82, 3-87, 4-159, 5-163, 6-196, 7-206, 8-207, 9-224

Bowling	O	M	R	W
Yohannan	17	3	56	2
Siddiqui	8	3	16	0
Kumble	28.4	6	81	6
Harbhajan Singh	24	9	59	2

INDIA FIRST INNINGS

SS Das	b Butcher	2
† D Dasgupta	b White	100
A Kumble	c Foster b Dawson	37
R Dravid	lbw b Ormond	86
SR Tendulkar	c Foster b Hoggard	88
* SC Ganguly	c Thorpe b Hoggard	47
VVS Laxman	c Hussain b Dawson	28
SB Bangar	c & b Dawson	36
Harbhajan Singh	lbw b Dawson	1
IR Siddiqui	b Hoggard	24
T Yohannan	not out	2
Extras	(lb 12, w 2, nb 4)	18
Total	(all out, 169 overs)	469

Fall of wickets 1-23, 2-76, 3-212, 4-290, 5-370, 6-378, 7-430, 8-436, 9-449

Bowling	O	M	R	W
Hoggard	32	9	98	3
Ormond	28	8	70	1
Butcher	7	1	19	1
Flintoff	34	11	80	0
White	25	8	56	1
Dawson	43	6	134	4

SECOND INNINGS 5 TO WIN

IR Siddiqui	not out	5
† D Dasgupta	not out	0
Extras		0
Total	(no wickets, 0.2 overs)	5
Did not bat	R Dravid, VVS Laxman, SR Tendulkar, *SC Ganguly, SB Bangar, A Kumble, Harbhajan Singh, SS Das, T Yohannan	

Fall of wickets -

Bowling	O	M	R	W
Hoggard	0.2	0	5	0

India won by 10 wickets

being played. But it was not just the fact that I was listening to cricket that made it appealing, it was also the way in which the game was covered. There were characters in the *TMS* box, and there was also a sense of fun and mischief.

An example of this came in the mid-1990s, involving the late, great Fred Trueman. It was on a Sunday morning during a break in play when I was travelling to Trent Bridge to play for Middlesex. As I drove into the ground the topic of conversation on the radio turned to David Lloyd, the England coach, and his desperate attempts to motivate his under-performing team. Bumble had strategically placed large placards around the dressing room with WIN, PRIDE, COMMITMENT, PASSION and DETERMINATION written on them. He had also resorted to playing recordings of Winston Churchill's speeches to the players in the hope that it may kick them in to action.

Knowing that this sort of thing wound Fred up hugely, Aggers asked him what he thought of it all. Well Fred set off, starting with something like, 'I just cannot understand what is going off in there.' My travelling companion left the car and went to the dressing room with the message that I would be along shortly. Another 15 minutes followed with Fred tearing in to this, that and everything. By that time I had tears rolling down my cheeks. I was late for the team meeting but I didn't care – it was absolutely brilliant. Fred finished by saying, 'When I was playing for England I didn't need motivating. I had them three Lions on me chest and that were enough for me. When I arrived at ground I'd knock on the opposition's dressing room door, stick me head round, and say, "Five of you get your pads on 'coz I'm on fire today."'

My first proper involvement with *TMS* came during the winter of 2001–02. My England career was over and Peter phoned me up to ask me whether I would like to cover the Test series in India before Christmas, and the one-day series against India and New Zealand that followed. I had acted as a summariser on a couple of occasions before and enjoyed it enormously, so I jumped at the opportunity.

At the age of 36, like most other players, I was wondering what I would do following my retirement. Coaching appeared to be favoured option, but that winter with *TMS* gave me a taste of what it was like working in the media. My first thought, and it is one that still remains with me, is that this wasn't a bad way of spending my post playing days. On the tours I spent a great deal of time talking with the *TMS* commentators, and in particular Jonathan Agnew. Aggers informed me that the BBC rarely took summarisers with them on overseas tours, and that getting a position with the written media would be the best way of becoming a regular both at home and abroad.

The opportunity came within weeks of my return to England when Paul Newman, then Sports Editor at the *Independent*, phoned me for a chat. Derek Pringle had moved from the *Independent* to the *Daily Telegraph*, and within a week I had been offered the chance to become Cricket Correspondent for a national newspaper.

During the five years I have been associated with *TMS* I have been amazed at the popularity of the programme. At the cricket dinners I go to I am constantly fielding questions related to *TMS* and the nature of the characters I work with. I am often asked if is it really as much fun as it sounds. Well, yes it is. Listeners suggest that the commentary sounds like mates relaxing in a bar chatting about the cricket and, in my opinion, that is just how it feels. A 30-minute summarising stint goes in a flash and it is with regret that you vacate the seat for the next person.

I believe that *TMS* benefits enormously from having trained journalists filling many of the top positions. With them comes skill, experience and different opinions, along with the desire to cut through the rubbish, ask the tough questions and get to the bottom of a story. I feel there is a tendency for former players to get too wrapped up in it all, get too analytical and take it too seriously. There are obviously times when commentators and summarisers need to be thoughtful and critical, but we should not forget that cricket is only a game and people tune in to be entertained by what they see and hear.

As a member of the ICC Cricket Committee, which attempts to come up with innovative ideas that take the game forward, I take a lot of unfair flak. Yes, we do visit Dubai for a couple of days each year, and we do stay in nice hotels. But, to the contrary of views held by Agnew, Blofeld, CMJ, Vic Marks and others, we do not sit around the pool on sun loungers, drinking cocktails all afternoon.

Working for *TMS* – if it really is work – continues to be an enormous pleasure, even when a newspaper deadline looms and I am yet to get a word down, and I hope to be part of the set-up for many years to come.

MY FIRST TEST MATCH

Shilpa Patel

It took me ten years to move from the ground floor of the Lord's pavilion to the rooftop. I suppose by the standards of the day that was pretty quick promotion for a woman. In the mid-1980s, I was in charge of the Bowlers' Bar which was just beneath the away dressing room – men only, of course. On 22 June 1995, I arrived at Lord's for the start of the Second Test against the West Indies. The stewards took some persuading to let me in and the early arrivals among MCC members were polite – but clearly startled. I had never seen so many raised eyebrows in such a short time but I knew where I was going. To the roof – to the *Test Match Special* box – to become Backers' production assistant.

I already knew Lord's well – it had become my second home long before my stint in the Bowlers' Bar. I grew up in a cricket loving family – indeed I regarded myself as no mean left-handed batsman in my younger days. It's strange what tricks time can play on the memory! I was lucky enough to witness at first hand Collis King winning the World Cup for West Indies in 1979 and Kapil Dev saving the follow-on in the First Test against England in 1990 with four towering sixes. I was a long-standing member of Middlesex County Cricket Club too, so I was

Shilpa Patel and producer Peter Baxter, 'Backers' to some, plan another day's play at Lord's in 2006.

England v West Indies Second Test

22–26 June 1995 Lord's, London   Umpires **DR Shepherd and S Venkataraghavan (Ind)**

ENGLAND FIRST INNINGS

* MA Atherton	b Ambrose	21
† AJ Stewart	c Arthurton b Gibson	34
GA Hick	c Lara b Bishop	13
GP Thorpe	c Lara b Ambrose	52
RA Smith	b Hooper	61
MR Ramprakash	c Campbell b Hooper	0
DG Cork	b Walsh	30
D Gough	c Campbell b Gibson	11
PJ Martin	b Walsh	29
RK Illingworth	not out	16
ARC Fraser	lbw b Walsh	1
Extras	(b 1, lb 10, nb 4)	15
Total	(all out, 99.4 overs)	283

Fall of wickets 1-29, 2-70, 3-74, 4-185, 5-187, 6-191, 7-205, 8-255, 9-281

Bowling	O	M	R	W
Ambrose	26	6	72	2
Walsh	22.4	6	50	3
Gibson	20	2	81	2
Bishop	17	4	33	1
Hooper	14	3	36	2

SECOND INNINGS

* MA Atherton	c Murray b Walsh	9
† AJ Stewart	c Murray b Walsh	36
GA Hick	b Bishop	67
GP Thorpe	c Richardson b Ambrose	42
RA Smith	lbw b Ambrose	90
MR Ramprakash	c sub b Bishop	0
DG Cork	c Murray b Bishop	23
D Gough	b Ambrose	20
PJ Martin	c Arthurton b Ambrose	1
RK Illingworth	lbw b Walsh	4
ARC Fraser	not out	2
Extras	(b 6, lb 27, w 2, nb 7)	42
Total	(all out, 99.1 overs)	336

Fall of wickets 1-32, 2-51, 3-150, 4-155 5-240, 6-290, 7-320, 8-329, 9-334

Bowling	O	M	R	W
Ambrose	24	5	70	4
Walsh	28.1	10	91	3
Gibson	14	1	51	0
Bishop	22	5	56	3
Hooper	9	1	31	0
Adams	2	0	4	0

WEST INDIES FIRST INNINGS

SL Campbell	c Stewart b Gough	5
CL Hooper	b Martin	40
BC Lara	lbw b Fraser	6
JC Adams	lbw b Fraser	54
* RB Richardson	c Stewart b Fraser	49
KLT Arthurton	c Gough b Fraser	75
† JR Murray	c & b Martin	16
OD Gibson	lbw b Gough	29
IR Bishop	b Cork	8
CEL Ambrose	c Ramprakash b Fraser	12
CA Walsh	not out	11
Extras	(b 8, lb 11)	19
Total	(all out, 112 overs)	324

Fall of wickets 1-6, 2-23, 3-88, 4-166, 5-169, 6-197, 7-246, 8-272, 9-305

Bowling	O	M	R	W
Gough	27	2	84	2
Fraser	33	13	66	5
Cork	22	4	72	1
Martin	23	5	65	2
Illingworth	7	2	18	0

SECOND INNINGS 296 RUNS TO WIN

CL Hooper	c Martin b Gough	14
SL Campbell	c Stewart b Cork	93
BC Lara	c Stewart b Gough	54
JC Adams	c Hick b Cork	13
* RB Richardson	lbw b Cork	0
KLT Arthurton	c sub b Cork	0
† JR Murray	c sub b Gough	9
OD Gibson	lbw b Cork	14
IR Bishop	not out	10
CEL Ambrose	c Illingworth b Cork	11
CA Walsh	c Stewart b Cork	0
Extras	(lb 5)	5
Total	(all out, 78.3 overs)	223

Fall of wickets 1-15, 2-99, 3-124, 4-130, 5-138, 6-177, 7-198, 8-201, 9-223

Bowling	O	M	R	W
Gough	20	0	79	3
Fraser	25	9	57	0
Cork	19.3	5	43	7
Martin	7	0	30	0
Illingworth	7	4	9	0

England won by 72 runs

delighted that Mark Ramprakash and Angus Fraser were in the England side for the first match in my new job, though they were to have contrasting fortunes.

My job initially was to be the *TMS* girl Friday – not to mention all the other days of the week. It involved greeting guests, answering phones, booking phonelines and hotels for future matches, collecting cakes from the pavilion door which had been delivered by appreciative *TMS* fans and generally administering unto almost every need of commentators, producers, scorers and engineers alike and dealing with anything else that might occur.

The commentary box itself would never have passed today's health and safety regulations. It was cramped and the roof leaked. There were no refreshments on tap – indeed we had to suffer the whiff of a good lunch being prepared for the players and the VIPs in Nancy's kitchen two floors below. Years earlier, John Arlott had the best idea. He brought his own. However, by 1995, the BBC would have taken a pretty dim view of claret on duty!

It all meant a lot of fetching and carrying for me, up and down stairs, dodging incoming batsmen and – potentially more dangerously – outgoing batsmen angry at yet another of those allegedly dodgy umpiring decisions. Mind you, the commentators were not in the best position to judge those decisions – action replays were in their infancy and the dear old broadcasting box was not quite behind the bowler's arm. What is more, the written press were in a different building so second opinions were hard to come by. How much luckier we all are now in the new media centre at the Nursery End.

But that day, my first, the *TMS* commentators were Jonathan Agnew, Christopher Martin-Jenkins and the voice of West Indies cricket, Tony Cozier. All three could not have been more tolerant and supportive of this new young lass skipping in and out, giggling sometimes when she shouldn't and, I fear, being of rather questionable value to the team – at least for a while. Equally kind and considerate were the summarisers. Trevor Bailey, a seasoned old pro – as a cricketer and a broadcaster – and for many years I had enjoyed the rich tones of Bailey and the Yorkshire growl of F.S. Trueman as they talked us through match after match. This time, though, it was not Trueman but the former Derbyshire and England fast bowler, Mike Hendrick who was in the summarisers' chair. Next to him was our indefatigable scorer, Bill Frindall whose voice, like his beard, has become more and more familiar with the passing of the years.

As for the match itself, England went into the game one-nil down after a nine-wicket thrashing at Headingley. Our record at Lord's in recent years had not been good so there seemed little cause for optimism – and England's first innings score of 283 looked a little below par. However, Gus Fraser, who nowadays is such a stalwart of *TMS*, knew how to make the most of the Lord's pitch and its slope. The 'foot-slogging yeoman', as *Wisden* described him at the time, cheered England supporters with 5 for 66 as West Indies were dismissed for 324. England's batsmen fared rather better in the second innings (though sadly not Ramprakash who bagged a pair) and set the tourists 296 to win. But it was a young England bowler who was to prove decisive. This was Dominic Cork's debut – and what an inspired selection it proved to be. Any thoughts of a West Indies victory vanished as Cork ripped through their batting. He finished with 7 for 43 and the West Indies were bowled out for 223, losing the match by 72 runs.

It was a gripping encounter – even for me who was supposed to be working. Lord's had been full for the first four days and, on the final afternoon, there were still well over 10,000 people in the ground. Up in the box, I had a bird's-eye view of the whole proceedings – but then so did so many others. The *TMS* box then – as now – was packed with visitors. There were BBC bosses (well, we could hardly keep them away!), assorted sporting and other celebrities and the occasional MCC member who decided to deliver a fruit cake in person. Our guest giving his 'View from the Boundary' that day was the distinguished actor, Michael Denison, who, like his equally distinguished actress wife, Dulcie Gray, was a lifelong cricket fan. Indeed, he was also a member of Middlesex CCC so we discussed Middlesex's championship prospects at some length. I remember we were quite optimistic – but then, all things seemed possible when you were looking down upon the great game from the roof of the pavilion at Lord's.

It is one of the great joys of cricket broadcasting that we are an international family. There has been a great tradition of shared commentaries over the years and even when that has not been possible, commentators have been swapped, preserving a crucial balance of impartiality.

Here is a selection of visiting commentators and expert summarisers who have worked with *Test Match Special* in England.

Australia

'He's everything to cricket,
Cricket's everything to him, you know.
The game is not the same
Without McGilvray.'

Opposite Alan McGilvray: a master of the art of radio broadcasting, McGilvray is the longest serving cricket commentator ever to grace the airwaves – from 1934 to his retirement in 1985.

Overleaf In the commentary box at Lord's in 1997 for the visit of Australia were (left to right) Peter Baxter, Jeff Thomson, Bill Frindall, Chris Cowdrey, Mike Selvey, Dennis Lillee, Neville Oliver, Jonathan Agnew, Christopher Martin-Jenkins and Graham Dilley.

It is a measure of the regard in which Alan McGilvray was held that the Australian Broadcasting Commission, as it then was, used that ditty to push their asset in the face of the arrival of Kerry Packer's Channel Nine television coverage of cricket.

Alan had played as an all-rounder for New South Wales first in 1933, and after the departure of Bradman to South Australia, he went on to captain the state. It was while in that role that he was introduced to broadcasting, giving close-of-play reports from Brisbane on a Sheffield Shield match in which he was playing. Commentary started with the 'synthetic' broadcasts mentioned in the first chapter, but after the war it became the real thing as he was sent by the ABC to cover the 1948 tour of England. For the 1953 and 1956 tours he had other media duties, but returned to the ABC – and with them, the BBC – becoming an ever-present until his retirement at the Oval in 1985, which he sealed with the simple line, 'Well, that's my story'.

In the commentary box McGilvray's voice was so quiet that one would have to wear headphones to hear him, as he placed an elbow on each side of the stand microphone that we used then, to support the large binoculars that bore a dire warning to anyone who might borrow them, not to adjust them.

His confidential, comprehensive style was very popular with the British audience, who showered him with plaudits on the day of his retirement.

For the next three tours the ABC sent Neville Oliver, an extrovert, red-haired Tasmanian, who went on to become head of ABC Radio's sports department. With Jim Maxwell and Tim Lane, both of whom have had tours of England for ABC Radio, Neville formed a commentary trio that allowed the ABC to have a strong response to the post-McGilvray era.

A number of former Australian Test players have also joined us in the *TMS* box. The dry, ironic drawl of the former opener Jack Fingleton started the era and it was a joy to us all to have Lindsay Hassett, who had been a regular on the ABC in Australia, with us for the Centenary Test of 1980, alongside the great all-rounder, Keith Miller. More recently players of the 1970s and 1980s such as Jeff Thomson, Dennis Lillee, Merv Hughes, Rod Marsh and Geoff Lawson have graced our airwaves.

Bangladesh

The two-Test tour of England in 2005 did present us with something of a problem, which was solved by being able to use the services of Dav Whatmore, Bangladesh's Sri Lankan/Australian coach. As the dressing rooms for both Lord's and the Riverside, where the Tests were played, were on the other side of the ground, his summaries were done via a radio microphone – an arrangement that (astonishingly) worked rather well.

At Lord's there was some discussion on the eve of the match about the changing of the name of the batsman, Javed Omar Belim. The discussion prompted the writing of a spoof press release to the effect that the wicketkeeper, Khaled Mashud, now

wished to be known as 'Bernard'. Looking suitably official, the press release was slipped in front of Blowers just before one of his sessions with Dav on the radio mic. Blowers mentioned it, reading out the statement and its call for 'Bernard' Mashud's wishes to be respected. Dav Whatmore gave a perfect pause before saying, 'I think you've been had, mate.'

India

Most Indian representation in the team has been in the form of expert summarisers, but Pearson Surita, a splendidly urbane resident of Calcutta, who first joined the programme in 1959 and, more recently, Harsha Bhogle, from Bombay, who has become a very familiar face on Indian television, are both notable exceptions who have taken on the ball-by-ball role. Pearson had a memorable verbal exchange with Don Mosey at the 1982 Test in Calcutta on the orientation of the pitch.

'It runs East-West,' he insisted. 'Always has done.'

'Then why,' demanded an increasingly frustrated Mosey, 'is there a gap in the stands over mid-wicket to prolong the light of the setting sun?'

We have been touched, too, by the nobility in the considerable presences of the Maharajkumar of

Right Monty Panesar's father (left) waits to hear what Bishen Bedi (front) has to say about his son at Chandigarh in 2006. Christopher Martin-Jenkins and scorer Jo King pretend they're not listening.

Opposite Pearson Surita: with his posh accent and slow delivery, he was a perfect exponent of the art of ball-by-ball commentary.

MY FIRST TEST MATCH

Harsha Bhogle

You can see why the talk star is a weird animal. Radio commentators have been known to puff on a pipe, plonk a drink in front of them, smear each other with chocolate cake, go hysterical over a joke only they could have cracked, and understood. I've seen them turn up in fluorescent green shirts, in tie and shorts, in yesterday's T-shirt – many of them could never have been in the prim and starchy world of television.

But they have all had something that television could never do justice to. They could spin a yarn, paint a picture, dissolve in laughter, call each other by the most unlikely nicknames and not miss a ball. *Test Match Special* pioneered this style; conversational, easy on the ear and

with a lot of bonhomie all around. It was addictive and if you aspired to enter the club, you needed to conform, in a lovely, happy kind of way. And *TMS*, long before television thought of it, made its commentators into stars. You may not have heard them but you had definitely heard of them.

So it was to an Indian growing up in Hyderabad, who struggled to pick up the accent amidst the intrusions of the neighbouring station and the constant static. By the time I began a career in broadcasting I had heard more of Arlott on cassette than on radio, had read Johnston more than I had heard him. And thanks to Peter Baxter and many admirers of *TMS*, had acquired a copy of the two books produced in 1981 and 1983. It was there that I first read the line, 'And after

England v India First Test

6–9 June 1996 Edgbaston, Birmingham Umpires **DB Hair (Australia) and DR Sheperd**

INDIA FIRST INNINGS

V Rathour	c Knight b Cork	20
A Jadeja	c Atherton b Lewis	0
SV Manjrekar	c Atherton b Lewis	23
SR Tendulkar	b Cork	24
* M Azharuddin	c Knight b Irani	13
† NR Mongia	b Mullally	20
SB Joshi	c Thorpe b Mullally	12
A Kumble	c Knight b Cork	5
J Srinath	c Russell b Mullally	52
PL Mhambrey	c Thorpe b Cork	28
BKV Prasad	not out	0
Extras	(b 3, lb 10, nb 4)	17
Total	(all out; 69.1 overs)	214

Fall of wickets 1-8, 2-41, 3-64, 4-93, 5-103, 6-118, 7-127, 8-150, 9-203

Bowling	O	M	R	W
CC Lewis	18	2	44	2
DG Cork	20.1	5	61	4
AD Mullally	22	7	60	3
RC Irani	7	4	22	1
MM Patel	2	0	14	0

SECOND INNINGS

V Rathour	c Hick b Cork	7
A Jadeja	c Russell b Lewis	6
† NR Mongia	c Hussain b Cork	9
SR Tendulkar	c Thorpe b Lewis	122
* M Azharuddin	b Mullally	0
SB Joshi	c Russell b Mullally	12
SV Manjrekar	c Knight b Lewis	18
A Kumble	run out	15
J Srinath	lbw b Lewis	1
PL Mhambrey	b Lewis	15
BKV Prasad	not out	0
Extras	(b 4, lb 9, nb 1)	14
Total	(all out; 70.4 overs)	219

Fall of wickets 1-15, 2-17, 3-35, 4-36, 5-68, 6-127, 7-185, 8-193, 9-208

Bowling	O	M	R	W
CC Lewis	22.4	6	72	5
DG Cork	19	5	40	2
AD Mullally	15	4	43	2
RC Irani	2	0	21	0
MM Patel	8	3	18	0
GA Hick	4	1	12	0

ENGLAND FIRST INNINGS

NV Knight	c Mongia b Srinath	27
* MA Atherton	c Rathour b Mhambrey	33
N Hussain	c sub (R Dravid) b Srinath	128
GP Thorpe	b Srinath	21
GA Hick	c Mhambrey b Prasad	8
RC Irani	c Mongia b Srinath	34
† RC Russell	b Prasad	0
CC Lewis	c Rathour b Prasad	0
DG Cork	c Jadeja b Prasad	4
MM Patel	lbw b Kumble	18
AD Mullally	not out	14
Extras	(b 16, lb 3, nb 7)	26
Total	(all out; 90.2 overs)	313

Fall of wickets 1-60, 2-72, 3-109, 4-149, 5-195, 6-205, 7-205, 8-215, 9-264

Bowling	O	M	R	W
J Srinath	28.2	5	103	4
BKV Prasad	28	9	71	4
A Kumble	24	4	77	1
PL Mhambrey	10	0	43	1

SECOND INNINGS 121 TO WIN

NV Knight	lbw b Prasad	14
* MA Atherton	not out	53
N Hussain	c Srinath b Prasad	19
GP Thorpe	not out	17
Extras	(b 8, lb 7, w 1, nb 2)	18
Total	(2 wks; 33.5 overs)	121
Did not bat	GA Hick, RC Irani, RC Russell, CC Lewis, DG Cork, MM Patel, AD Mullally	

Fall of wickets 1-37, 2-77

Bowling	O	M	R	W
J Srinath	14.5	3	47	0
BKV Prasad	14	0	50	2
A Kumble	5	3	9	0

England won by 8 wickets

Trevor Bailey it will be Christopher Martin-Jenkins,' and actually wondered what it must have been like to be CMJ that day! A bit like Eric Hollies when Bradman was walking back? The overpowering anti-climax?

So on a thankfully hot day at Trent Bridge in 1990 it wasn't too difficult for me to recognise either Peter or CMJ. It was the afternoon before India's first one-day game and, as someone who had done a bit on All India Radio and the Indian TV network Doordarshan, I wanted to be on *TMS*. I followed them around, trying to catch their eye and hoped the tiny conversation that followed could take the place of an audition. But it didn't happen.

Luckily for me I was in Australia during the 1992 World Cup and, having worked with the ABC, was part of a motley group that came together. I met Peter, of course, (he made me, a confirmed T-shirt and sneakers guy, wear a jacket to Iain Gallaway's for dinner!) but I also met Mike Selvey and Jonathan Agnew who I had last seen marking his run up at the Gymkhana ground in Secunderabad in 1984; a run-up so long I thought he would hit the sight screen first bounce!

But I didn't really get to be a real *TMS* person till India's tour in 1996. I got my tie from Henry Blofeld with whom I had spent some time in a television commentary box. He announced it on air, which was a great moment. The tie was made by David Bairstow who was also working on that tour; sadly it was the only time I got to meet him.

Peter seemed to get a bit stuck with the initials HB thereafter and inevitably I found myself following the cheerful, popular voice of Henry. And, as you know, things happen when Henry is on air and at Bristol six years later (again HB following HB!) I actually had to issue a little warning – something along the lines of, 'I'm afraid this is the other HB and that means for the next 20 minutes birds are unlikely to do graceful pirouettes in front of third man, stunning waitresses will cease to carry glasses of beer, good heavens there may be no buses or trains moving anywhere. The other HB will be back on in about 40 minutes at which point the world will resume its romantic ways.'

That tour was also the only time I met Fred Trueman and Trevor Bailey. I was a little apprehensive about Trueman after all that I had heard, but he was wonderful, polite and predictable. Bailey on the other hand (Trevor? Did I know him well enough to be on first name terms?) spoke with his eyes shut and made me grow rather tense every time the bowler was at the top of his mark! I remember wondering if he would recognise me if we ran into each other a few minutes later!

The World Cup of 1999 was a time to make friends with two fine broadcasters all over again. Jeremy Coney joined us at Trent Bridge, only a little late after he and his guitar were spotted asking for a lift on the way. And Donna Symmonds was more than just a bit peeved to discover that a caller had identified a voice in Peter's quiz as belonging to her when it was, in fact, the Kenyan captain Maurice Odumbe.

By 2002, of course, Chris Cowdrey and Graeme Fowler had arrived to join the perennially cheerful Vic Marks and all three added significantly, and in their own way, to the mirth; Fowler's deep knowledge of kitchen sinks coming in very handy during a particularly elaborate discussion on 'throwing the kitchen sink' at something! And television commitments meant I didn't have to lug Peter's ISDN kit around. If that isn't on your CV it is highly recommended. You put in a power cord, snap on a telephone jack and even as you fiddle around with the phone you hear this polite voice saying, 'Are you ready to do 60 seconds in the next 3 minutes? And how do you pronounce your last name?'

I wish *TMS* more strength, may it give more joy though I guess it might be asking for too much if one were to request that the cakes be low-cal!

MY FIRST TEST MATCH

Gerald de Kock

Though it took me a while to realize it, my original dream of playing this great game for a living at the highest level was derailed almost before it began due mainly to my lack of talent, but also to my introduction to the delights of listening to the game on the 'wireless' of which there was one in every room of the house I grew up in.

When I first became aware of the game in the 1970s there was no such thing as television in South Africa so the radio commentaries of the great Charles Fortune, played a big role in introducing the game to me. My parents were friends of 'Mr Fortune' and his wife Daphne. Regular bridge evenings were interrupted by a snotty

nosed, skinny kid wandering in to try and engage the great man in conversation; needless to say he was not amused by my invasions and he dismissed me with a withering, schoolmasterly stare.

I did, once, get to visit him in the commentary box at Wanderers during a match between the Derrick Robins XI and a South African XI in the mid-1970s, the height of the isolation era. Maybe it was then that the seed was planted.

Gerald de Kock: in the middle of his hat-trick of commentaries in July 1995 – the rugby World Cup final in Johannesburg, the Second Test against the West Indies at Lord's and the Wimbledon tennis championships – in three consecutive days.

SOUTH AFRICA FIRST INNINGS

AC Hudson	c Gooch b Gough	6
G Kirsten	c DeFreitas b Hick	72
WJ Cronje	c Crawley b Fraser	7
* KC Wessels	c Rhodes b Gough	105
PN Kirsten	c Rhodes b Gough	8
JN Rhodes	b White	32
BM McMillan	c Rhodes b Fraser	29
† DJ Richardson	lbw b Gough	26
CR Matthews	b White	41
PS de Villiers	c Rhodes b Fraser	8
AA Donald	not out	5
Extras	(lb 9, nb 9)	18
Total	(all out, 118.5 overs)	357

Fall of wickets 1-18, 2-35, 3-141, 4-164, 5-239, 6-241, 7-281, 8-334, 9-348

Bowling	O	M	R	W
DeFreitas	18	5	67	0
Gough	28	6	76	4
Salisbury	25	2	68	0
Fraser	24.5	7	72	3
Hick	10	5	22	1
White	13	2	43	2

SECOND INNINGS

G Kirsten	st Rhodes b Hick	44
AC Hudson	lbw b Fraser	3
WJ Cronje	c Fraser b Gough	32
* KC Wessels	c Crawley b Salisbury	28
PN Kirsten	b Gough	42
JN Rhodes	b Gough	32
BM McMillan	not out	39
† DJ Richardson	c Rhodes b Fraser	3
CR Matthews	b Gough	25
Did not bat	PS de Villiers, AA Donald	
Extras	(b 8, lb 10, nb 12) 30	30
Total	(8 wks dec, 102.3 overs)	278
Did not bat	PS de Villiers, AA Donald	

Fall of wickets 1-14, 2-73, 3-101, 4-141, 5-208, 6-209, 7-220, 8-278

Bowling	O	M	R	W
Fraser	23	5	62	2
Gough	19.3	5	46	4
DeFreitas	14	3	43	0
Hick	24	14	38	1
Salisbury	19	4	53	1
White	3	0	18	0

ENGLAND FIRST INNINGS

* MA Atherton	c Wessels b Donald	20
AJ Stewart	b Donald	12
JP Crawley	c Hudson b de Villiers	9
GA Hick	c Richardson b de Villiers	38
GA Gooch	lbw b de Villiers	20
C White	c Richardson b Donald	10
† SJ Rhodes	b McMillan	15
IDK Salisbury	not out	6
PAJ DeFreitas	c Wessels b Donald	20
D Gough	c & b Donald	12
ARC Fraser	run out	3
Extras	(b 2, lb 5, nb 8)	15
Total	(all out, 61.3 overs)	180

Fall of wickets 1-19, 2-41, 3-68, 4-107, 5-119, 6-136, 7-141, 8-161, 9-176

Bowling	O	M	R	W
Donald	19.3	5	74	5
de Villiers	16	5	28	3
Matthews	16	6	46	0
McMillan	10	1	25	1

SECOND INNINGS 456 RUNS TO WIN

* MA Atherton	c McMillan b de Villiers	8
AJ Stewart	c Richardson b Matthews	27
JP Crawley	c Hudson b McMillan	7
GA Hick	lbw b McMillan	11
GA Gooch	lbw b Donald	28
C White	c Wessels b Matthews	0
† SJ Rhodes	not out	14
PAJ DeFreitas	c G Kirsten b Matthews	1
D Gough	retired hurt	0
IDK Salisbury	lbw b Donald	0
ARC Fraser	lbw b McMillan	1
Extras	(b 1, lb 1)	2
Total	(all out, 45.5 overs)	99

Fall of wickets 1-16, 2-29, 3-45, 4-74, 5-74, 6-82, 7-85, 8-88, 9-99

Bowling	O	M	R	W
Donald	12	5	29	2
de Villiers	12	4	26	1
Matthews	14	6	25	3
McMillan	6.5	2	16	3
Cronje	1	0	1	0

South Africa won by 356 runs

Still, on 24 July 1994 I walked into the Lord's pavilion and up the grand, creaking staircase to the *TMS* commentary box it was with a sense of excitement and a little disappointment. You see, I would far rather have been unpacking my kit one floor below in the visitors' dressing room, sharing pre-match banter with Kepler and the boys, than sweating profusely in a jacket and tie on a blazing summer's morning as I sat down nervously alongside one of my boyhood idols, Barry Richards, and Aggers to discuss South Africa's chances in their first Test Match at the ground since readmission.

The ground was familiar enough. Lord's was the first port of call on my initial visit to London 11 year earlier and I had made the pilgrimage every visit since, but never had I been into the imposing pavilion. I was also familiar with *TMS* having spent the summers of 1983 and 1984 misguidedly pursuing my dream of playing the game in the leagues in Birmingham. Among my duties were mowing of the outfield and rolling the pitch, and it was while perched atop a big yellow Bomag roller that I heard the broadcast of the debut of a certain J.P. Agnew against the mighty West Indies at the Oval in 1984.

Sadly, I can recall little of my first session as a commentator on *TMS* as, rather like SA opener Andrew Hudson, nerves got the better of me and all I remember was a tap on my right shoulder by Peter Baxter as I chatted well into CMJ's 20-minute slot.

My first meeting with a South African icon took place in that little commentary box. Following the commotion surrounding his dress, the jacketed but tieless Archbishop Tutu was eventually granted access to the pavilion and joined a somewhat surprised Aggers for a memorable period on air. To meet the man who had fought, peacefully, for the rights of all South Africans was truly humbling, and to do so while South Africa were playing a Test Match at Lord's was deeply ironic.

The relaxed, jovial atmosphere soon settled my nerves as did the South African team who outplayed England to win by some distance. I recall Barry and I being on air during the somewhat confusing final moments of the match on the fourth afternoon. England lost their ninth wicket on 99 and we were not sure whether the injured Darren Gough would come out to bat. He didn't and the match was over. South Africa had won by 356 runs.

For Barry and I and the Atherton 'dust-in-pocket' incident was long forgotten as we were swept along by the rare emotion of a great South African performance. Those were heady days for us South Africans in our fledgling democracy, and the sight of the new, multi-hued flag waving defiantly from the balcony beneath us as coach Mike Procter celebrated was as intoxicating as it was confusing, we hardly knew which way the flag should fly!

My colleague, Kotie Grove, was the Afrikaans language commentator and was housed in a broom cupboard next to the toilets on the first floor of the Warner Stand. During the Saturday of the match I popped down to visit him after lunch. He had just come to the end of a stint and handed back to the studio in Johannesburg, when play was interrupted by a streaker. A little taken aback Kotie, said to me, in Afrikaans, 'My donder, hier kom 'n ou met a lang slang!' A direct translation of which is, 'My thunder, here comes a guy with a long snake!' Little did he know that the studio presenter back in Johannesburg had not closed the fader to Lord's, and Kotie's words were broadcast to the somewhat sensitive Afrikaans community in crystal clear FM!

In 1995 South Africa experienced another unforgettable moment when the Springbok rugby team won the World Cup at Ellis Park. I was fortunate enough to be commentating for SABC Radio that day. But I had little time to celebrate as I flew to London that night as a member of the SABC's TV commentary team at the Wimbledon championships starting on the Monday.

Having arrived in London on Sunday morning a little worse for wear. I decided to visit a few friends at Lord's where England were engaged in another desperate fight for survival against the West Indies. I bumped into Peter Baxter at the back of the pavilion and he invited me to the *TMS* box to chat about the World Cup final the day before. He then offered me the chance to pursue what would be an unusual broadcasting hat-trick, by broadcasting a ball of play, as it happens it was two balls as a streaker, again, appeared from the Mound Stand!

The hat-trick was duly completed in SW19 on the Monday, completing a 48-hour whirlwind that began at Ellis Park in Johannesburg on Saturday afternoon, continued at Lord's on Sunday and ended at Wimbledon on Monday.

Thank you *Test Match Special* for the moments, memories and friendships.

Vizianagram in 1959 – known to our team as 'Vizzy' – and, in 1974, the Maharajah of Baroda, who asked, in the spirit of the modern egalitarian India, to be introduced as 'Fatesingh Gaekwad, the former Maharajah of Baroda', but showed the common touch by agreeing that, as this was something of a mouthful, he could thereafter be addressed as 'Prince'.

Among other, more recent Indian summarisers have been former wicketkeeper/batsman Farokh Engineer, who was such a success at Lancashire and who almost had to be restrained from falling out of the commentary box window when India won the World Cup in 1983. Since then two of the stars of that World Cup-winning team have been welcome additions to the commentary box: Sunil Gavaskar and Ravi Shastri.

New Zealand

Not until 1973 did our counterparts in New Zealand send a commentator to join the TMS team for a tour of England. That year former provincial cricketer, soccer player and racehorse owner, Alan Richards from Auckland, made the first of his five trips to England to commentate. His successor – Bryan Waddle from Wellington – had a completely contrasting style from the quiet, efficient Richards. Having been a DJ, Bryan has a sound radio background and in between the battles he has with his bosses for the money to support the coverage he plans, is busy as a newshound and presenter. A brusque manner can disguise an impish sense of humour, though an attempt to practise that on his fellow Kiwi, Jeremy Coney, during the 2004 series came to grief. England's 'super-sub', Gary Pratt, had taken the field and, in attempt to make Coney laugh, Bryan said, 'He's one of the Durham Pratts.'

Opposite Jeremy Coney: the amiable Kiwi punches the air in celebration after hitting the winning run to give New Zealand their first ever victory on English soil in the Second Test at Headingley in 1983.

'I think that's a little harsh,' replied Coney, neatly turning the tables on the now-corpsing Waddle.

Former New Zealand captain, Coney, combines a wonderful sense of humour with incisive comment and a splendidly enquiring mind, fuelled by an ongoing succession of university courses. He follows in the footsteps of the first New Zealand summariser on TMS, Bill Merritt, a former Test leg-spinner, who joined the programme for the 1958 series.

Pakistan

Omar Qureshi had an interesting career around Pakistan cricket, which included managing the national side and a substantial amount of writing and broadcasting. For the 1962 and 1967 tours of England he was a ball-by-ball commentator with TMS, but apart from him representatives of Pakistan in the commentary team have been summarisers.

In 1971 the series was divided between two Pakistan experts – Khan Mohammed and Wazir Mohammed, both of whom had played their Test cricket in the 1950s. One of Wazir's three Test-playing brothers, Mushtaq, joined us in 1987 and was with TMS for three Pakistan tours. Even after 57 Test Matches and a long career with Northamptonshire, Mushy's love of the game saw him still playing league cricket for Old Hill in the West Midlands well into his 50s.

Khalid 'Billy' Ibadulla was another who spent a long time in county cricket – in his case for Warwickshire. He did a series for TMS in 1974, entertaining the commentators to post-match refreshments at his then lodging – the groundsman's flat overlooking the Colts' Ground at Edgbaston. Billy was used to the British way of life, but another who did one series, the great leg spinner, Abdul Qadir, was less so. It led to a few misunderstandings, but all were taken in very good part.

We were fortunate in 2006 to secure – briefly – the services of Pakistan's great all-rounder and World Cup-winning captain, Imran Khan. After he returned to his political duties, the splendid Rameez

Raja took his place. Rameez, both in England and Pakistan, has made the switch from sessions on television and radio with tremendous facility and is admirably even-handed in his comments, even riding through the controversies of the forfeited Test at the Oval.

South Africa

Charles Fortune, originally a schoolmaster from Gloucestershire, was the first man to be sent by the SABC to join the BBC commentary team as early as 1951. At the time he dominated South African sports broadcasting and was also used in Australia on Ashes series before the BBC sent its own commentator. He did once earn an official BBC rebuke for using the airwaves to report his car stolen. From 1951 to 1965 he covered every South African tour of England. After that there were none to report for 29 years.

When they returned to the international fold in 1994 after the abolition of apartheid, the SABC's principal commentator was Gerald de Kock, who had been coming to Wimbledon to commentate for years. Even before that he was no stranger to England, having played Birmingham League cricket in his youth. Gerald gradually moved more to television in South Africa and then the poacher turned gamekeeper when he became the South African team's media liaison officer, pulling off the near-impossible task of being trusted by both team and press.

For the first South African Test in England for a generation, we invited someone whose Test career had probably been minimised by the isolation of his country, Barry Richards. Hampshire followers were the beneficiaries of the fact that he only played four Tests before the barrier came down, but he frequently showed them what he might have done at the highest level.

Gerald de Kock's place in our commentary team was taken for the 2003 tour by Neil Manthorp, an energetic Capetonian, who runs his own press agency and on that tour, too, Allan Donald, retired from a career of terrorising batsmen, charmed listeners and fellow commentators alike as our expert comments man.

Sri Lanka

When Sri Lanka first came to England to play Test cricket, their part was taken in the commentary team by Gamini Goonasena, whose cricket career had pre-dated Sri Lankan Test status, but who had played 12 years of county cricket with Nottinghamshire, including four years for Cambridge University.

Since then, the beautiful island's principal exports to the *TMS* team have been the two Roshans. In 2002, former Test batsman Roshan Mahanama acted as our expert summariser. He has since been elevated to the ranks of ICC Test Match referee. Roshan Abeysinghe shuttled between the SLBC commentary box and ours for the three Test series in 2006. He is a Colombo businessman who has also devoted much energy into the founding of a cricket club in one of the less fashionable suburbs of the city, where they have brought on a number of very talented young players.

West Indies

The pioneers, Ken Ablack and Gerry Gomez, have been mentioned earlier in this book. For the second Test of that maiden *TMS* series of 1957, the delightful Jamaican, Roy Lawrence, made his debut, going on to cover another three West Indies tours of England and thereafter, having settled in Harrogate, was always a popular visitor to the box during Headingley Tests.

He was followed by one of the great radio commentators of any era – Tony Cozier. It is a measure of the regard in which he is held that

Opposite Viv Richards: making his commentary debut with Somerset colleague Vic Marks at Antigua in 1994.

television companies, who these days only seem to use ex-international players as commentators, still employ him regularly. From his home in Barbados, he always appears to have read and heard everything. He played a shameful part in the famous 'leg over' incident, recounted by Jonathan Agnew in these pages, when he sat quietly in the corner and carried on writing, rather than baling out his helpless colleagues, reckoning that it was safer not to risk a 'corpse' himself.

In the Caribbean in 1998, we were aware that one of the local radio commentary teams included a more attractive broadcaster than is usual. Donna Symmonds, a lawyer from Barbados, had made appearances on earlier tours, but was more of a regular now and so in Trinidad she was invited to join us on *Test Match Special*. In doing so she became the first female commentator we had used. She followed that by coming to join us for the World Cup in England the following year and then, with Tony Cozier, was part of our team for the West Indies tour of England in 2000. However, she was finally lured to television in time for the 2003 World Cup in South Africa.

Among former West Indian Test players who have graced the box since Gerry Gomez have been Sir Everton Weekes, the last – and some would say the greatest – of the Three Ws on whom so many bowling attacks broke, the former Guyana and Lancashire fast bowler, Colin Croft, whose genial smile now belies what an awkward prospect he was for batsmen of the 1970s and Gordon Greenidge, half of two devastating opening partnerships – for the West Indies with Desmond Haynes and for Hampshire with Barry Richards. On recent tours we have had the great Sir Viv Richards, wearing his passion for West Indies cricket on his sleeve, but a generous and friendly companion who carries his celebrity lightly for someone who used a wonderful arrogance to impose himself on opposition bowlers.

Zimbabwe

In the few Tests that England have played against Zimbabwe, we have been joined by a couple of their former Test players as summarisers. Andy Pycroft's career lasted just long enough to give him a handful of their early Tests and we have shared his services with cricket administration and with television. On Zimbabwe's 2003 tour of England, their former fast bowler and rebel against the regime, Henry Olonga, proved a very popular addition. He remains – happily – the only member of the *Test Match Special* team to have sung to an audience in the Long Room at Lord's.

In 1996 producer Peter Baxter arrived at the Queens Club in Bulawayo to find that there was no commentary box. Within 24 hours he had constructed one (above right) ... and they say that cricket's relaxing! But his efforts were dwarfed by a nearby construction for a taxidermist which came complete with an elephant's head (right).

MY FIRST TEST MATCH

Donna Symmonds

Test Match Special is a signature brand in the world of cricket commentary. To be a part of it allows you to see and feel it at first-hand and, perhaps, add something to the image – good or bad. What a treat! On the other hand, how intimidating to be involved with such a celebrated broadcast since few would dispute that it has set the standard for most of those that have followed, even though many have been in another medium. I was given that opportunity in Trinidad & Tobago in 1998 and then the following year in England and Ireland for the 1999 World Cup.

I have to make a distinction between the two first time experiences because *Test Match Special* 'on tour' and *Test Match Special* 'at home' are truly different entities.

I did not know a certain Jonathan Agnew (hereinafter called Aggers or I won't know who I am referring to) before the 1998 the Test series between England and the West Indies. That was a good thing because, had I known him, I doubt I would have believed him when he said that Peter Baxter wanted to see me in the BBC commentary box for me to do a stint during the Second Test at Port-of-Spain. Why? Well, Aggers is one of the wiliest practical jokers around and, one way or the other, he will get you. And he did get me on my second day – I think – luring me

Donna Symmonds: makes her *TMS* debut in Trinidad in 1998 flanked by Vic Marks and Jo King.

West Indies v England Second Test

5–9 February 1998 Queen's Park Oval, Port-of-Spain, Trinidad   Umpires **SA Bucknor and S Venkataraghavan (Ind)**

ENGLAND FIRST INNINGS

* MA Atherton	c Lara b Ambrose	11
AJ Stewart	lbw b Benjamin	50
JP Crawley	c SC Williams b Ambrose	17
N Hussain	not out	61
GP Thorpe	c D Williams b Hooper	8
AJ Hollioake	run out	2
† RC Russell	c SC Williams b McLean	0
AR Caddick	lbw b Walsh	8
DW Headley	c D Williams b Ambrose	11
ARC Fraser	c D Williams b Benjamin	17
PCR Tufnell	c Lara b Benjamin	0
Extras	(b 6, lb 10, nb 13)	29
Total	(all out, 109.0 overs)	214

Fall of wickets 1-26, 2-87, 3-105, 4-114, 5-124, 6-126, 7-143, 8-172, 9-214

Bowling	O	M	R	W
Walsh	27	7	55	1
Ambrose	26	16	23	3
McLean	19	7	28	1
Benjamin	24	5	68	3
Hooper	9	3	14	1
Adams	3	0	8	0
Chanderpaul	1	0	2	0

SECOND INNINGS

* MA Atherton	b Walsh	31
AJ Stewart	c Hooper b McLean	73
JP Crawley	lbw b McLean	22
N Hussain	c & b Walsh	23
GP Thorpe	c Lara b Walsh	39
AJ Hollioake	c Lara b Ambrose	12
† RC Russell	lbw b Ambrose	8
AR Caddick	c D Williams b Ambrose	0
DW Headley	not out	8
ARC Fraser	c Hooper b Ambrose	4
PCR Tufnell	c D Williams b Ambrose	6
Extras	(b 5, lb 15, w 1, nb 11)	32
Total	(all out, 94.5 overs)	258

Fall of wickets 1-91, 2-143, 3-148, 4-202, 5-228, 6-238, 7-239, 8-239, 9-246

Bowling	O	M	R	W
Benjamin	15	3	40	0
McLean	12	1	46	2
Ambrose	19.5	3	52	5
Walsh	29	5	67	3
Hooper	19	8	33	0

WEST INDIES FIRST INNINGS

SL Campbell	c Russell b Headley	1
SC Williams	c Atherton b Fraser	19
* BC Lara	c Atherton b Fraser	55
CL Hooper	b Fraser	1
S Chanderpaul	c Thorpe b Fraser	34
JC Adams	lbw b Fraser	1
† D Williams	lbw b Tufnell	16
CEL Ambrose	c & b Fraser	31
KCG Benjamin	b Fraser	0
NAM McLean	c Caddick b Fraser	2
CA Walsh	not out	0
Extras	(b 12, lb 5, nb 14)	31
Total	(all out, 73.1 overs)	191

Fall of wickets 1-16, 2-42, 3-48, 4-126, 5-134, 6-135, 7-167, 8-177, 9-190

Bowling	O	M	R	W
Headley	22	6	47	1
Caddick	14	4	41	0
Fraser	16.1	2	53	8
Tufnell	21	8	33	1

SECOND INNINGS 282 RUNS TO WIN

SL Campbell	c Stewart b Headley	10
SC Williams	c Crawley b Fraser	62
* BC Lara	c Russell b Fraser	17
CL Hooper	not out	94
S Chanderpaul	c Thorpe b Tufnell	0
JC Adams	c Stewart b Fraser	2
† D Williams	c Thorpe b Headley	65
CEL Ambrose	c Russell b Headley	1
KCG Benjamin	not out	6
Extras	(b 10, lb 8, nb 7)	25
Total	(7 wks, 98.2 overs)	282
Did not bat	NAM McLean, CA Walsh	

Fall of wickets 1-10, 2-68, 3-120, 4-121, 5-124, 6-253, 7-259

Bowling	O	M	R	W
Headley	16	2	68	3
Caddick	16	2	58	0
Tufnell	34.2	9	69	1
Fraser	27	8	57	3
Hollioake	5	0	12	0

West Indies won by 3 wickets

into a bogus overseas interview, which was fodder for all present then and maybe even now when they want a good chuckle and aren't being set-up themselves!

Aggers and I were part of a ball-by-ball radio commentary team for a communications station in Trinidad & Tobago. Vic Marks was also sharing his views as one of the panel of summarisers. The First Test in Jamaica had been abandoned after ten overs and one ball had been bowled. The state of the pitch at Sabina Park in Kingston was directly responsible for this disappointment. Fortunately, time allowed the tour schedule to be rearranged and both England and the West Indies agreed to play back-to-back Test Matches at the Queen's Park Oval in Port-of-Spain, Trinidad. Interestingly, the side batting last in each of the Tests won the game by a three-wicket margin in two fairly low-scoring matches and moved on to Guyana with the series even at one win apiece and all to play for. So we all had a great deal to talk about and nearly ten days of working together.

I joined TMS again in Barbados during that series and was intrigued by the presentation, the use of statistics and the interaction between the presenters and summarisers who did not appear to conform to any set format but let their personalities and views mesh or clash as the game unfolded. The producer paced the programme remarkably well with interviews, features and information. As far as I can remember Sir Everton Weekes, Trevor Bailey and Mike Selvey provided the comments with Aggers, Christopher Martin-Jenkins, Henry Blofeld, Peter Baxter and me sharing the running call.

My impression of it all was that this was a professional presentation but very enjoyable because fun was not excluded. I expected and looked forward to the same atmosphere when I went to participate in the 1999 World Cup with Test Match Special. It was all there, but there was also so much more. After my first few matches in England, it was obvious that the programme had a phenomenal following who participated by email, letters, cards, telephone and wonderful gifts of cakes, biscuits, flowers and paintings. Requests for information about all of us followed and, I must say, that suggestions for improvement and criticism were not absent from the copious correspondence.

While the professionalism and fun were still present, when Test Match Special cranked up at home, there was a different feel to the thing. I was more conscious of an immense tradition and of the crafted mix of voices and styles which created an unmistakable sound, updated as times and demographics change. A substantial amount of information was available and supplied to listeners but not to the exclusion of fine broadcasting, full of quality and content. What comes through so clearly to the listener is not just the substance of the material, but a genuine esteem and commitment to the game of cricket.

When TMS is talked about the super lyricists are always mentioned and now I know why. I felt encouraged to display my vocal art just as they were and I did so. Sadly, this type of approach does not appear to be prevalent, or even encouraged, elsewhere.

Test Match Special definitely has an advantage at home due to the strength of the county game and the number of overseas players it has always attracted. A wealth of resources in terms of the expert input exists and there is neither a shortage of former captains from many countries nor of present and past English and overseas players. This permits flexibility and a broad cultural range of opinions to permeate the commentary and makes the performance very inclusive. Thankfully, the need to reach the widest number and range of supporters of the game still seems to be important to TMS in producing a well-rounded cricket radio show.

Yes, there will always be those who want a new slant, greater information, further interaction, different presenters and summarisers, more action, less action, more and less of other things. But for me Test Match Special's longevity is proof of its adaptability and ability to make itself relevant as time passes. Long may this continue which will allow me to keep on listening. I am a fan.

7

FRED TRUEMAN
AND TREVOR BAILEY

by Henry Blofeld

Arthur and CB, Norman and Freddie, Fred and Trevor, *Test Match Special* summarisers, like fast bowlers, seem to operate best in pairs. When the programme began after the Second World War – it became *Test Match Special* in 1957 – Arthur Gilligan and Charles Fry were the two voices of wisdom who had their moment at the end of every over. 'What do you think, Arthur?' became a catch phrase to rival Wilfred Pickles's 'Give 'im the money Mabel'. It almost invariably produced the mildest of replies. C.B. Fry was amazingly fluent, extremely erudite and a law unto himself, but always great value. The genial and courteous Norman Yardley then complemented the more rumbustious, forthright views of Freddie Brown just as the no-nonsense Yorkshireness of Fred Trueman blended so well with the crisp and decisive thinking and diction of his great friend Trevor Bailey.

Above right Never short of a word or two, Fred Trueman (left) and Trevor Bailey dispensed their expert comments in different ways. Trevor's approach was laconic, while Fred favoured a rumble of thunder.

Opposite Arthur Gilligan: a superb cricketer, most notably for Sussex and England, whose experiences in Test and County cricket made him a popular summariser in the years after the war especially in tandem with another popular ex-player Victor Richardson.

A crucial and special feature of *Test Match Special* has been the easily identifiable and distinctive voices of the main participants. Who will ever forget the charmingly avuncular voice of Arthur Gilligan, the classical erudition of CB of whom the famous cricket historian, Harry Altham, once wrote, 'an arresting personality, and a brilliant conversationalist, Fry could, alike in form and in feature, have stepped straight out of the frieze of the Parthenon', the amiable and suggestive tones of Norman Yardley, the swashbuckling and yet always good humoured advice dished out by Freddie Brown, the Yorkshire pithiness and common

sense of 'What's going off out there?' Trueman and the inscrutably decisive 'Can't bowl. Can't bat,' Bailey.

Gilligan, Fry, Yardley and Brown all captained England in styles that were strongly similar to the way they broadcast. Gilligan would have sent a man down to third man with an apologetic gentleness. Fry would have issued his instructions with a vice-regal gesture, Yardley would have done it in a manner that suggested discussion, but with his mind firmly made up. Brown would have dispatched the fielder rather as if he was warming up for a robust performance on the quarterdeck.

Fiery Fred was never a candidate for the England captaincy, not that he would have refrained from offering advice, but he was in charge of Yorkshire when they beat the Australians at Sheffield in 1968 and never let anyone forget it. Much as he would loved to have done it, the job was never given to Trevor although he will always have been a most useful guide and counsellor to any incumbent he played under.

The combined knowledge and experience of these players made them fascinating to listen to. It is the purpose of this piece to discuss the contributions of Fred and Trevor, but if it had not been for the pioneering contributions of Arthur and CB followed by the example of Norman and Freddie who developed the art of summarising still further they would have found it more difficult, at the outset at any rate, to have fitted so seamlessly into the commentary.

I came into TMS at the time of the changeover from Norman and Freddie to Fred and Trevor. The only time I worked with the first two was in the one-day series against Australia in 1972, which was the first ever one-day series in England. The two matches I was given, at Lord's and Edgbaston, were also the only occasions I shared the commentary box with two other redoubtable performers, the former and mildly irascible Australian opening batsman, Jack Fingleton, and the commentator, Alan Gibson. By the time I came to Old Trafford for my first Test Match with TMS, Fred and Trevor were in as firm possession of the summarisers' seats as John Arlott and Brian Johnston were of the lead commentary positions.

I am eternally grateful to Fred and Trevor for allowing me such a relatively easy passage in my nerve-ridden start to the business of commentary. They nobly tolerated the young upstart that I was and made me realise straightaway the importance of the summariser to the commentator and also how essential it is to strike up the right sort of rapport between you. In my early days I must have asked them some pretty stupid questions and also have made some extremely facile remarks, but, by and large, they both let me down with the gentlest of bumps. I learned early on that the one thing that I should not do was to take the summariser on. However much I may have disagreed with something they had said, who was I to have the temerity to query the view of such experienced Test cricketers? They were very good too, in not making me look a complete fool when I had described a wicket and had either not seen something crucial or had described it wrongly.

They also taught me the folly of trying to lead your summariser. It was never sensible to ask him if he agreed with your interpretation of an incident. The safer *modus operandi* is to set out the state of affairs as it happened or as you saw it and then to ask the summariser his view of the situation. There was one incident not long after I began, I was on the air with Trevor towards the end of a boring Test Match against Australia at Lord's in 1975. There had been some rain during the match and on the last day Australia were batting out time without any hope of a result. Greg Chappell was playing a typically elegant innings and the strokes were flowing classically and easily off his bat. There was one glorious off drive that went through extra cover for four. I waxed eloquent about it and suggested that if ever there was such a thing as the ultimate coaching book which, I suggested, might be found in Heaven, if we were lucky enough to get there, there would be more photographs of

Opposite Blowers's nightmare: Greg Chappell plays a classic *on* drive against England at Lord's in 1975.

Greg Chappell playing that stroke that anyone else. I went on to suggest that Trevor might like to give his views at the end of the over.

When that moment arrived, I gave the score and stopped talking. Trevor distinctly cleared his throat and then said with great emphasis, 'Of course, the stroke that Greg Chappell is *best* known for is the on drive.' The emphasis he put on the word best said it all. It was time for a red face and a considerable helping of humble pie.

But Trevor never minded if you mobbed him up about his own rate of scoring when he played for England. He had not been known as Barnacle Bailey for nothing. Probably his most famous innings of obstructive blocking was played at the Gabba in Brisbane in 1958–59. He occupied the crease for no

Trevor Bailey: cuts the ball between the slips during his 163-run, fifth-wicket partnership with Willie Watson against Australia at Lord's in 1953.

less than seven hours and 38 minutes while amassing 68 runs. Sadly this display of monumental patience did not have the desired effect because Australia went on to win by eight wickets with more than a day to spare. His career also included innings of 26 in 251 minutes and 8 in 125 minutes, which would have tried the patience even of Job.

Of course, there was also that brave partnership at Lord's in 1953 when Trevor and Willie Watson put on 163 for the fifth wicket, frustrating the Australian bowlers for 248 minutes and heroically preventing them from winning the Second Test in that series. Trevor's resourceful defence did not confine itself to batting either. In the Fourth Test that year at Headingley Australia were heading for an almost certain victory which would have put them one-up in the series with only one match to go. Trevor then bowled six overs down the legside at his lively medium pace from which they were only able to score nine runs. This, after he had batted for a small

MY FIRST TEST MATCH

Christopher Martin-Jenkins

It seems a trifle indulgent and pretentious to write about my first Test as a commentator at Lord's in 1973, as if, somehow, I were playing in it. The excitement of taking part in the ball-by-ball description, however, did not seem far short at the time of what it might have been had I actually buckled on pads and gone out to face Lance Gibbs in his prime on a turning pitch in hot sunshine, with Gary Sobers at leg-slip, legs spread wide and predatory arms at the ready. He took six catches in that game and one of the first surprises on checking the scorecard against my memory is that only one of them was off Gibbs.

The game seems in my mind now like a happy, sunlit blur. It was full of incident and it proved to be something of a watershed in English cricket: the end of Ray Illingworth's career as captain and the start of a long period of domination by West Indian teams over English ones. Before their short series in the second half of the summer West Indies had played 20 Test Matches in four years without a win. Not far round the corner was their momentous series in Australia, when Jeff Thomson and Dennis Lillee outgunned their own fast bowlers. The Packer revolution and World Series Cricket soon followed, bringing no-holds-barred aggression and the realisation by Clive Lloyd and others that hostile fast bowling held the key to relentless success in international cricket, against Australia, England and everyone else.

England v West Indies Third Test

23–27 August 1973 Lord's, London

Umpires **HD Bird and CS Elliott**

WEST INDIES FIRST INNINGS

RC Fredericks	c Underwood b Willis	51
† DL Murray	b Willis	4
* RB Kanhai	c Greig b Willis	157
CH Lloyd	c & b Willis	63
AI Kallicharran	c Arnold b Illingworth	14
GS Sobers	not out	150
MLC Foster	c Willis b Greig	9
BD Julien	c & b Greig	121
KD Boyce	c Amiss b Greig	36
VA Holder	not out	23
Extras	(b 1, lb 14, w 1, nb 8)	24
Total	(8 wks dec, 168.4 overs)	652
Did not bat	LR Gibbs	

Fall of wickets 1-8, 2-87, 3-225, 4-256, 5-339, 6-373, 7-604, 8-610

Bowling	O	M	R	W
Arnold	35	6	111	0
Willis	35	3	118	4
Greig	33	2	180	3
Underwood	34	6	105	0
Illingworth	31.4	3	114	1

Gary Sobers powers his way to a majestic unbeaten 150 on his last appearance in a Test Match in England.

ENGLAND FIRST INNINGS

G Boycott	c Kanhai b Holder	4
DL Amiss	c Sobers b Holder	35
BW Luckhurst	c Murray b Boyce	1
FC Hayes	c Fredericks b Holder	8
KWR Fletcher	c Sobers b Gibbs	68
AW Greig	c Sobers b Boyce	44
* R Illingworth	c Sobers b Gibbs	0
† APE Knott	c Murray b Boyce	21
GG Arnold	c Murray b Boyce	5
RGD Willis	not out	5
DL Underwood	c Gibbs b Holder	12
Extras	(b 6, lb 4, w 3, nb 17)	30
Total	(all out, 73 overs)	233

Fall of wickets 1-5, 2-7, 3-29, 4-97, 5-176, 6-176, 7-187, 8-205, 9-213

Bowling	O	M	R	W
Holder	15	3	56	4
Boyce	20	7	50	4
Julien	11	4	26	0
Gibbs	18	3	39	2
Sobers	8	0	30	0
Foster	1	0	2	0

SECOND INNINGS FOLLOWING ON

G Boycott	c Kallicharran b Boyce	15
DL Amiss	c Sobers b Boyce	10
† APE Knott	c Murray b Boyce	5
BW Luckhurst	c Sobers b Julien	12
FC Hayes	c Holder b Boyce	0
KWR Fletcher	not out	86
AW Greig	lbw b Julien	13
* R Illingworth	c Kanhai b Gibbs	13
GG Arnold	c Fredericks b Gibbs	1
RGD Willis	c Fredericks b Julien	0
DL Underwood	b Gibbs	14
Extras	(b 9, w 1, nb 14)	24
Total	(all out, 65.3 overs)	193

Fall of wickets 1-32, 2-38, 3-42, 4-49, 5-63, 6-87, 7-132, 8-143, 9-146

Bowling	O	M	R	W
Holder	14	4	18	0
Boyce	16	5	49	4
Julien	18	2	69	3
Gibbs	13.3	3	26	3
Sobers	4	1	7	0

West Indies won by an innings and 226 runs

The Lord's Test in August 1973, staged at the end of the season because New Zealand had played at Lord's in June, was the last Test played by Sobers, Gibbs and Rohan Kanhai in England. Each of those outstanding players marked it with a special performance. It was said at the time that it would also be remembered as the 'bomb scare' Test because of the 85 minutes of play lost after Billy Griffith's calm, insistent voice had cut through the noise made by 28,000 excited spectators on Saturday afternoon, requesting all present to leave their seats and to evacuate the ground.

An IRA bombing campaign was in full spate at the time and no chances were taken when MCC received a coded warning. In fact many spectators chose not to leave the ground, some of them sunbathing on the outfield instead while the players stayed in the middle for some time before returning to their hotel across the road while Dickie Bird and Charlie Elliott, the umpires, relished the responsibility of guarding the pitch. All was good humour and good order. Up in the box, led by Brian Johnston, we disobediently chatted on through the drama, albeit not without in my case a feeling of slight unease until the police had inspected our eyrie at the top of the pavilion.

We were just embarking then on a long period when grounds for great matches in England would invariably be full and certainly so at Lord's. The Gillette Cup had officially started with great success in 1963 and we were at the dawn of the era of one-day international cricket. Like many an England player since I had cut my 'commentating' teeth in county cricket and one-day internationals – making my commentary debut in the first international played in England, against Australia at Old Trafford the previous summer.

England won that match and one of the other two but in Tests the side that had regained the Ashes under the shrewd Illy's command in 1970–71 had begun to crumble. At Lord's for that Third and final Test of the series the attack of Bob Willis, Geoff Arnold, Tony Greig, Illingworth himself and Derek Underwood was, even in the absence of John Snow, at least as good as the West Indies combination of Keith Boyce, Vanburn Holder, Bernard Julien, Sobers and Gibbs. But after Geoff Boycott and Dennis Amiss England's middle order – Brian Luckhurst, Frank Hayes, Keith Fletcher and Tony Greig, could not and did not match the brilliant West Indies line-up. After Roy Fredericks and, when fit, Lawrence Rowe, came Kanhai, Lloyd, Alvin

Kallicharran and Sobers. Julien and Boyce made a fairly formidable pair at Nos.8 and 9 in the batting order.

Boyce was in his brief, spectacular prime in this series and he made the difference between the sides. The wiry Barbadian bowled faster and more fiercely than anyone to take 19 wickets in three games at 15 runs each. At Lord's he took four in each innings but the basis of victory was the gargantuan first innings total of 652 for 8 declared, scored while Jim Fairbrother's hard, bouncy pitch was at its truest.

On the first day the West Indies scored more than 100 runs in each session, not too common then. Kanhai scored his fifth hundred against England in three hours and finished Thursday's play with 156 not out and a standing ovation after quicksilver stands with Fredericks and Lloyd. The next day Sobers and Julien took over, Sobers making his 26th Test hundred with familiar long-handled strokes that often seemed to go through 360 degrees; Julien, elegant through the covers, his first.

The declaration came early enough for England's fate to become probable by the close of the second evening at 88 for 3. That became 233 all out on Saturday and, after the bizarre stoppage in mid-afternoon, Boyce led the decisive thrust shortly before the close by getting out Amiss, Alan Knott and Boycott in his last four overs. The spinners did the damage on a dry pitch in the later stages, Gibbs adding three second-innings wickets to his two in the first but Fletcher, who had saved the day at Lord's against New Zealand earlier in the summer, emerged with credit again this time, top scoring with 68 in the first innings and 86 not out in the second.

Combining my commentaries with news reports galore for various BBC programmes, as I had all summer in my role as acting Cricket Correspondent in succession to 'BJ', I had to mention at the end of the game not just the cricket but the gloating nature of some of the celebrations by the huge crowd of West Indies supporters who invaded the pitch at the end. Then, as now, as always, cricket could never be isolated from the social forces that whirled around it. If truth be told though, I and my fellow commentators – the equally youthful and enthusiastic Tony Cozier in the company of the masterly old hands Johnston, John Arlott, Norman Yardley, Trevor Bailey and (summarising) Jim Swanton – preferred to stick to the cricket. And how we enjoyed it.

matter of 262 minutes in England's second innings while scoring 38 runs. At the end Australia, needing 177 for victory, were 30 runs short with six wickets in hand and the series remained all square.

It was these defensive skills of Trevor's that enabled England to be in the position to win the Fifth Test at the Oval and regain the Ashes for the first time since the Bodyline tour of 1932–33.

Above The Boil appeals for lbw against Australia's Keith Miller at Melbourne in 1950.

Opposite Fred Trueman, Trevor Bailey and Tony Lewis in full cry in TMS's al fresco commentary position in Sydney in 1983.

Whenever Trevor was reminded of these sterling performances, a wry smile and a knowing shake of the head told of the huge enjoyment and satisfaction they had given him. He was, therefore, in one sense hardly the crowd's best friend, but surely when he almost single-handedly prevented Australia from winning a Test Match or indeed a series he should have been their greatest hero.

Trevor's ability to bat for long periods while remaining almost runless, may have given him a rather lopsided reputation. He undoubtedly saved more matches for England than he won. For all that, it should never be forgotten that one morning in 1954 at Sabina Park in Kingston after the West Indies had won the toss and batted on what looked like a belter of a pitch, Trevor found a little moisture and took 7 for 34, bowling out a formidable West Indian batting side for 139. England went on to win the match – in which Gary Sobers made his debut for the West Indies – by 9 wickets and in doing so drew the series 2–2.

Trevor's first-class career went from 1946 to 1967 and in this time he made 28,642 runs at 33.42 and took 2,082 wickets at 23.13. These are the figures of a formidable all-round cricketer who played 61 times for England before bringing his extraordinary knowledge of the game into the *Test Match Special* box.

Sometimes in his comments he would advocate greater aggression from the batsmen in the middle and this would sometimes produce moments of great amusement in the box. Alan McGilvray, for so long Australia's leading commentator, never let Trevor get away with it when he made exhortations of this sort. Maybe Alan had particularly strong memories of having to commentate through long stretches of Trevor's runlessness, But Trevor always took any light chiding he may have received in this direction with good humour.

As a critic he was severe when he felt that a participant was doing an appalling job or was simply not up to it at Test Match level. If a newcomer had played a less than distinguished innings or had had a nightmare when put on to bowl and you asked Trevor for his opinion, it was then that he would

come out with those devastating one-liners of 'can't bat' or 'can't bowl' or maybe 'can't field' if a catch had gone down. There were never any grey areas with Trevor which made him such good value – and he was not often wrong in his opinions either, a point which is sometimes forgotten.

I daresay that while talking on *Test Match Special* most of us over the years have broken every known rule of broadcasting on an hourly basis. We interrupt, we speak over the top of each other, we deal too much in in-jokes and give ourselves a licence to do just about anything we want and largely get away with it. Our producer Peter Baxter's grey hair is probably the result of how close to the line we usually go. In the past, in one aspect in particular, we almost certainly went a step too far. I am certain that Lord Reith and his successors never perceived of alcohol as a natural accompaniment to on-air broadcasting, and yet in the *TMS* box we pretty successfully turned a blind eye to this.

Of course, John Arlott set an irresistible example in that department and it became generally accepted that commentary was actually enhanced by the occasional glass of champagne. We were exhorted to open the bottles carefully so that there was not a thunderous pop when the cork came out, though

this would undoubtedly have had our audience on the edge of its collective seat. As time went by though we became more adept at opening the bottles silently. The champagne would be poured and the glasses handed round.

It was this stage that Trevor would give the game away. When a glass of bubbling liquid was put in front of him, he would say in unmistakeable tones of ringing enthusiasm and emphasis, 'Aaaah. The medicine.' I fear our listeners were soon able to put forward the correct interpretation to those memorable words. Fred, on the other hand, never came out of his corner quite so strongly and was known on occasions to leave his glass almost completely untouched.

Trevor was known to some, especially Brian Johnston, as the 'Boil'. This nickname came about when, in his days at Cambridge, Trevor went on a football tour to Europe with the University side that also included his Essex and England team-mate, Doug Insole. They were playing a game in Switzerland and when Cambridge took the field, the chap on the public address system called him Boiley. Insole called him the Boil from then on and it soon spread.

While Trevor's entrance to the box each morning was always smiling and jolly, with a pronounced

'Goooooood moooooooooorning' to everyone, Fred Trueman's was always a little bit more like Lawrence Olivier making a stage entrance at a rather anxious point during the battle of Agincourt. First, there was often a gruff word or two from without which was highly audible and then the commentary box door would burst open admitting Fred. He would be in full voice talking over his shoulder as he came in. Those of us who were there received a resounding yet cursory 'morning all'. There was usually a bit of clutter in his hands that needed to be put down. Sometimes there would be a friend with him who might be carrying a box or two of his latest book that he needed to autograph before flogging them somewhere during the lunch interval.

Fred's arrival usually gave the box a bit of a shake up. It would not be long before he turned to one of us and asked whoever it was if he had heard the one about …? When the answer came in the negative, he bounded back on stage and unleashed what was always a splendid story, although at times he would have had the Lord Chamberlain reaching for his red pencil.

Then there was his pipe. Gnarled and curling almost into the shape of an Indian 'hookah', and accompanied by a pouch or tin of tobacco and a box of Swan Vestas matches he would drop it with aggression onto the long desk covered with green

Voted Pipeman of the Year in 1974, Fred celebrates with a bowlful from the selection he has stored in his top pocket at a reception at the Savoy in London.

baize onto which the commentators and summarisers lent while in full flow. Soon afterwards and in mid-conversation he would pick it up and start to ram the tobacco into the bowl. This was always quite a performance. When this had been done the match would be struck and applied and the first puffs of evil smelling smoke would curl from his lips and from the pipe itself. It was quite a performance and it was clear that it made him feel much better.

Fred, like Trevor, was never lost for a word when his moment came. When I began to commentate, the summariser automatically came in at the end of an over or if a wicket fell and the commentator brought him in if something happened which needed explaining. Nowadays, and Aggers was the first to do this, commentary has become more of a constant dialogue between commentator and summariser. It is an example of how almost everything in life is exposed to a constant evolutionary process. It is not that one way is better than the other, but just that they are different.

Fred always seized his moment. Some would have said that he was a little too critical of modern players and was too prepared to say that it was a better game played as it was in the days when he marked out his long run. Nonetheless, whatever he said was full of pith and moment. For a time it was unwise to bring Yorkshire's opening batsman Geoff Boycott into the conversation because Fred would then unleash a volley of verbal bouncers and yorkers. However, it gives me great pleasure to say that well before Fred so sadly died they had become bosom pals. To ask his comments on the latest efforts of the Yorkshire committee was also likely to lead him into a ferocious *cul de sac* as would mention of the MCC committee or any of its leading lights such as Gubby (G.O.) Allen or Freddie Brown. Fred would then begin to soliloquise and it would be difficult to stop him in time for the next ball or over.

Not surprisingly, Fred, the first bowler ever to take 300 Test wickets, had a healthy disregard for amateurs, but there were exceptions and perhaps the most notable one was Trevor himself. Fred's first

England tour, to the West Indies in 1953–54, did not always see him at his best and he was docked his good conduct money for both words and deeds which were considered to be too extravagant. He did not go to Australia the following winter and he was also not selected for the tour to South Africa in 1956–57.

Soon after the touring Party for South Africa had been announced Yorkshire visited Southend for a game against Essex. Fred was not a happy man and was anxious to relieve his frustration. Before lunch on the first day he found himself bowling at Trevor and he unleashed a particularly fierce bouncer that Trevor was unable to avoid. It hit him a nasty crack on the head and he went down in the crease. Being Trevor, he thought that if he could make a bit of thing of it and stay down for some while he would not have to face another over from Fred before lunch. He had just worked this out when he was surprised to see Fred's gargantuan figure looming over him. He said, 'Sorry Trevor lad. There's plenty of others I would rather have hurt than you.'

Fred was at his best in the summariser's chair when bad light or rain had stopped play. When that happens, as any follower of *TMS* will know, we carry on talking about anything and everything and some of our listeners even write in and say how much better we are when there is no cricket being played. It was at times like this when Fred, with his pipe at maximum smog level, would reminisce about the Test Matches he had played in when he first came on the scene in the early 1950s. His memory for detail was extraordinary. He never forgot a wicket he had taken and his memory of the strengths and weaknesses of opposing batsmen was faultless. He always spoke with a lively sense of humour too, even if he did occasionally see events of the past through glasses that were a trifle too rose-coloured.

He first came into the England side for the series against India in 1952, playing his first Test Match in front of his home crowd at Headingley. His was a remarkable debut. India, in their second innings, lost their first four wickets before any runs had been scored and Fred had taken three of them. It is not unfair to say that some of India's leading batsmen were none too happy when Fred pitched the ball short and sent it whistling past their ears. There was a certain amount of backing away to leg.

In that series Fred took 29 wickets and one of the Indian batsmen who was particularly alarmed was H.R. Adhikari. Later, in the Indian Army, he rose to the rank of Lieutenant Colonel. He retired from the military in the 1970s and was immediately asked to manage the Indian touring side to England. During the wet Old Trafford Test Match in 1971 Brian Johnston brought Adhikari into the minute wooden commentary box that was tucked away into the top of the scoreboard at the Stretford End. He introduced us all to the Colonel and when he came to Fred he said, 'Fred, of course you remember Colonel Adhikari?' Fred looked at the Colonel, shook him by the hand and said, 'Ay Colonel, and glad to see yer got some o' yer colour back.'

Fred had been a truly great fast bowler. No one in the history of the game could have bowled a better late outswinger. He was not an out-and-out fast bowler. He was capable of genuine pace but preferred to bowl within himself and this meant that he was able to use his top pace as a surprise weapon. His main attribute was the extraordinary rhythm of his approach to the wicket, followed by his classical action. It was all a gloriously supple, flowing process and it meant that unlike so many fast bowlers, he put his body under very little pressure. This was the reason that he was so seldom affected by injury in a career that stretched from 1949 to 1972. In this time he took 2,304 wickets at an average of only 18.29 runs per wicket. He was at his best in the second half of his Test career, in the late 1950s and early 1960s. By then, he had learned the full value of variety, and on a number of occasions destroyed formidable Australian and West Indian batting sides.

The image of Fred coming in to bowl will always remain with those who saw him. As he walked back

to his mark both shirtsleeves would be rolled up for they seemed to unroll with almost every ball. He would turn and break into his lovely purring run up to the wicket with his thick mane of dark hair flopping energetically. Then he opened himself for the final stride before delivery. The back foot would initially come down well behind the return crease (for most of his career the no-ball was decided by the position of the back foot which had to land behind the return crease). But once Fred's right foot had hit the ground there was a considerable drag which meant that by the time the ball left his hand his right foot was well over the return crease so he was able to bowl from less than the regulation 22 yards.

When the no-ball rule was changed to the position of the front foot (which then had to land behind the popping crease) Fred had some trouble in adapting. But that change in the Laws was made in 1962 close to the end of his career. Having such natural talent I have no doubt that Fred would have adapted comfortably enough to the new ruling if it had come about when he was just starting.

Fred soon acquired the nickname of 'Fiery Fred' for obvious reasons. He was a fierce competitor against all comers. Most seasons Yorkshire would play three-day matches in May against both Oxford and Cambridge Universities and Fred gave the undergraduates no favours. The arrival of a new batsman wearing a colourful striped cap prompted the usual Fred mutterings about, 'F***in' jazz hat', which you may be sure would soon be taking evasive action as the ball buzzed past the batsman's head.

As a batsman Fred adopted the traditional habits of tail-enders of his vintage and threw his bat at everything. This sometimes produced a splendid display of cricketing fireworks. His innings seldom went on for very long but he gave great entertainment while he was at the crease. He was by no means a negligible batsman though, and he had three first-class hundreds to his name. He was also the most versatile of fielders, whether in the deep or up round the bat with the close-catchers. He was one of those cricketers that people would pay good money to go and see. It was not just about taking wickets or

Opposite Fred watches anxiously as Colin Cowdrey catches Australia's Neil Hawke to earn him his 300th Test wicket during the Fifth Test at the Oval in 1964.

catches and hitting the ball as hard as he possibly could: it was the figure he cut when going about it all. How lucky we were to have him with us in the commentary box and what fun he provided.

Because of his forthright, table-thumping style, Fred often found himself the victim of verbal practical jokes. When some England batsman had played a particularly hideous stroke and as commentator you suggested to Fred that he had been rather unlucky, Fred's apoplexy would leap into the room with every listener. He invariably took the bait. There was one occasion when he and I found ourselves in complete agreement on something. I said something like, 'That's a matter, Fred, of two great minds thinking alike and rightly so too considering that we took 307 Test wickets between us.' At this Fred came explosively out of his corner to remind listeners that I had never played in a Test Match, let alone taken a wicket. Then he suddenly realised that as he had taken 307 Test wickets I was not claiming to have taken any. We had a big laugh about that one.

He was not by nature the most modest of men. I remember him saying longingly on one occasion that he wished he had had the chance to bowl at Viv Richards because he knew exactly how to get him out. He liked to claim that he had dismissed the three great West Indian batsmen, Frank Worrell, Clyde Walcott and Everton Weekes in the same innings. The record books suggest he got them all in the same Test, but not in the same innings – a feat, incidentally, achieved by his commentary box friend and colleague Trevor Bailey, at Lord's in 1957.

There were also times when, after listening to him for a few minutes, you began to doubt that he had ever bowled a straight ball in his life. But that was Fred and it was impossible to take offence at his endearing invincibility even if it more than once raised a healthy smile.

Fred and Trevor were the greatest of friends and collaborated on some books together. I think Trevor did most of the writing and, having recorded Fred's often outspoken views on the players under consideration, then added his own more measured

comments. In commentary styles they were very different although both, in their different ways, gave forth opinions that brooked no argument. By and large, Trevor distributed praise or condemnation with a certain good-humoured sarcasm, while Fred announced himself with a fair amount of spluttering interspersed with the odd roll of thunder. Sometimes Fred felt that he had perhaps gone too far in criticising a player and would try and make it up by saying, 'Aye, but he's still a luvly lad'.

Opposite Short and sweet: never long at the crease while batting, Fred Trueman was a good batsman but threw the willow at everything, as here for Yorkshire against Middlesex in 1955, because he was always keen to have a bowl at the opposition.
Above Fred, resting his eyes, at Lord's in 1992.

They did, however, have one thing in common which may ultimately have counted against them when the BBC decided that they had served their term of duty. They were both inclined to make the listener think that the standards of the modern generation of player were lower than the standards that Test and county cricketers achieved in their own playing days. Were they right or was it simply a case of distance lending enchantment? I don't suppose we shall ever know.

Fred spoke to his audience on *TMS* exactly as he batted and bowled. He told it as he saw it and never took prisoners. He would whistle the ball around his listeners' ears just as he would have done to the batsmen at whom he bowled. With bat in hand he always took the long handle just as he did now when

facing the microphone. Trevor, on the other hand, was more skittish in the commentary box than he ever was on the field of play. He always talked good sense, but every now and then he would say something that made you think that his twinkling footwork had taken him two or three paces down the pitch and played a forceful follow-through. The forward defensive prod was less in evidence than it had been when he had his pads on. Trevor's address for much of his life was, 24 The Drive. It was often said, much to his amusement, that it should have been 24 The Forward Defensive.

Fred and Trevor's days at the *Test Match Special* microphone sadly came to an end after the series against New Zealand in 1999. Both were getting on in years and it was felt that young listeners might not have been aware of all these two had done for England. Younger summarisers were the order of the day and one unhappy side-affect of this was that it has left CMJ and me as the two old lags in the box.

Dinner at the Swan Hotel in Bucklow Hill ahead of the 1992 Test Match against Pakistan: (left to right) David Lloyd, Mike Hendrick, Brian Johnston, Fred Trueman, Christopher Martin-Jenkins and Jonathan Agnew.

Jonathan Agnew

I suspect the majority of people that might have been in my shoes when I opened the rather battered door to the Headingley commentary box for the first time for the First Test against the West Indies on 6 June 1991 would admit to feeling enormous trepidation. I had met Brian Johnston once before, and he was already inside the surprisingly cramped wooden room, closely inspecting the early delivery of cakes. Meticulously, he placed them in order of preference in one corner. Bill Frindall who, again, I barely knew was setting up his vast array of scoring equipment. It would have been enough for any fan of *Test Match Special* to go weak at the knees, let alone those of the new BBC Cricket Correspondent,

whose duty is to observe and preserve the great tradition of one of the most prestigious jobs in cricket.

I had been taken by surprise during an interview for the BBC on the day I was appointed to succeed Christopher Martin-Jenkins. The line of questioning focused heavily on the history and tradition not of cricket, but of the previous correspondents, Brian, Christopher (twice) and, briefly, Don Mosey. I remember thinking to myself that there appeared to be more to this new job than I had imagined, but since I had barely ever listened to *Test Match Special*, perhaps it was not surprising.

My father was a farmer, and I do recall him carrying a radio with him wherever he went when a Test Match

England v West Indies First Test

6–10 June 1991 Headingley, Leeds   Umpires **HD Bird and DR Sheperd**

ENGLAND FIRST INNINGS

* GA Gooch	c Dujon b Marshall	34
MA Atherton	b Patterson	2
GA Hick	c Dujon b Walsh	6
AJ Lamb	c Hooper b Marshall	11
MR Ramprakash	c Hooper b Marshall	27
RA Smith	run out	54
† RC Russell	lbw b Patterson	5
DR Pringle	c Logie b Patterson	16
PAJ DeFreitas	c Simmons b Ambrose	15
SL Watkin	b Ambrose	2
DE Malcolm	not out	5
Extras	(lb 5, w 2, nb 14)	21
Total	(all out, 79.2 overs)	198

Fall of wickets 1-13, 2-45, 3-45, 4-64, 5-129, 6-149, 7-154, 8-177, 9-181

Bowling	O	M	R	W
Ambrose	26	8	49	2
Patterson	16.2	8	97	3
Walsh	14	7	31	1
Marshall	13	4	46	3

SECOND INNINGS

* GA Gooch	not out	154
MA Atherton	c Dujon b Ambrose	6
GA Hick	b Ambrose	6
AJ Lamb	c Hooper b Ambrose 0	0
MR Ramprakash	c Dujon b Ambrose	27
RA Smith	lbw b Ambrose	0
† RC Russell	c Dujon b Ambrose	4
DR Pringle	c Dujon b Marshall	27
PAJ DeFreitas	lbw b Walsh	3
SL Watkin	c Hooper b Marshall	0
DE Malcolm	b Marshall	4
Extras	(b 4, lb 9, w 1, nb 7)	21
Total	(all out, 106 overs)	252

Fall of wickets 1-22, 2-38, 3-38, 4-116, 5-116, 6-124, 7-222, 8-236, 9-238

Bowling	O	M	R	W
Ambrose	28	6	52	6
Patterson	15	1	52	0
Marshall	25	4	58	3
Walsh	30	5	61	1
Hooper	4	1	11	0
Richards	4	1	5	0

WEST INDIES FIRST INNINGS

PV Simmons	c Ramprakash b DeFreitas	38
DL Haynes	c Russell b Watkin	7
RB Richardson	run out	29
CL Hooper	run out	0
* IVA Richards	c Lamb b Pringle	73
AL Logie	c Lamb b DeFreitas	6
† PJL Dujon	c Ramprakash b Watkin	6
MD Marshall	c Hick b Pringle	0
CEL Ambrose	c Hick b DeFreitas	0
CA Walsh	c Gooch b DeFreitas	3
BP Patterson	not out	5
Extras	(lb 1, nb 5)	6
Total	(all out, 54.1 overs)	173

Fall of wickets 1-36, 2-54, 3-58, 4-102, 5-139, 6-156, 7-160, 8-165, 9-167

Bowling	O	M	R	W
Malcolm	14	0	69	0
DeFreitas	17.1	5	34	4
Watkin	14	2	55	2
Pringle	9	3	14	2

SECOND INNINGS 278 RUNS TO WIN

PV Simmons	b DeFreitas	0
DL Haynes	c Smith b Pringle	19
RB Richardson	c Lamb b DeFreitas	68
CL Hooper	c Lamb b Watkin	5
* IVA Richards	c Gooch b Watkin	3
AL Logie	c Gooch b Watkin	3
† PJL Dujon	lbw b DeFreitas	33
MD Marshall	lbw b Pringle	1
CEL Ambrose	c Pringle b DeFreitas	14
CA Walsh	c Atherton b Malcolm	9
BP Patterson	not out	0
Extras	(lb 1, nb 6)	7
Total	(all out, 56.4 overs)	162

Fall of wickets 1-0, 2-61, 3-77, 4-85, 5-88, 6-136, 7-137, 8-139, 9-162

Bowling	O	M	R	W
Malcolm	6.4	0	26	1
DeFreitas	21	4	59	4
Watkin	7	0	38	3
Pringle	22	6	38	2

England won by 115 runs

was on. I loved cricket, of course, but tended to watch the television, usually blacking out a room for the five days and then going out and playing with my brother on the lawn. Clearly, when I joined Leicestershire in 1978, we were involved in our own matches during the summer to the extent that I can honestly say I have absolutely no recollection of either John Arlott or Brian commentating.

I really believe this was a blessing because I started the job without being weighed down by the stifling pressure that many others would have felt. However, it was with some anxiety that I shook Fred Trueman by the hand. He had barged rather late into the box with his pipe billowing smoke like an autumn bonfire, and my only previous experience of the great man had been to read some rather uncomplimentary observations he made about my bowling a few years before. It was now, with hindsight of course, that I could admit he was right all along, and Fred was nothing but warm and gentle with me whenever we shared a microphone together.

England won that Test Match – a happy start for the new correspondent – with Graham Gooch making as good a century as you could see in difficult conditions and my old friend Phillip DeFreitas getting amongst the wickets. I did not commentate, but at Peter Baxter's sensible suggestion acted as an 'expert' summariser until I bedded in. Since I was sharing that position with Fred and Trevor Bailey, I did feel rather inadequate!

Gradually I settled in, and was able to gain first-hand experience of working with all the commentators. Again, this was a really useful part of my development as everyone had their own style and brought their personality into their descriptions. What struck me most was how relaxed the whole thing was – and still is, for that matter.

The final Test of that series – my last as summariser – produced one of the greatest howlers ever broadcast on radio. I always feel rather uncomfortable whenever the incident, which has simply become known as the 'leg over', beats all comers in classic commentary competitions because this was not strictly commentary. I suppose it illustrated just how quickly I had been made to feel at home by everyone on the programme that I deliberately let slip the immortal observation that Ian Botham 'failed to get his leg over', even if the line had been fed to me by John Etheridge of the *Sun* a few minutes before. The impact

it made on Johnners, of course, was immediate and devastating: I will never forget the look of absolute horror on his face as he glanced at me, before burying himself in the scorecard, furiously blinking back tears of laughter.

The dialogue is well known, and never reads as well as it sounds, but I do recommend listening out for a couple of incidents that might otherwise go unnoticed. The first is during the initial silence, when my line hits Johnners between the eyes. A clatter of china is audible in the background, and is the sound of Bill slamming his tea cup into its saucer as, like Brian, he is completely taken aback.

The second – and you have to strain your ears for this – is during one of the later silences when both Brian and I are unable to speak. I still have a clear memory of Peter looming into view from the back of the box, looking horrified, hissing, 'Will somebody *say* something'.

It is a little known fact that Brian was not entirely thrilled with his performance when he packed up and left for home that evening. He felt he had been unprofessional. I was left in the box scribbling my morning reports fearing the worst – it might not have been such a great idea to infuriate the main man in one's first season. It was only the following morning, when the first wave of letters from delighted listeners started to arrive, that I was able to persuade Brian to go down into the engineers' room at the Oval and hear it for ourselves. From that moment Brian was sold.

Graham Gooch plays a magnifcent on drive to the boundary on his way to a match-winning 154 not out at Headingley.

8

TMS ON TOUR
by Jonathan Agnew

Test Match Special is never more challenging than when we head off to foreign soil on England's winter tours. I include the listener in that opening remark, because the quality of the broadcasting line will sometimes make hearing what is said something of a trial, and every now and then it will drop off completely. This is the moment the unfortunate soul in the continuity studio in London absolutely dreads. It is probably 4.30 a.m. on the fourth night on duty, he has been forcing himself to stay awake, feels ghastly, and suddenly he has to commentate off the television: not easy, I can tell you.

All I can offer in mitigation is that if you were actually to see some of the conditions and surroundings we are attempting to broadcast from, it is often nothing short of miraculous that we get a word out of the place at all.

For the last 26 years – when, for the first time, a producer was sent on an England tour – it has been Peter Baxter's privilege to get *Test Match Special* on the air. I have worked with Peter for the last 16, and have

Opposite top Peter Baxter surveys the scene in the commentary box at Nagpur in 2006.

Bottom It's always an anxious moment as the lines are installed: World Cup 1987 at Jaipur.

learned that it is usually a good policy to lie low throughout the day preceding the Test Match. This is the situation in much of the cricketing world, but particularly in the Caribbean and Asia where there seems to be a shared view that minor essentials, such as broadcasting circuits and telephones, should be installed as late as possible and, every now and then, after the first ball of the match has been bowled.

Peter and I have got to know the routine pretty well now. On the day before the Test I wave him off at about 8 a.m., rather like a fussy mother seeing her child off to school at the garden gate, and he heads to the ground full of optimism. It is usually about ten hours later, after I have interviewed the captains and done my match previews, that a broken man returns to the hotel with the usual stories of missing telecom engineers and filthy commentary boxes that have no clear view of the pitch or the scoreboard. It remains a triumph, therefore, when we hit the airwaves next day even if there is often a local engineer behind us brandishing a screwdriver at what appears to be the contents of a recently exploded party popper, which in fact is our broadcasting circuit to London.

Modern telecommunications such as ISDN have made the process of broadcasting easier once the line has been established. In the grand old days of

four-wire circuits, it required a chain of operators to flick their appropriate switches to get through to London. Again, it was never a good idea to be too close to Peter when, for the first time, he would ambitiously call out from Eden Gardens, 'Good morning Calcutta Telecom. This is the BBC in Eden Gardens. Please put this line through to London.' There would invariably be no response at all: a depressing situation when one considered that it was currently impossible to broadcast 3 miles from the ground, which left 5,000 still to go, and the circuit had to be switched through Bombay before finally reaching the Telecom Tower in London.

Happily, there is never any shortage of help, however. On that occasion in Calcutta in 1993, the local radio station supplied us with four lovely female engineers who did their best to assist in the commentary box throughout the five-day Test. Unfortunately it was not an easy arrangement, as Peter revealed later in his grateful letter of thanks. He speculated how it might have been even better had either we been able to speak Bengali, or the ladies at least a few words of English.

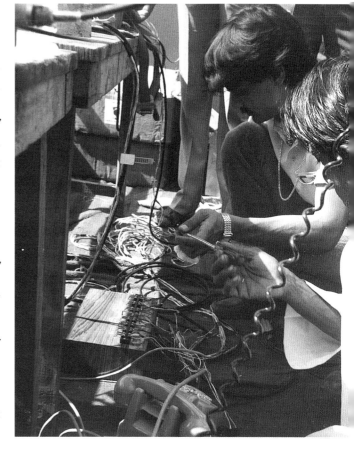

No matter where you are in the world, you are at the mercy of the local telecom engineers. Even in South Africa it is possible to have problems. It took me an entire Test Match to convince a caller to my telephone in the Johannesburg commentary box that I was not the local blood bank, and the local telecom company installed an ISDN circuit – that had been destined for my hotel room – in the basement car park, resulting in my offerings for the BBC being accompanied by the sound of squealing tyres, revving engines and slamming doors.

I will never forget the urgency with which I sought the toilet moments after the Jamaica Test of 1998 was abandoned because of a dangerous pitch. Barging into the little gents' cubicle near our commentary box, I was surprised to discover Henry Blofeld commentating in full flow, as it were, on the eventful proceedings into his mobile telephone. There was nothing to stop me and having relieved myself very noisily and flushed the toilet I glanced at Henry's face. Needless to say, it was a picture.

On one tour of New Zealand, the local company in New Plymouth thoughtfully installed my telephone in the ladies toilet. Granted, the view of the spectacular little ground from within was surprisingly good but, overall, filing reports from there was fraught with difficulty. So, too, my first ever mission for the BBC, which occurred when I was working for the now defunct *Today* newspaper on the 1990–91 tour of Australia. Peter had asked me to stand in during one match in Ballarat to fill the void between him returning home and the then BBC correspondent, Christopher Martin-Jenkins, arriving in Australia. This time the line was installed in the groundsman's shed and, again, the view was excellent. This time, though, the problem was a massive and indisputably ferocious German shepherd dog with which I was supposed to share a small area that had been partitioned off from the rest of the shed. The only answer was to run for it and having managed to slam the door between the two rooms just in time, my debut on the *Today* programme

was punctuated by the sound of the beast snarling, growling and feverishly scratching at the door.

They do seem to have rather a thing about dogs in Ballarat. It was here that we were subjected to possibly the most mundane lunchtime entertainment in living memory when poor old Guitas, the 'Frisbee-catching Wonder Whippet' gamely went through his paces for the entire interval. Indeed, there appears to be a tireless quest throughout Australia for what they believe to be the best interval filler in the world.

'Chase the Sheila' proved to be a favourite with the locals the last time we were Down Under. This is a race around the perimeter of the ground, roughly along the lines of fox and hounds, which involves male athletes of all sizes and physical conditions, and one unfortunate woman. She is given a head start of 20 yards or so, and then, it appears, she is

forced to dash for freedom as the pack of men pursue her, presumably with the aim of running her to ground. Happily, I can report that all the Sheilas we saw that year were successful in outpacing their predators so the inevitable question of what happened next was averted. Probably just as well.

The most difficult times Peter and I have experienced together were towards the end of the 1990s when the BBC did not have the commentary rights. Talk Sport, a national commercial radio

Opposite The All India Radio technical support staff trying to contact London for *TMS*, Calcutta 1993.

Above When Talk Sport had the rights to Test Matches during the late 1990 things got rough for *TMS*. (Left to right) Robin Jackman, Mike Selvey and Aggers were reduced to broadcasting *Test Match Special Report* by torchlight in Durban on the 1999–2000 tour.

station, went through a phase of buying the broadcasting rights for four winter tours, which meant that while I was allowed to do a limited number of news flashes for the entire output of BBC radio, we were often not even guaranteed a seat in the grounds.

This reached a remarkable climax in Galle, Sri Lanka, in 2001 when we were physically locked out of the ground. We had a feeling that there might be trouble during the first day, but hoped that it might go away. Sadly, we arrived for the second to find the gates locked, and our entrance barred, so I headed for the old Dutch fort, which overlooks the ground at the sea end (and which spared the lives of a number of cricketers when the tsunami struck the area in 2004). From the splendid ramparts among bemused iguanas and saffron-robed monks, we had a workable view of the cricket ground and scoreboard just across a busy road and, thanks to the modern miracle that is the satellite telephone, I was able to broadcast in perfect quality for the bulletins on Radio 4 and Radio Five Live breakfast programmes. Peter, meanwhile, maintained a determined, dignified and solitary vigil at the gates until common sense prevailed, and we were finally allowed back into the ground.

I wonder what some of my predecessors – the pioneers of BBC cricket reporting – would make of much of the above. How things have changed since the winter of 1932–33 when French commercial radio stations, of all things, broadcast reports and even some 'synthetic' commentary on the infamous Bodyline tour of Australia. Jim Swanton became the first full-time reporter to travel for the BBC when he pestered them to go to South Africa in 1938–39. Ten years later, John Arlott commentated on some exciting climaxes to the Tests in South Africa, and there were brief periods of commentary from Australia in 1950–51 and on subsequent tours it became the practice to take the last session of play for the day. But it was not until 1977 that *Test Match Special* could really claim to have hit the airwaves when CMJ, Henry and Robin Marlar described England winning the series on the last day of the Test in Madras. From then come my first memories of

listening to *TMS* at night via a small radio buried under the pillow at school during the 1977 Centenary Test in Melbourne. Little did I think then that I would be subjecting listeners to the same nocturnal torture 14 years later.

The one piece of kit that has really made a difference from those days to this is the satellite telephone. It is possible literally to broadcast, day or night, from just about anywhere that has a reasonably uninterrupted view of the sky. At most hotels we get the choice of the area around the swimming pool – which is definitely the preferred option, unless it is the Centre Point Hotel, Nagpur where the pool is essentially a giant underground skip in that it has no water and is full of broken toilets and other assorted builders' rubbish – or the hotel roof. Although the view can be impressive up there, roofs, in my experience, are not the most glamorous of locations, and are usually only accessible via narrow and dark, stone stairwells. At the Shiza Hotel in Multan, we sent back reports among rows of slate grey hotel towels that had been pegged out between the rattling air conditioning ducts. From the roof of the Meghdoot Hotel in Kanpur, you easily pick up the gentle, early evening lowing of the water buffalo in the street below, and see the flickering flames of the funeral pyres lighting up the night sky on the banks of the Ganges. The Piccadilly Hotel in Chandigarh offers a glimpse of the Himalayas, while for those who might now be developing a real penchant for hotel roofs, I recommend the Old Holiday Inn in Sydney. This places you almost directly under the Harbour Bridge and with a superlative view across the water of the Opera House. Not a bad place from which to broadcast.

One peril of the satellite telephone is that radiation from the panel that one aims into space to pick up the signal can, apparently, make you sterile if you stand in front of it for too long. At least, this is

the excuse we make to prevent people from getting in the way and knocking out our signal. I carefully imparted this information to a member of the Zimbabwean Police Force as we awaited England's arrival at Harare airport in 2004. A large fellow with a kindly smile, he had spent rather too much time hovering around for my liking, and I could tell from the splats in my headphones that he might inadvertently cut us off at any moment.

Apparently shaken by the news, he disappeared for a few minutes only to reappear and, squatting low with his hands on his knees, straddled the panel. 'What on earth are you doing?' I shouted at him, at

which point he gestured towards his nether regions and, with a huge grin, replied, 'No more kids!'

Of course, modern communications mean that we are constantly available for work: there is no escape! On what had been billed as a quiet day beside the hotel pool in Cairns in 1998, Radio Five Live were being particularly persistent for my liking. 'That's it!' I said to Peter at the end of another piece. 'If they ring again, I'm doing it from the jacuzzi!' Ten minutes later, the inevitable happened, and I am not sure to this day if Peter Allen knows that his carefully recorded interview was undertaken amid a mass of foaming bubbles and a group of startled Japanese tourists.

The nature of touring has certainly changed dramatically since those early days of tearful farewells at Tilbury Docks, followed by a month at sea. Come to think of it, what a wonderful experience it must have been to be the BBC reporter in those days. There was certainly no means of firing up a satellite dish on

Above On the roof of the Piccadilly Hotel, Chandigarh in 2006, Aggers waits while Kevin Howells sends a report to Radio Five Live.

Opposite Enough's enough: Aggers sends yet another report for Radio Five Live from the jaccuzi, Cairns, 1998.

the boat, so four weeks of peace and quiet, while watching the cricketers go through their not especially taxing training routines on deck. Fantastic!

The tours were much longer then, of course, with an incredible amount of cricket played between the Test Matches. For example, England's tour of Australia in 1951–52 on which there were occasional passages of radio commentary for the first time, consisted of no fewer than five warm up matches before the First Test – and these were five-day games in Perth, Adelaide, Melbourne, Sydney and Brisbane. Compare that with England's latest Ashes trip on which the build-up consisted of two three-day games and a limited-overs jolly in Canberra. In 1951–52 there was at least one five-day first-class match between every Test. In 2005–06, Andrew Flintoff's team had just one game that was not a Test Match between the First Test and the last!

Even in the early 1990s, when I first started, there was more cricket played on all the tours, and often the most enjoyable part of a trip to Australia was the up-country game or two that England would play in order to get match practice – and also to raise the profile of cricket in the more remote towns of that colossal continent. The locals always tried so hard, not merely to be welcoming, but to win the game

that for the majority was the highlight of their playing careers. I have a vivid memory of Miles Obst, a little-known farmer from the Geraldton area of Western Australia, bowling his guts out in 1990 to take 4 for 36 for the Country XI. This effort was all the more spectacular for the fact that a massive plague of locusts was munching its way through his wheat crop at the time and yet, for Obst, nothing was more important than having his one and only bash at an England cricket team.

The public address announcers can be just a little biased and full of their own importance on these occasions. I recall a match in Lawes, south-east Queensland, during which the tinny speaker crackled into life, 'Ladies and gentlemen, there's a bowling change. This is Stormy Gale coming on at the Piggery End. Let's hope he puts the wind up the Poms!'

Tours of the subcontinent are much easier now – particularly Pakistan, which I have never found anything but the most helpful and welcoming country. India remains chaotic which, from a cricketing point of view, is a frustration. The BCCI is making an astonishing amount of money from the game, but never seems to put much back into its infrastructure – particularly towards the upkeep of the stadiums, which are largely filthy, structurally unsafe and inhospitable places. The toilet facilities at Indian grounds are nothing short of disgusting health hazards, and certainly not to be recommended to travelling supporters. Despite that, the tour of India in 1993 remains my favourite of all time.

A strike by the domestic airline played havoc with England's carefully laid plans, and this was not helped either by a religious uprising in Ayodhya: a town very close to Lucknow, the venue of one of England's warm up games. This gave rise to a bizarre match from which spectators were banned, and the town was sealed off. The concrete stadium was full of armed police, who were supposed to be guarding the cricketers with their backs to the game in the event of infiltrators scaling the walls from outside. Of course this lasted only an hour or two, and it was not long before they sat in the stands, with the officers leading the applause as Navjot Singh Sidhu hit John Emburey for a number of huge sixes. The armed presence remained with us throughout our stay, though, with guards placed outside our rooms in the hotel, which incidentally is the only one in the world in which I have stayed to boast a cattle grid at its front door.

The highlight of the hastily-revised travel plans was a rail journey from Bhubaneswar, on the east coast, to Calcutta: a trip of only an hour or so by aircraft, but one that took all night by sleeper. The first-class cabin consisted merely of padded shelves, one above the other, and we were entertained throughout the journey by a family of mice scampering about in the semi-darkness. The real delight, though, was sharing the ordeal with the players who also reclined in our creaking carriage and, like us, were thoroughly bemused by the whole unforgettable experience. It is difficult to imagine a similar situation being allowed these days.

To complete a remarkable tour, we were held up by armed highwaymen during an eight-hour marathon bus ride from Calcutta to Jamshedpur. It is true that they were not necessarily the most committed of bandits, and they ran off when our travel guide shouted at them to go away. Then, having finally made it to Jamshedpur, the crowd rioted and we drove back again.

Travelling through the Caribbean brings its own uncertainty. It is not the easiest business getting from one country to another and we have often found ourselves at the mercy of one island-hopping airline whose initials have been affectionately turned into the acronym for Luggage In Another Terminal. This came true on one occasion when the team and media were all crammed into a small machine with two propellers bound for Trinidad from St Vincent. As we thundered down the runway, those of us on the right-hand side of the aircraft could see much of our luggage still sitting firmly on the ground, where

Opposite On the Bhubaneswar to Calcutta express in 1993, Jonathan Agnew (top) tries to stop the air conditioning with a sock while cricket writer Mark Baldwin wonders if it's all worth it.

it remained for 36 hours. Trouble was, the selection of suitcases that made the journey was entirely random and resulted in a number of the team going out for dinner the following night wearing white cricket flannels, cricket socks and training shoes along with a smart, casual top half!

In Barbados, it is very tempting to travel to the Kensington Oval by Mini Moke. These are not necessarily the largest or the most comfortable of cars, but they are brilliant fun with the roof off, and if it rains you get wet and the water drains through a plughole in the floor. Carrying a full set of golf clubs in the back of a Moke is ambitious, but this did not deter Christopher Martin-Jenkins from bouncing back after 18 holes on a course on the west coast to our hotel on the other side of Bridgetown with the clubs, that he had very generously been lent by a local, perched perilously across the back seat. Returning to the hotel, he was aghast to discover a completely empty bag behind him – each and every one of the many bumps and potholes along the way having sent at least one club flying out of the car and onto the road. An embarrassed plea during the local cricket commentary the following day asked for the return of any golf clubs that might have been found on the highway.

Stories of CMJ on tour abound, but my favourite concerns his car journey as navigator for Mike Selvey from Montego Bay, in the north west of Jamaica, over the Blue Mountains to Kingston. Because of the time difference with London, it is necessary to speak with the office early in the day from that part of the world, and it was with rapidly mounting desperation that Chris tried repeatedly to dial his sports editor on his mobile telephone. After numerous failures, he handed the handset to Mike, who made the literally unbelievable, but hilarious discovery that it was not a telephone at all, but the television remote control from CMJ's hotel room!

Right Aggers with the BBC line to London, Jamaica, 1994.
Overleaf Photographer David Munden captures the moment when Mother Theresa almost told Aggers to 'sod off', Calcutta, 1991.

I have learned to expect the unexpected on my travels. In 1994, England's first cricket match in the sprawling township of Soweto, near Johannesburg, was a historic occasion in many ways. It was the first tour of South Africa by an England team for 29 years, and although the opening match had more than just a little of a political edge to it, any cynical views were quickly hushed by the arrival, by helicopter, of the president, Nelson Mandela. Naturally enough, this brought the game to a standstill as the president, who was in the middle of his election campaign, slowly walked around the boundary edge waving to the crowd. I caught the attention of one of the press officers and said, 'Look, I know this is ridiculous, but what chance is there of me being able to interview Mr Mandela?'

Bearing in mind that we feel chuffed to have a one-on-one audience with Duncan Fletcher these

days, I was amazed when he told me to stand where I was, and he would see what he could do.

And so it was that Nelson Mandela, in one of his characteristic Mdiba shirts, strolled casually over and, with the press corps gathered breathlessly behind me, gestured for me to start the interview.

What struck me was how incredibly calm he was. He also spoke very slowly and deliberately. After five or six questions, I stood aside and the written press boys had their moment with one of the great icons of our lifetime. I glanced anxiously at my good friend and Press Association photographer, Rebecca Naden, and she gave me the thumbs up: she had taken a snap for me! (Just wish I had not been wearing sunglasses. Forgot I had them on.)

Just about everything involving South Africa at that time was viewed as 'historic' – certainly by the tireless Ali Bacher, one of the great survivors in cricket politics. I had been in Calcutta in the autumn of 1991 to watch South Africa's first tentative step into world cricket after decades of isolation. There were truly amazing scenes in the cricket-crazy city as hundreds of thousands of people lined the streets and gave Clive Rice's team a tremendous welcome.

My phone rang early one morning before the opening match, and I instantly recognised the voice of Chris Day, the South African media liaison manager. 'The team has been invited to meet Mother Theresa in one of her missions. Do you fancy coming along too?' I was in the lobby before he had put the telephone down. Unfortunately I was not alone. Such was the naivety of South African cricket at the time – and the genuine desire to be helpful – that there were scores of television personnel, photographers and a healthy gathering of newspaper hacks all bustling to get a place on the trip.

We crammed into a decrepit bus and lurched around the streets of Calcutta before stopping outside an anonymous building with a dirty stone façade and steps leading up to the front door. Venturing inside, I was confronted by absolute bedlam. Television crews were pushing and shoving people aside, voices were raised and tempers flared

as everyone tried to get close to Rice and Mother Theresa, who gathered for a team photograph. Deciding that a low profile was the best course of action, I waited until the melee had died down at which point I noticed that Mother Theresa appeared to be handing out pieces of paper to those who filed past her.

I joined the queue just as a raucous Afrikaans-speaking television broadcaster started to shout a report into his camera a few feet from Mother Theresa. This was the last straw, and the moment her saintly poise temporarily deserted her. Angrily, she started to bundle us out. As I went past she handed me a card, on which was printed a prayer, and a flashgun went off. The picture, taken by David Munden, stands proudly in my sitting room today and visitors always remark on it. What they do not know, of course, is that if there was ever a moment in her life when Mother Theresa came close to telling somebody to sod off, that was it.

If *TMS* on tour sounds like a lot of fun, that is because it genuinely is. There are ups and downs, of course, and the biggest downside is the amount of time we spend away from home every winter. Christmas is particularly difficult, and although we all do our best to get through the day, the truth is it is all very depressing. It is a shame that the traditional drinks party with the players, which was always held before lunch on Christmas Day and was the highlight of the festivities, has fallen by the wayside. Members of the press would put on a skit which, now and then, was quite amusing, and it was a really good time for us all to mix with the players – who would be in fancy dress – and bury any differences. Now we go our separate ways throughout the day and make the best of it.

But that apart – and the occasional, but devastating encounter with alien stomach bugs along the way – it is not a bad lot. I take great heart in the thought that somewhere out there is a youngster, listening to *Test Match Special* through the night, whose enthusiasm for cricket is fired by what we are doing and who, one day, will get his or her chance to carry the baton.

MY FIRST TEST MATCH

Tony Cozier

The summer of 1966 was a great time to be a West Indian in England. Even though by then well ensconced as citizens of the Mother Country, the hundreds of thousands who had streamed in from the soon-to-be-independent Caribbean colonies over the previous decade were still West Indians by birth and upbringing. Cricket was their passion and the presence of a powerful, charismatic team in their adopted land for the second time in three years was an antidote to the tedium of their jobs on the buses and tubes, in hospitals and post offices.

In 1963, they had been uplifted by the 3-1 triumph of the team under Frank Worrell that made such an impression the previously unalterable itinerary was adjusted to have the West Indies back again three years before they were due. Once more the outcome was 3-1 and, while *Wisden* commented that the team 'failed by a

Above Tony Cozier (centre) and other assorted journalists from the Caribbean arrive in London to cover the West Indies tour in 1966.
Right A more relaxed Tony Cozier enjoys himself at his annual beach party at home in Barbados in 1994.

long way to reveal the power' of its predecessor, it made little difference to their supporters.

Certainly the comparison didn't figure much in the copy of the young reporter covering the tour for West Indian papers and who, by good fortune, was to start a 40-year association with the remarkable BBC radio programme known, and loved, as *Test Match Special*. By virtue of a soft-hearted father, who himself had reported for the Caribbean press on the historic 1950 tour of England and

England v West Indies Fourth Test

4–8 August 1966 Headingley, Leeds

Umpires **JS Buller and CS Elliott**

WEST INDIES FIRST INNINGS

CC Hunte	lbw b Snow	48
PD Lashley	b Higgs	9
RB Kanhai	c Graveney b Underwood	45
BF Butcher	c Parks b Higgs	38
SM Nurse	c Titmus b Snow	137
* GS Sobers	b Barber	174
DAJ Holford	b Higgs	24
CC Griffith	b Higgs	0
† JL Hendriks	not out	9
WW Hall	b Snow	1
LR Gibbs	not out	2
Extras	(b 1, lb 12)	13
Total	(9 wks dec, 164 overs)	500

Fall of wickets 1-37, 2-102, 3-122, 4-154, 5-419, 6-467, 7-467, 8-489, 9-491

Bowling	O	M	R	W
Snow	42	6	146	3
Higgs	43	11	94	4
D'Oliveira	19	3	52	0
Titmus	22	7	59	0
Underwood	24	9	81	1
Barber	14	2	55	1

'The summer of 1966 was a great time to be a West Indian in England.' Supporters celebrate after West Indies victory at Headingley which put them 3-0 ahead in a five-match series.

ENGLAND FIRST INNINGS

G Boycott	c Holford b Hall	12
RW Barber	c Hendriks b Griffith	6
C Milburn	not out	29
TW Graveney	b Hall	8
* MC Cowdrey	b Hall	17
BL D'Oliveira	c Hall b Griffith	88
† JM Parks	lbw b Sobers	2
FJ Titmus	c Hendriks b Sobers	6
K Higgs	c Nurse b Sobers	49
DL Underwood	c Gibbs b Sobers	0
JA Snow	c Holford b Sobers	0
Extras	(b 12, lb 11)	23
Total	(all out, 78.3 overs)	240

Fall of wickets 1-10, 2-18, 3-42, 4-49, 5-63, 6-83, 7-179, 8-238, 9-240

Bowling	O	M	R	W
Hall	17	5	47	3
Griffith	12	2	37	2
Sobers	19.3	4	41	5
Gibbs	20	5	49	0
Holford	10	3	43	0

SECOND INNINGS FOLLOWING ON

G Boycott	c Hendriks b Lashley	14
RW Barber	b Sobers	55
BL D'Oliveira	c Butcher b Sobers	7
TW Graveney	b Gibbs	19
* MC Cowdrey	lbw b Gibbs	12
† JM Parks	c Nurse b Gibbs	16
C Milburn	b Gibbs	42
FJ Titmus	b Gibbs	22
K Higgs	c Hunte b Sobers	7
DL Underwood	c Kanhai b Gibbs	0
JA Snow	not out	0
Extras	(b 8, lb 1, nb 2)	11
Total	(all out, 71.1 overs)	205

Fall of wickets 1-28, 2-70, 3-84, 4-109, 5-128, 6-133, 7-184, 8-205, 9-205

Bowling	O	M	R	W
Hall	8	2	24	0
Griffith	12	0	52	0
Sobers	20.1	5	39	3
Gibbs	19	6	39	6
Holford	9	0	39	0
Lashley	3	2	1	1

West Indies won by an innings and 55 runs

was now publisher of the Barbados *Daily News*, some persistent persuasion and an agreement to look after my expenses when I got there, I had wangled my way to England for the 1963 trip. YMCAs and the sofas of a few sympathetic student friends took care of the accommodation. Reports for the half-hour magazine show on the BBC Caribbean Service helped boost fragile finances.

Three years on, I had moved on a bit. Probably boosted by the 1963 BBC reports (the BBC has always enjoyed a formidable reputation in the Caribbean), I was included on the commentary team for the five Tests of the 1965 Australian tour in the West Indies and had also picked up a few assignments with regional and international papers. So my second tour to England wasn't so penny-pinching. Indeed, I was able to afford marriage in the interim and put it to the bride that, by way of a novel honeymoon, we could spend the summer in London, with intermittent trips to other cities for the Tests and, perhaps, a match or two in the simultaneous football World Cup. We rented a cosy bedsit off the Bayswater Road and I could even afford a nifty little Vauxhall Viva to get around in those days of negligible petrol prices and open roads.

I wasn't quite sure what Jillian made of the idea but it is the kind of existence she has put up with for 40 years and there has only been the occasional, audible grumble. I am sure it has something to do with the fact that, for several of those years, her husband and, by extension, she too has been part of the fun, and the family, that is *TMS*.

The link began by chance. Since Kingston was hosting the 1966 Commonwealth Games in August, it meant Roy Lawrence, head of sports at the Jamaica Broadcasting Corporation and *TMS*'s West Indian commentator since the 1957 tour, was needed back home, consequently missing the Headingley Test. I'm certain it was on the irrefutable recommendation of E.W. Swanton that I received a call to fill in. Hugely influential as Cricket Correspondent of the *Daily Telegraph* and *TMS* summariser, Swanton was a regular winter resident of Barbados with, it was said, an eye on the Governor-General's post. There were factors that must have counted in favour of Lawrence's Barbadian substitute.

It might have been an intimidating assignment for an inexperienced 26-year-old placed alongside such imposing luminaries as Swanton himself, Robert Hudson, Brian Johnston and the former England captain, Norman Yardley,

all familiar names and voices on BBC's ball-by-ball commentaries that had been beamed back to the West Indies since the 1939 tour.

It proved nothing of the sort. That the West Indies won the Test by an innings surely helped. So did the phenomenal all-round performance of the great Gary Sobers, a close friend, who scored 174 (one of three scores over 150 in the series), took 8 wickets for 80 with his menacing left-arm swing, besides, according to *Wisden* 'directing the men with masterly skill'.

But it was more than victory that made a nervous novice feel at home. What was immediately obvious was the comforting, relaxed air, engendered principally by Brian Johnston's cheery personality and impish sense of humour. I can't recall if I was the butt of any of his favourite pranks in that match but, if not, he subsequently made up for it – by asking a question on air as soon as you'd taken a bite out of one of the glut of cakes that became one of his trademarks or by strategically placing the kettle to boil just below your chair with the delayed shock of steam boiling the back of your thigh.

Johnners' credo was simple and set the tone for the broadcast. *TMS*, he said, 'is like a group of friends at a cricket match. We sit together, swap jokes and, if someone has a good tale to tell he's encouraged to tell it. Most importantly, we all think that cricket is fun.'

So it was then and has remained whenever I have been part of the 'group of friends', on nine West Indies tours of England, in three World Cups and, more recently, on my own patch in the Caribbean where I've been able to return some of the hospitality shown on the other side.

It's not to say there haven't been dissenting views. *TMS* would have been a distant memory had that been so. Throughout the long period of West Indian domination, I found myself repeatedly on the ropes, throwing punches in the face of accusations of intimidatory bowling and of slow over-rates. Strangely, the topic has not been raised much recently since the West Indies have been on the receiving end of similarly hostile English bowling, crumbling to double-figure totals and enduring whitewashes.

But, whatever is happening on the field and even with a changing cast, *TMS* has upheld Brian Johnston's maxim that 'cricket is fun'. That is surely what has preserved its global popularity and made it such a joy to be part of.

MY FIRST TEST MATCH

Jim Maxwell

Many of my earliest sleepless nights were blamed on cricket. The static from the short wave signal was so annoying that you had to hang in for that sudden burst of discernible commentary, and the all-important score.

While BBC listeners enjoyed John Arlott's colourful, poetic descriptions, ABC audiences heard a combination of pure Arlott, or when the technical gods were growling, Arlott short wave, until 1964.

My transistor radio was the size of a small brick, and as I manoeuvred it to find better reception, I heard an Australian voice, a silvery tone that became my spotlight on the game. Alan McGilvray's commentary was always accurate, insightful and embellished with a detailed replay,

'that was a half volley from McKenzie, and Dexter straight drove it for four, one of the hardest shots in the game'.

Arlott and McGilvray, and later Brian Johnston, were the main messengers, radio was the only medium of choice, until the first live television pictures from England were shown from the Oval in 1972.

My first taste of being part of the *TMS* team came in England in 1983, when Peter Baxter skilfully organised the World Cup coverage. Any nervousness I felt was quickly overcome when Brian Johnston insisted that I should enjoy myself in the box. Johnners chuckled, I smiled, more puns and double entendres, and there was an immediate sense of being at ease alongside

Australia v Zimbabwe World Cup Group B (60-overs match)

9 June 1983 Trent Bridge, Nottingham   Umpires **DJ Constant and MJ Kitchen**

ZIMBABWE

AH Omarshah	c Marsh b Lillee	16
GA Paterson	c Hookes b Lillee	27
JG Heron	c Marsh b Yallop	14
AJ Pycroft	b Border	21
† DL Houghton	c Marsh b Yallop	0
* DAG Fletcher	not out	69
KM Curran	c Hookes b Hogg	27
IP Butchart	not out	34
Extras	(lb 18, w 7, nb 6)	31
Total	(6 wks, 60 overs)	239
Did not bat	PWE Rawson, AJ Traicos, VR Hogg	

Fall of wickets   1-55, 2-55, 3-86, 4-86, 5-94, 6-164

Bowling	O	M	R	W
Lawson	11	2	33	0
Hogg	12	3	43	1
Lillee	12	1	47	2
Thomson	11	1	46	0
Yallop	9	0	28	2
Border	5	0	11	1

AUSTRALIA

GM Wood	c Houghton b Fletcher	31
KC Wessels	run out	76
* KJ Hughes	c Omarshah b Fletcher	0
DW Hookes	c Traicos b Fletcher	20
GN Yallop	c Pycroft b Fletcher	2
AR Border	c Pycroft b Curran	17
† RW Marsh	not out	50
GF Lawson	b Butchart	0
RM Hogg	not out	19
Extras	(b 2, lb 7, w 2)	11
Total	(7 wks, 60 overs)	226
Did not bat	DK Lillee, JR Thomson	

Fall of wickets   1-61, 2-63, 3-114, 4-133, 5-138, 6-168, 7-176

Bowling	O	M	R	W
Hogg	6	2	15	0
Rawson	12	1	54	0
Butchart	10	0	39	1
Fletcher	11	1	42	4
Traicos	12	2	27	0
Curran	9	0	38	1

Zimbabwe captain Duncan Fletcher pulls Jeff Thomson to the boundary in his innings of 69 not out.. He then took 4 for 42 with the ball to ensure a historic victory for his country.

Zimbabwe won by 13 runs

broadcasters who were far more experienced than a broadcasting green horn like me.

Despite Australia's abysmal showing, the experience of working with Trevor Bailey, Peter Parfitt, Colin Milburn, Zimbabwean Bob Nixon, Tony Cozier, CMJ, Henry Blofeld, the prompter cum scorer Bill Frindall and an ecstatic ('I got 16 to 1') Farokh Engineer at India's surprise victory, was lapped up.

There were other *TMS* tastes, at the 1996 World Cup, describing the West Indies extraordinary defeat by Australia in the semi-final at Chandigarh huddled in a makeshift, shoebox commentary position with Peter Baxter, Mark Nicholas and Bryan Davis, and for the first part of the 2001 Ashes series, before handing over to my accomplished colleague Tim Lane for the remainder.

In 2003 another co-production of international voices at South Africa's World Cup had a *TMS* flavour, fed out on long wave or the emerging medium of digital radio. Brian Johnston's influence lived on strongly, with colour and comment from Aggers, Blowers, Jenkers, Backers, Selvers, and the singular Angus Fraser, collectively watching England's hapless performance, as Australia won the Cup just ahead of a High Veldt storm.

The flavour of champagne moments and cake spotting was still fresh in my mind from the Johnston days when I joined up for the whole 2005 Ashes tour. It was memorable. The rapturous singing from the stands, fired up by the rendition of 'Jerusalem' every Test Match day, the dramatic tension of the contest, and the end-of-play scurry to get live interviews with the combatants, swayed into liaison by Peter Baxter's shrewd assistant, Shilpa Patel. Like actors aroused by a full house, the *TMS* team could work off the crowd, and the commentary flowed easily, and at last triumphantly at the Oval when Jonathan Agnew interviewed Michael Vaughan and every other victorious Englishman.

In the fancy dressed crowd the celebration had been previewed prior to play on the final day when my roving mike encountered a group of 19th century mother country police surrounding a Ned Kelly lookalike. 'So, what will happen to Ned if England regain the Ashes today?' I inquired. 'We'll hang him, of course.'

The 2005 tour coincided with the news that London would host the 2012 Olympics. My tourer up and down the motorways for three months was a Renault, with Paris number plates. It was also left-hand-drive. Perhaps I hadn't read the fine print when I collected the car at Heathrow. England had just scorched Australia in a one-dayer at Headingley, and as we moved towards our parked cars in the adjacent football ground, I noticed a note under the windscreen wipers, 'I hope you French are enjoying the cricket!! Bad luck about the Olympics.' And after the umpires had a bad day at Trent Bridge another note read, 'do you have any decent umpires in France?'

Fortunately the motorway umpires remained silent. My regular passenger and *TMS* co-commentator Geoff Lawson often inquired, 'What's the speed limit?' as he watched the needle hit 150. Well it was a kph speedometer, and how fast is 70 mph on conversion. So here's a tip for your next Ashes tour – get a left-hand-drive car with foreign plates.

Another *TMS* innovation features celebrity interviews during the Saturday lunch breaks. This required some interior design skill at Trent Bridge, because the box resembled a food hall, choc a bloc with pork pie hampers as rival bakers outdid each other for naming rights.

Having eaten or donated the stash to some hungry person outside there was enough room for the engineer, Dave Savage to set up the microphones to get the best result from Aggers' chat with the former leader of the Stranglers, Hugh Cornwell, and his live rendition of 'Golden Brown'. It was an acoustic triumph, and Hugh followed up in Australia when he paid us a visit in the ABC box at the SCG the following summer.

At Old Trafford I was asked to interview Michele Verroken, former boss of the British Sports Anti Doping Agency. Luckily we had a chat beforehand, so I was prepared.

Radio is a wonderful medium for imagination, and deception. On cue Michele asked me to undergo a live drugs test. Recent instances of male athletes' samples confirming that they were pregnant prompted a see-all testing procedure, ensuring that smuggled vials could no longer corrupt the test. So as I imaginatively made to strip off for the test, using up time to collect a wine bottle, taking care not to spill my sample inappropriately, listeners heard the effect of gentle dripping into a glass. As the box broke up with laughter, Michele did a quick test, which I passed, but then declared that I might have an alcohol problem. Even reality television would have struggled to pull that off, but on *TMS* radio anything's possible.

Aggers, flanked by Bill Frindall (left) and Mike Selvey, describes the action from the Fifth Test in Sydney as England's 2006–07 defence of the Ashes ends in a 5-0 whitewash.

9

A VIEW FROM
THE BOUNDARY

An interview with the playwright, Ben Travers, author of the Whitehall farces, was the catalyst for our Saturday lunchtime feature, 'A View from the Boundary', which has now been going for just over half the life of *Test Match Special* itself. During a fascinating interview he recalled the tour of Australia in 1928–29 where, as a friend of the England captain, Percy Chapman, he observed a historic series at first

hand. When he came up the stairs of Lord's in 1980 in sprightly fashion at the age of 94, he also told us tales of having seen W.G. Grace at the crease and gave us an account of Gilbert Jessop's famous 75-minute century against Australia at the Oval in 1902.

The rules we set ourselves were that the guests should be celebrities from a field other than cricket, who had a love of the game. We had to make one exception to our rule when the former Australian opening batsman, Jack Fingleton, stood in at Old Trafford in 1980, but he was – as ever – very entertaining.

Opposite The England team that Ben Travers saw against Australia at the Oval in 1902: (back row, left to right) George Hirst, Arthur Lilley, Bill Lockwood, Len Braund, Wilfred Rhodes, Johnny Tyldesley; (front row) C.B. Fry, Stanley Jackson, Archie MacLaren, Ranji, Gilbert Jessop.

Ben Travers

VIEW FROM THE BOUNDARY

'Well, of course he [W.G. Grace] was a great hulk of a chap. He was the great predominant figure of cricket in his time – more so than any other individual since. He had rather an odd stance in that he … had his left heel on the ground and cocked his toe up, and he also awaited the ball, when the bowler was halfway through his run, with his bat off the ground … some modern batsman … have done that, but W.G. started it, or at least he did it in his day …

'At the other end Jessop went absolutely crazy. This menace Saunders, who'd already dismissed all our star batsmen, Jessop hit him for four fours in the square leg to long-on district. Hugh Trumble was bowling at the other end. Jessop hit him onto the awning in the pavilion. The ball came back. He hit him there again next ball. And so he went on. The enthusiasm was tremendous.

'I was there [in Australia], very luckily, in 1928–29 when I saw Bradman play his first innings for Australia against England in Brisbane. It was a great tour. Of course England had a wonderful side. Percy Chapman was captain and Jardine making his first tour and Farmer White; they were the three amateurs. Then there were Hobbs and Sutcliffe. I always say, Brian [Johnston], that the greatest Test innings I ever saw was played by Jack Hobbs at Melbourne in the first few days of 1929, the Third Test Match, and he made 49. I think that 49 was the greatest innings I ever saw.'

LORD'S, 1980

this was an ideal slot for Brian Johnston. He knew so many of the guests anyway.

All the interviews have been done live in the commentary box except four of them which were recorded in special circumstances. The first of these was for the MCC's Bicentenary in 1987, when we managed to secure an interview with the twice-President, His Royal Highness, the Duke of Edinburgh. That was recorded in Prince Phillip's study at Buckingham Palace. He has been 'Twelfth Man' of the Lord's Taverners since its foundation in 1950 and, as President of the National Playing Fields Association, the cause of protecting our sports grounds is very dear to his heart. As an occasional off-spinner, his proudest moment was to take the wicket of Tom Graveney in a charity match at Arundel in Sussex.

Ben Travers may have been the inspiration, but he was not the first. That privilege went to Ted Moult, the farmer turned quiz panellist, who came to Trent Bridge from his farm at Swadlincote in Derbyshire. The original plan was that the interviewing would be shared around among the various members of the commentary team, but it quickly became plain that

Above Brian Johnston keeping tabs on the latest episode of his favourite soap *Neighbours* at Old Trafford, 1992.
Right Mick Jagger takes a slot for Guyanese radio during the 1998 England tour. A big supporter of *TMS*, he assisted our broadcasting during that same tour and appeared on 'A View from the Boundary' the following year.

The fact that the multi-millionaire, J. Paul Getty III, was prepared to do an interview was such a coup that we were only too happy to accede to his request to record it at his flat overlooking Green Park in London. He and Brian had become firm friends and shared an unlikely passion for the television soap *Neighbours*. Paul Getty was a great benefactor of cricket, responsible for much of the financing of the rebuilt Mound Stand at Lord's and creating his own cricket ground at Wormsley in the Chilterns. He made Brian his match manager.

With the intense publicity surrounding them, it was certainly understandable that we had to record the interviews with two genuine stars of the music world. Mick Jagger was recorded rather unusually in Dennis Amiss's office, then chief executive of Warwickshire, behind the sightscreen at Edgbaston. Also unusually, but not uniquely, we had two interviewers as both Mike Selvey and Jeff Thomson were keen to speak to him. Sir Mick was enough of a *TMS* fan to have made sure that our commentary on the 1998 series in the West Indies was relayed on the Internet via his own website. Another knight of rock,

Sir Elton John, was interviewed onstage by Jonathan Agnew as he prepared for a concert in aid of Andrew Flintoff's benefit. The interview was broadcast during the First Test of 2006. Elton had clearly seen a lot more of Sky's coverage of county cricket than Aggers and showed himself to be something of a fanatic. When we broadcast the interview, we included one part of the concert, when Flintoff himself joined Elton on stage for a rendition of 'Rocket Man'. It was enough to convince us that Freddie will not be leaving cricket for a recording contract in the near future.

Our list of guests (see pages 194–5 for a full list) shows that actors are way out ahead in terms of the professions represented, but there is a healthy selection of politicians, too, who have appeared in the commentary box on a Saturday lunchtime. Sir John Major's love of cricket is well documented. After all, he chose the Oval as his luxury for his *Desert Island Discs* and that is where he went on the afternoon of the day he was voted out of office as Prime Minister. His various entries in our visitor's book chart an interesting career. Under the address

Sir Elton John

'I liked one-day internationals when they started them but there are too many of them now. They wear out the players and cricketers are playing too many games. Tests are far more interesting, they are more of a chess game. Test Match cricket is far more worthwhile and relaxing.

'I do think you see the best cricket in Tests and I like the fact that you can play for five days and no one wins …

'… Every musician I've ever known would like to be a sportsman and every sportsman I've known wants to be a musician. They're both great levellers and there is a feeling of togetherness – sport and music, more than anything, bring people together.'

LORD'S, 2006

VIEW FROM THE BOUNDARY

column we have, 'the Treasury', 'the Foreign Office', '11 Downing Street', '10 Downing Street' and 'President, Surrey CCC'. It was as Foreign Secretary that he was interviewed by Brian Johnston, revealing that he had been known to have Test Match scores gravely brought to him during the great meetings of state.

Our other Prime Ministerial guest actually joined us while in that office. John Howard, Prime Minister of Australia, had to come to the Lord's commentary box twice during the day of his visit. His security people were alarmed that the lunchtime session had been too well advertised to the photographers, but impressively, he came up himself to apologise and agreed to return in the tea interval when a more ordered protocol could be prepared. He gloried in having been described by Mark Taylor as 'a cricket tragic'.

Lord Hattersley, before he was ennobled, was with us – appropriately for a Yorkshireman – at Headingley. After being given the usual BJ welcome,

Above Bill Frindall at work in the Lord's commentary box complete with his three stopwatches (one for each batsman and one for the innings as a whole), calculator and scorebooks. His efforts captivated Lord Tebbit during the politician's visit to the commentary box in 2001.

Opposite Former Prime Minister John Major joins the crowd at Trent Bridge for the Third Test against Australia in 2001.

he was slightly taken aback when he returned home later that day to be greeted by his wife saying 'Hello, Hatters!' Peter Hain, so prominent in his younger days in the anti-apartheid movement, was the choice for his native South Africa's first tour of England since 1965. He explained the painful irony he felt that his efforts had helped to deny him the chance to see for so long his own South African cricket heroes in action. For one of our team, Barry Richards, it was a particularly strained meeting, as his own Test career had been cut to just four matches by South Africa's international ban. But Peter was such a cricket enthusiast and even so was convinced that the end result had been the right outcome. Eventually even Barry was won over.

It was good to find that Kate Hoey, surely one of the best Ministers of Sport, was such a cricket fan. She, like John Major, has been on the Surrey committee and perhaps fell foul of New Labour thinking when she chose to attend a Lord's Test Match on FA Cup Final day. And not many days of a Trent Bridge Test go by without Ken Clarke being seen on the committee balcony. He took the wise precaution of becoming the local MP.

It is perhaps not surprising that someone of Jamaican birth should be passionate about his cricket, and the former TGWU leader, Bill Morris, is certainly that. He would probably fail the 'Tebbitt Test' when the West Indies are playing England, but would do so with the greatest diplomatic geniality. And Lord Tebbitt himself proved to be absolutely fascinated with the work of Bill Frindall, sitting at his shoulder for a period to observe at close hand the recording of dot and run.

We have also had a couple of very distinguished Episcopal visits. Christopher Martin-Jenkins's meeting with the Bishop of Durham was preceded some years before by Lord Runcie, the former Archbishop of Canterbury. He had happy memories of going to Aigburth, Liverpool, before the war to see Lancashire play and of seeing the likes of Hammond, Bradman and George Headley. Brian Johnston commented afterwards on the toughness in his make-up which was not generally manifest in

his public image, but which had helped make him a decorated tank commander in the war.

Lord Runcie had played his last game of cricket with a cameo appearance for the Archbishop of Canterbury's XI against the Governor of the Bank of England's XI, some time before another of our guests took that office. Mervyn King, a lifelong follower of Worcestershire, has subsequently become so involved in the game that he is President of the 'Chance to Shine' project, bringing cricket into state schools.

It is not too long a walk from Mervyn King's office in Threadneedle Street to the NatWest Bank headquarters where the late Lord Alexander used to

preside as Chairman. As Robert Alexander QC, he represented Kerry Packer when he took on the cricket establishment in 1977 over World Series Cricket. Of course, Alexander won the case and you might think he would not have been forgiven, but he had plenty to tell us about all that, when he took his 'View'.

George Shearing – as he said, 'Not a blind pianist, but a pianist who happens to be blind' – was such a hero of the then secretary of MCC, John Stephenson, that he insisted on accompanying him to the Lord's commentary box himself. George showed a wonderful sense of humour after going on to add that, 'I may get blind after I've done my work.' Talking of going round without a white stick, he recalled a Dr Spanner in New York who did the same. He was always having accidents, though, and acquired the nickname, 'the Scar-Spangled Spanner'.

At least George Shearing didn't bring his piano to the commentary box. Hugh Cornwell, formerly of the Stranglers, didn't bring his guitar either, but he

Below Music has often been a feature of 'A View from the Boundary', but perhaps the most exciting moment was when Hugh Cornwell sang 'Golden Brown' at Trent Bridge in 2005.
Opposite Lord Alexander watches the action at Lord's in the company of Jonathan Agnew and Mike Selvey before giving his 'View' in 1997.

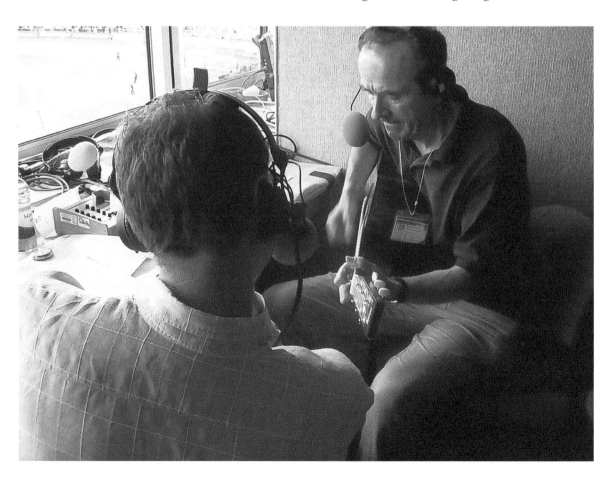

was game enough to agree to borrow Mike Selvey's to give us a wonderful live rendition of 'Golden Brown'. And if Julian Bream, the classical guitarist, did not play for us, he did create a wonderfully evocative image of life at a Test Match, when he told of an attempt to visit the gents in a tea interval. The urinals under one of the stands were made of stainless steel, which, when in mass use, created a curious drumming sound. The tea interval simply was not long enough to cater for all the would-be clientele and play had re-started before the gentlemen had all had their turn. Suddenly there

Above With impressionist Rory Bremner in full flow as Richie Benaud during his 'View', the *TMS* team sneaked the real Richie into the box. It must have been a weird experience, for both of them.

Opposite Entertainer Max Boyce: instructed listeners how to get home to Wales without losing radio reception in any of the tunnels and so avoid missing any of the Test Match.

was a shout from the crowd and a voice at the door announced, 'Botham's out!' As if a mighty conductor had waved his baton, the drumming sound ceased, only to start again with apologetic dribbles.

Artists' agents can be a difficult obstacle to overcome in the securing of a guest. Attempts to arrange a visit from David Essex in 1989 were not proceeding very well and a call to his agent was meeting the usual blank, when the man suddenly said, 'Hang on a minute.' A new voice came on the line. 'Hello. David Essex here. What's this about?' He was keen enough to delay a family holiday to come on and he finished with a duet of 'Underneath the Arches' with Johnners.

He wasn't the last to do that, either. Brian's last 'View' was with Roy Hudd at the Oval in 1993 and, with their shared love of music hall, it was almost inevitable that they would play out on that old Flanagan and Allen number.

Brian Johnston had been given the 'This is Your Life' treatment in 1983 and at the reception afterwards, the word was dropped by Richard Stilgoe that he would be very keen to take a 'View' himself. In the event he asked if we had a spare pass for a friend and that friend turned out to be Peter Skellern and the two of them, after an entertaining half hour were also required to provide music – without the aid of instruments.

We've had a few laughs along the way, surely no more than when Michael Bentine was with us for an anarchic session at Lord's. After describing how he was cured of his stutter at Eton by being taught to speak with 'a swing-and-a-rhythm-and-a-pause-and-a-run', he talked of being rejected as a wartime pilot because of poor eyesight: 'When they caught me trying to get the guide dog into the front turret, there was murder.'

At Edgbaston one day Rory Bremner was doing his 'default imitation' of Richie Benaud, so we sneaked Richie into the box behind him, much to Mr Bremner's consternation. The great Welsh fly-half, Barry John, also came to Edgbaston and as he was leaving mentioned that his driver would quite like to

do the spot. 'Oh, yes,' we said, 'What's his name?' 'Max Boyce,' was the answer. And that made for another hugely entertaining session, which included his poem of how, 'Llanelli beat the All Blacks – and all the pubs ran dry' and the details of how to pick a route home to listen to *Test Match Special* without losing reception in any tunnels.

Only one man has been on twice: the actor, Robin Bailey, who appeared the first time with Peter

Tinniswood. Robin had played Uncle Mort in Tinniswood's TV series *I Didn't Know You Cared* and the Brigadier in various *Tales From the Long Room*. His second appearance was at rather short notice. Terry Wogan had cut it rather too fine to reach Lord's by the lunch interval and Robin was, as usual, watching the Test Match from the top deck of the pavilion and nobly answered the call. Terry, laid-back as ever, appeared in time for the tea interval, so we had two 'Views' that day – another unique occasion.

When Michael Atherton and Alec Stewart each reached the landmark of a hundred Test Matches in the same match at Old Trafford in 2000, we had

VIEW FROM THE BOUNDARY

Michael Grade – BBC Chairman

'The whole object of getting this job was to get into the *Test Match Special* commentary box and it's the only way you can achieve it …

'At my prep school I was the first XI scorer. I was the first XV touch judge and the first XI linesman. I am a professional spectator. I love cricket. I could turn a leg-break. I still can – in the garden. I never got out; I could stay all day, but I couldn't score any runs. If you read the *Eagle* and you were a member of the Eagle Club, after four o'clock you could get into Lord's free. And I loved it …

'One of the benefits of this extraordinary Ashes series is that cricket has moved to the centre of everybody's radar screen and the ripple effect of that across coverage in the newspapers and so on will be felt, hopefully, for years to come.

'Sport for the media is about stars and the sports that go into decline are the sports that can't produce stars who capture the public imagination.'

THE OVAL, 2005

their fathers on the programme together. Micky Stewart, of course, had not only played Test cricket himself, but had been coach of the England side when Alec came into it, but Alan Atherton came from a different background altogether as a headmaster. Both were intensely proud of their sons' achievements, though it had taken Micky longer to be allowed to admit it.

Nigel Havers appears unable to get a word in while Blowers holds forth. But his enthusiasm for the tactical side of the game revealed itself during his interview. 'Cricket is rather like being at war,' he said, 'you lull the opposition into a false sense of security, then you attack them without knowing. It's just like being in the trenches.'

Among the many actors who have been on, there have been two from *The Archers*. Charles Collingwood, it turned out, is rather miffed that his character, Brian Aldridge, is not a cricketer. Michael Lumsden is more fortunate in his role of Alistair Lloyd, the vet, who is captain of the Ambridge team. Another drama that has provided us with a pair of guests is *Only Fools and Horses*, with Trigger and Boycey – otherwise Roger Lloyd Pack and John Challis. *The Vicar of Dibley*, too, can claim a pair, because Roger Lloyd Pack, who also plays Owen in that show, followed Clive Mantle, who won the heart of the vicar as David Horton's brother, Simon. Clive Mantle revealed that he is a regular at Edgbaston, as is

VIEW FROM THE BOUNDARY

David Troughton – but then he goes to see his son, Jim, who plays for Warwickshire.

We've had two of the *Monty Python* team on the show. John Cleese, who sat all day in the Headingley commentary box, riveted to the game. He talked, among other things, about the Somerset side of his childhood which included the likes of Harold Gimblett, Arthur Wellard and Bertie Bewes, and his excitement when the county had its days of glory with Botham, Richards and Garner. Eric Idle appeared too, having just recently written a musical called *Behind the Crease*, from which he sang us a number called 'Oh, Jolly Good Shot'.

Michael Craig revealed that he had once been out in an actor's match at Stratford, caught Peggy Ashcroft, bowled Lawrence Olivier. Nigel Havers' revelations included the news that for a bedroom scene with a beautiful actress he prepares two lines – one for each eventuality – either 'Forgive me if I get aroused,' or 'Forgive me if I don't get aroused'. If that provided the sex in 2005, Michele Verroken, the expert on illicit doping in athletics, dealt with the drugs in the next game, which leads us back to Hugh Cornwell who provided the rock and roll in the next Test.

It sounds unlikely, but Dennis Skinner – alias 'the Beast of Bolsover' – chose his own interviewer … And it was Henry Blofeld. Starting with backgrounds poles apart, they charmed each other, while the chief memory of Vic Marks' meeting with actor, Peter Davison, was of the question whether, when playing Tristan the vet, he had actually had to insert his arm that far into a cow. Aggers, meanwhile, found himself fixed by the steely eyes of the Jackal, when he interviewed Edward Fox, establishing early on his distaste for most things European.

Brian Johnston found the tables turned on him to celebrate his 80th birthday. The choice of interviewer was taxing, as it had to be someone Johnners would believe was a genuine guest. And on the day he sat there, expecting to interview Ned Sherrin, until the moment when the studio announcer handed over to Ned. After an initial, 'What's happening?', he handled the shock well – and next season we got Ned back to talk about his passion for Somerset cricket.

It has been a very mixed bag, but of such diversity are our 'Views from the Boundary' made up. The list of guests overleaf is as complete as we can make it:

Politicians

Lord Brooke
Ken Clarke
Peter Hain
Alan Haslehurst
Roy Hattersley
Kate Hoey
John Howard
Boris Johnson
John Major
Bill Morris
Jim Prior
Iqbal Sacranie
Dennis Skinner
Ian Sproat
Norman Tebbitt

Musicians

Julian Bream
Hugh Cornwell
David Essex
Benny Green
Max Jaffa
Mick Jagger
Elton John
James Judd
Vic Lewis
George Shearing

Peter Skellern
Ian Wallace

Stage and screen

John Alderton
Robin Askwith
Robin Bailey
Michael Bentine
Max Boyce
Rory Bremner
Tim Brooke-Taylor
Ian Carmichael
John Challis
John Cleese
Kevin Connelly
Charles Collingwood
Michael Craig
Leslie Crowther
Bernard Cribbins
Alan Curtis
Peter Davison
Michael Dennison
Bella Emberg
John Fortune
Edward Fox
William Franklyn
Stephen Fry
Jaye Griffiths
Nigel Havers
Frazer Hines
Karl Howman
Roy Hudd
Eric Idle
Michael Jayston
Penelope Keith
Christopher Lee
Roger Lloyd Pack
Michael Lumsden
Clive Mantle
Derek Nimmo
Peter O'Toole
Bill Pertwee
Robert Powell

Jane Rossington
Willie Rushton
Colin Salmon
Stephen Tomkinson
David Tomlinson
David Troughton

Broadcasters

Robin Day
Michael Charlton
John Ebdon
Michael Grade
Brian Johnston
Henry Kelly
John Kettley
Trevor McDonald
Patrick Moore
Ted Moult
Barry Norman
Nick Owen
Michael Parkinson
Ned Sherrin
Richard Stilgoe
Chris Tarrant
Brian Turner
Richard Whiteley
Terry Wogan

Writers

Alan Ayckbourne
Oz Clarke
Lord Deedes
Richard Gordon
Ian Hislop
Darcus Howe
Miles Kington
David Nobbs
Harold Pinter
Tim Rice
Peter Tinniswood
Leslie Thomas
Ben Travers

Artists
David Shepherd
Bill Tidy

Sports persons
Rob Andrew
Jimmy Armfield
Ian Balding
Peter Beardsley
Bill Beaumont
Jack Buckner
Jack Fingleton
Neal Foulds
Josh Gifford
Dusty Hare
Geoff Hurst
Barry John
Mark Lawrenson
Gary Lineker
Peter Scudamore
Micky Stewart
Nobby Stiles
Graham Taylor
Michele Verroken
Sid Waddell

Keith Wood
Billy Wright

Religious
Lord Runcie
Michael Turnbull,
Bishop of Durham

Others
Lord Alexander
Alan Atherton
General Robin Brims
Rod Eddington
Duke of Edinburgh
David English
Major Ronald Ferguson
Paul Getty
Mervyn King
Sir Bernard Lovell
John McCarthy
Jill Morrell
Al Pinner
Ian Richter
Sir John Stevens

Opposite top Mervyn King, Governor of the Bank of England, rehearses his 'View' flanked by Roger Knight, Secretary of MCC, and Pip Kirtley, mother of James.

Opposite bottom Professional politician Lord Brooke had no need for such preparation at Trent Bridge in 2006.

Above left Michael Grade, then Chairman of the BBC, explains to CMJ at the Oval in 2005 that the only reason he took the job was to get free tickets to the Test Match.

Above right Actor Stephen Tompkinson looks as relaxed as he would be on a Hawaiian beach before his interview.

10

CHAMPAGNE MOMENTS

It all started in the Grill Room of the Savoy Hotel in London. Brian Johnston was dining there one night in late 1988 when the manager approached him with an idea. The following year, 1989, the hotel would be celebrating its centenary and seeing Brian in the restaurant had given him the thought that they might do something involved with cricket to mark the occasion. They chewed over a few ideas and a plan emerged to celebrate a special moment – one incident in a Test Match that captured the imagination – a brilliant shot, a brilliant ball, a catch, a run-out, a particularly sporting bit of behaviour or a career landmark. Whatever it was, the player would receive a bottle of the Savoy's house champagne and they were even happy for the BBC to exercise its usual caution about using their name ... the Champagne Moment was born.

The first recipient was Australia's Merv Hughes. In the First Test at Headingley that year, he bowled Chris Broad with a slow leg-break, which amused the bowler – if not the batsman – hugely. It set the tone for the award, which often takes the element of

Opposite Australian pace bowler Merv Hughes was the first winner of the Champagne Moment for the ball with which he bowled Chris Broad at Headingley in the First Test in 1989.

surprise into account. The second award also had quirkiness about it when a member of the Lord's ground staff, Robin Sims, held a catch on the fine leg boundary to dismiss Allan Border. He received his champagne in a little presentation ceremony in Brian Johnston's garden, just up the road from Lord's. Nor was Sims the only man to win champagne as a substitute. Not long afterwards, Craig White, deputising at square leg in Brisbane, took a fine catch and the bubbles.

At the end of the season the Savoy announced that, happy as they were with the way it had gone, their centenary year was over and they would not be continuing with the award. Evidently, however, the champagne-dispensing community has its own intelligence system because a call soon followed from Rupert Cleveley of Veuve Clicquot. He enquired whether we would be interested in continuing the award under their sponsorship. At this point we felt the safest approach was to make it an official matter and so they were directed through the channels of the Test Match sponsors, Cornhill, and their public relations agency, Karen Earl.

From that moment until this very day the winner of the Champagne Moment wins a magnum of Veuve Clicquot. Nominations are written on a piece

─Shane's sure of champagne start to New Year─

Top of the town . . . Shane Warne was the toast of Sydney yesterday.   Picture: MIKE KEATING

of paper pinned on the commentary box wall. Several of them will be frivolous – CMJ going to the wrong ground, Blowers' third 'kicking horse' of the morning, Aggers' 20th plug for his own Radio Five Live close of play programme and the like. As the match nears its conclusion, a vote is taken amongst the commentary team, although we've sometimes opened the nominations to our audience to email their thoughts too, and a decision is taken.

Above Not all publicity is good publicity as Shane Warne found out to his cost in 1994 after being hauled across the coals for being photographed with a bottle of *TMS*'s Veuve Clicquot – awarded for his hat-trick in the Melbourne Test – instead of the sparkling wine that sponsored the Australian team.
Opposite Peter Baxter hands over the bubbly to Freddie Flintoff for catching Brian Lara in both innings in the Test in Jamaica in 2004.

After Brian Johnston died in 1994, a listener wrote in to suggest that we should now rename the award after him. Many sponsors might have been wary of watering down their contribution like that, but Veuve Clicquot embraced the idea without hesitation. And today, any deadlock in the voting brings the question, 'What would Johnners have gone for?'

Sometimes Champagne Moments select themselves. We have had four hat-tricks in the 18 years of the award when very little discussion has been needed to make the choice. Shane Warne was the first of them in Melbourne at the end of 1994. Photographed receiving his vintage magnum by Sydney Harbour bridge a few days' later, he incurred the wrath of team management, because they were sponsored by an Australian sparkling wine. Hardly the same thing! Dominic Cork won it at Old Trafford a few months later for a hat-trick of West Indian wickets in his second Test Match, and on England's next tour of Australia, it was Darren Gough who took three in three. Most recently, Matthew Hoggard's hat-trick in Barbados in 2004 tightened England's grip on the series-winning match.

Sometimes a player reaches a significant statistical landmark that just has to be recognised as a Champagne Moment. Shane Warne's 600th wicket, despite being something of a scrambled affair, at Old Trafford in 2005 was such a one, and how could we deny the award – twice – to Brian Lara for breaking the record for the highest individual Test score. Remarkably, both were in Antigua and separated by ten years.

With that sort of talent, it is inevitable that just getting Lara out often wins the champagne. Andrew Flintoff held two good catches to dismiss him in both innings in Jamaica in 2004 and then had him caught at slip at Old Trafford later the same year. Two magnums for Freddie!

A less well-known Test record, but still one worthy of reward, is the total number of sixes hit in a career. Chris Cairns broke that record at Lord's in 2004 in an extraordinary innings of 82, made from only 47 balls. His knock included four sixes, which took him to a new Test career record tally of 85. A few other players have won it for their ability to hit sixes. Nick Knight kept England right in the hunt for victory in Bulawayo in the 1996 Test, recalled in this book by Simon Mann, when he hit Heath Streak for six in the final over. Ian Bell reached a hundred before lunch against Bangladesh at Chester-le-Street with a six in 2005. And in 2006 two hits off Muralitharan

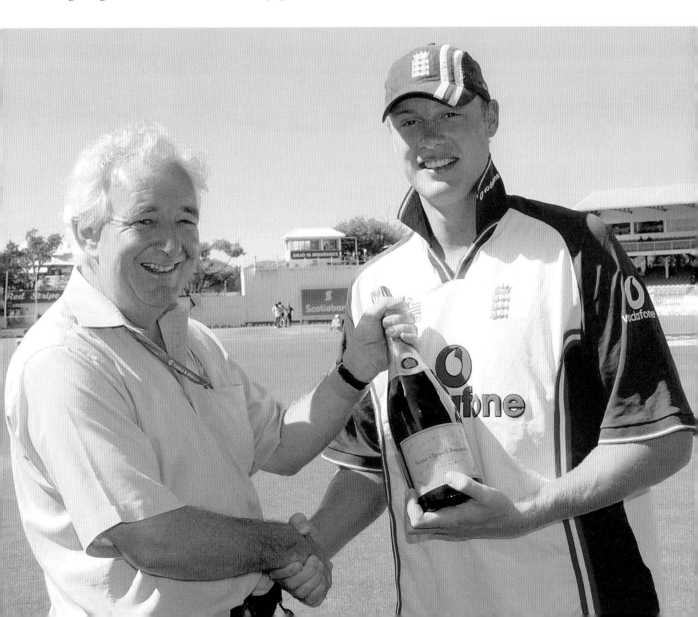

won champagne: Kevin Pietersen played an extraordinary reverse sweep at Edgbaston and Monty Panesar surprised us all with a more orthodox left-hander's sweep in the next Test at Trent Bridge. Andrew Flintoff hit a huge six off the hapless Omari Banks into the pavilion at Edgbaston in 2004 to go to his 150 against the West Indies. In the same series, Chris Gayle set a Test record by hitting six fours off one over from Matthew Hoggard at the Oval.

Of course, sometimes the award seems destined for one player whose performance is then trumped later in the same game. One such example came in Christchurch, New Zealand in 2002. Graham Thorpe seemed certain to have won the award with the third fastest Test Match double-century of all time, but within a few hours, Nathan Astle wrenched the bubbly away from him with the fastest double-hundred by a considerable distance. It came from only 153 balls and his eventual 222 included eleven sixes – one short of the record for a Test innings.

Remarkable shots – and remarkable deliveries – have won the 'moment' too. Top of the latter list would have to be the 'Gatting ball'. It was Shane Warne's first ball bowled in an Ashes Test Match and it came in the First Test of the 1993 series at Old Trafford. We were all intrigued to see how this much-vaunted leg-spinner would get on and his first ball to Mike Gatting pitched well outside the leg stump and hit the off. The split second of stunned silence, from both the batsman and the crowd, was echoed 11 years later at Lord's when Ashley Giles turned a ball sharply out of the rough to bowl Brian Lara. And Michael Vaughan must still smile about the ball that won him a magnum at Trent Bridge in 2002 – another that turned sharply out of the rough, this time to bowl Sachin Tendulkar.

Bowlers sometimes get the nod for little personal milestones, like Steve Harmison's first ten-wicket match haul at Old Trafford in 2006, or Simon Jones' fifth wicket in an innings in Trinidad in 2004. Alex Tudor won it for his first Test wicket at Perth in 1998 and Mark Ramprakash for his first in Guyana earlier the same year, though he had to share it with the man who just as remarkably took the catch at square

leg – Phil Tufnell. Ramprakash got a magnum to himself in the next Test in Barbados, when he went to a fine century with a fitting shot for four. Andrew Flintoff won it at Edgbaston in 2005 for an entire over that saw Langer out to the second ball and Ponting, after being thoroughly worked over, caught behind off the last. It checked Australian resurgence in that superbly exciting match.

Overseas players who do not know of our Champagne Moment tradition are often taken by surprise when they win it. The South African batsman, Andrew Hudson, was quite bowled over to receive a magnum for a fine catch to dismiss Michael Atherton in Durban at the end of 1995. Andre Adams took a crucial and brilliant catch off his own bowling to help to win the 2002 Auckland Test for New Zealand and found Messrs. Agnew and Marks thrusting champagne into his hands in the post-match melee. Inzamam-ul-Haq made a valiant attempt to dive over his stumps at Headingley in 2006, when he lost his balance. He didn't make it, but the dismissal gave us all such amusement that we had to vote for it. And the Champagne Moment at Lord's in 1993 was not the shot that brought Michael Slater to his hundred on the ground where he used to be part of the ground staff, but the celebratory kiss on the Australian badge on his green helmet. In that act he set something of a trend.

The significance of a century to a career or a match often wins the award, rather than the quality of the shot that brings up the three figures. Geraint Jones went to his first Test hundred at Headingley in his third Test with a single and Mahela Jayawardene needed overthrows to get there at Lord's in 2006, but both deserved their bottles.

Some great catches have been mentioned already – and as we know catches win matches … and bubbly.

Opposite Mike Gatting looks completely stunned as he is bowled by Shane Warne with his very first ball in an Ashes Test Match at Old Trafford in 1993. Now known as the 'Gatting ball', it was a moment well worthy of winning a bottle of the finest champagne. **Overleaf** Monty Panesar's majestic sweep off Muttiah Muralitharan in the Test at Trent Bridge in 2006 won him his first bubbly.

Pictures of Andrew Strauss' airborne stretch to dismiss Adam Gilchrist have widely shown the suitability of his winning the champagne at Trent Bridge in 2005. That catch was not only brilliant but also significant in the course of the match – winning the vote on both counts. Similarly, Damien Martyn's mid-wicket boundary catch to dismiss Kevin Pietersen at Lord's in the First Test of that Ashes series could also have qualified either way.

Paul Collingwood is regularly nominated for run-outs and catches. In 2006 at Lord's he won the magnum for an astonishing leap at third slip to

dismiss Pakistan's Faisal Iqbal. Mark Butcher also leapt like a salmon in Trinidad in 1998, to give Angus Fraser Carl Hooper's wicket. In the same series the Barbadian, Roland Holder, dived spectacularly at square leg to remove Nasser Hussain in Antigua and Glenn McGrath's smile when he pulled off the boundary catch that ended Michael Vaughan's innings in Adelaide in 2002 was repeated a few weeks later when he received his large bottle of Veuve Clicquot.

There was one occasion when we certainly – in retrospect – got it wrong. Early in 2000, at Centurion

Park in South Africa, Nasser Hussain agreed to a deal proposed by his opposite number, Hansie Cronje, to revive the final Test, which seemed to have been destroyed by rain. Each side would forfeit an innings and South Africa, who had already secured the series, would set England a target. Perhaps because of the relief we had of not describing a dreary draw, we felt that this enterprising spirit deserved the champagne to be shared by the two captains. Subsequently, the scandal of Cronje's commitment to match fixing for bookmakers was exposed and the champagne of that moment turned very sour.

There are places, of course, where obtaining the bubbly to present to the winners has proved impossible. The subcontinent has defeated us so far. Zimbabwe customs, too, proposed such a ridiculous tariff on it that prizegiving had to wait till our return to England. West Indian deliveries have been interesting. On one occasion a Mini Moke had to be taken to a dockside warehouse in Barbados, to be loaded with a crate of the stuff, adorned encouragingly with the familiar orange label. On another tour, with no previous warning, the irascible England manager of the time opened his conversation with, 'If you don't get that case of champagne out of my room quickly, I shall drink it myself.' After that approach, it was almost a pity to have to present some of it to members of his team. But a more friendly reaction came from the former Sussex captain and then England tour manager, John Barclay, when a similar delivery had come to his room on a tour of South Africa. 'I say,' he informed me, 'my room is so full of champagne crates that I can hardly get into it – and I think some of it's yours.'

In South Africa, Australia and New Zealand, the local agents can generally be relied upon to get the magnums to us, though with so much travel involved, a bit of forward planning is required. Aeroplane hand luggage has sometimes been weighed down by the prize for the next Test Match.

It is, of course not a very serious presentation, but it is one that catches the imagination of many of our listeners and – we hope – the spirit of *Test Match Special*.

Opposite Inzamam-ul-Haq rests on the ground for a moment before collecting himself and leaving the Headingley field in 2006. He was awarded the Champagne Moment for trying to avoid treading on his stumps in a less-than-graceful fashion. Needless to say, he failed.

Above Aggers keeps his eye on the prize at St Vincent airport in 1994, making sure that whatever gets left behind en route to Trinidad, it's not the case of Veuve Clicquot earmarked for that series of 'moments'.

Overleaf The best of the lot? Umpire Steve Bucknor, Andrew Flintoff and Brett Lee watch as Andrew Strauss stretches to catch Adam Gilchrist during England's magnificent Test victory at Trent Bridge in 2005. The catch won the match as well as the champagne.

11

THE AUDIENCE SPEAKS

In the days before emails, a cardboard box of post would arrive in the commentary box every morning from the secretary's office at each ground. This swelled unusually one year at Headingley when a pre-ordered sandwich service was offered by the club. It was a good enough idea, but the organisers decided – originally – to call the service 'Test Match Special'. I fear that a number of orders that were sent up to our box found us reluctant to make sandwiches and arrived back with the caterers too late to be of any use.

These days the vast majority of our correspondence is electronic. That revolution came too late for Brian Johnston. What would he have made of its immediacy? In the days of the pen the biggest pile of post – by a distance – was always his. The only exceptions to that rule came on the days when first John Arlott and then Alan McGilvray retired. Brian was a model of courtesy in trying to answer all his mail – if not on the air, then on postcards. On the rest day of a Test Match he would

often find a quiet spot in a park or garden and sit there working through a mountain of correspondence.

It was that innate politeness that ultimately led to the tradition of supplying cake to the commentary box. Brian received a cake once on behalf of the rest of us and felt it was such a kind thought that he thanked its provider on the air. Others evidently felt that cake was the way to our hearts and so the custom was born and at its height we would often have to visit a local children's hospital to see if they could make more deserved use of such generosity.

The ultimate cake was delivered in 2001, when we were summoned to the Committee Room at Lord's to receive a cake from Her Majesty the Queen. She said that she had heard that we had a fondness for cake and admitted that it was made, 'Not personally, but specially'. We were able to confirm that the Buckingham Palace kitchens produce a very fine rich Dundee.

There have been quite a few other memorable cakes. Lord's is always good for at least one sensational fruit offering. Brian Johnston, as President of the 'Riff-Raff Club' (a very informal formal group), once received a magnificent cake adorned with an almost life-size icing model of a pair of his co-respondent shoes. He never had the

Opposite top The Long Room at Lord's was witness in 2001 to the Queen's delivery of a fine Dundee Cake to the members of the *TMS* team. On hand to accept it were (left to right) Peter Baxter, Henry Blofeld and Christopher Martin-Jenkins.
Bottom The cake made in celebration of ten years of the Riff-Raff Club. Brian Johnston deemed it so fine that it was never eaten.

heart to eat it and it was trotted out frequently at his parties as an exhibit.

Brian did seem to encourage cake sending with his aired thanks, which prompted John Arlott once, with his tongue firmly in his cheek, to say, 'Send your letters and cakes to Brian. He loves them. For the rest of us, perhaps, something more useful – like champagne.' He was extremely sheepishly embarrassed when, half an hour later, two chilled bottles of the best arrived in the box.

More recently Jonathan Agnew's preoccupation with the moles in his lawn gave rise to a marzipan mole rising from a chocolate cake. There have been cakes that have looked like headphones on a large cricket ball, any number of bats and cricket pitches, an impressive female bust (whatever that had to do with *TMS*), Welsh lardy cake, Scotch pancakes, Irish Guinness cake and – thanks to friends of Mushtaq Mohammed – a very pungent curry cake.

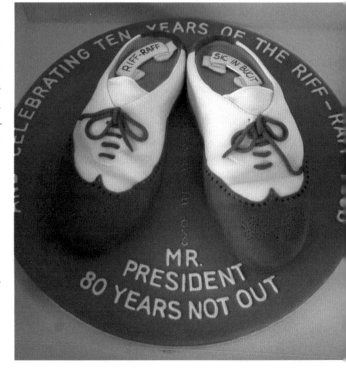

But it has not all been cake. Blowers regularly receives local bus timetables and for Old Trafford, tram schedules. For those terrible grounds where he is out of sight of any public transport, he has even been sent Matchbox toys of buses.

Our listeners write about anything that comes up in commentary box conversation and often to complain that we do not give the score often enough. If you have just tuned in, it is of course infuriating to have to wait for three balls even for an update, but we find it hard to believe that attention has not wandered when some insist that the score was not given for half an hour. They write, of course, to tell us what they think of us, too and often in quite vitriolic terms, though the usual approach is, 'I love the programme and all the commentators except …' and that blank is filled by a different name every time. It is, actually, quite extraordinary how the preferences and hatreds even themselves out throughout the commentary team.

On the last day of the deciding Ashes Test at the Oval in September 2005, emails came in literally at the rate of one every second from all round the world. Most of them were congratulatory – not just for England's achievement, but for the radio team as well. A year later the Oval Test again ended with the emails flooding in with polarised opinions on the unique events that led to the forfeiture of a Test Match. Most gratifying were those like the thanks from Andrew Waddle, 'Great interviewing by Simon Mann and chat from Aggers and CMJ. Great comments!' And from David Williams, 'The ongoing coverage of this sad episode in Test cricket is first-class radio journalism. A good example of informed, experienced journalists making reasoned judgements and conducting in-depth interviews. The rest of the media world could learn a lot about professionalism by tuning into TMS.'

With no explanation coming over the public address system as to what had delayed the resumption of the match, many were grateful for what little we could do to explain the situation as we saw it. Sadly, Gillian Reynolds, of the *Daily Telegraph*, chose instead to write

Opposite Christopher Martin-Jenkins chats on the telephone completely unaware of the 'breasts' cake on the shelf behind him.
Above The drama of the 'forfeited' Test at the Oval in 2006 brought in a huge amount of positive correspondence from listeners. With tempers and confusion rising at pitch level – here Mohammad Yousuf shows the 'tampered' ball to a cameraman – and no explanation forthcoming, the *TMS* team did a superb job in working out exactly what was happening.
Overleaf There were plenty of plaudits too for *TMS*'s coverage of England's Ashes victory in 2005 which saw unprecedented levels of interest in cricket not only at home but all around the world.

a rather churlish piece suggesting that we should have known even more, but she was – not for the first time – the only critical voice.

One interesting note came from a gentleman who knew the whereabouts of the ball from 1992 at Lord's when another ball-tampering accusation was made. He had been shown it, he said – but then asked us not to reveal his secret.

A constant source of criticism, however, is the level of volume of various sound effects. Remarks such as, 'Why do you have to put the effects microphone in the beer tent?' are a regular feature. We do not, of course, put the effects microphone in the hospitality tents and indeed work with the crowd noise largely suppressed. On noisy days the outside microphones are all but closed. Much of the problem is caused by the difference between the various methods of reception. On digital radio the sound should be crisp and clear, but complaints from those listening on long wave are often caused by the compression on the network that causes a surge of sound whenever a commentator pauses. We are, of course, always working to improve this defect.

Over the 2005 and 2006 seasons, a recurring theme was the allocation of television rights, particularly whenever an ECB official has been on the air with us. It is a subject about which our colleagues at Sky get very irate when we discuss, failing to appreciate that the principle of whether television coverage of cricket should be free-to-air is entirely divorced from the excellent job that they do. But it is a subject that gets our audience very worked up.

Lee Mellor, from Stoke-on-Trent made the point in 2006, 'Last summer I had work colleagues chatting to me about cricket and asking me the score. This year not one person has made a cricket related comment. Is it the terrestrial TV loss, or has this series not captured the imagination?'

Traffic troubles at the Rose Bowl came to a head with the Twenty20 International there in 2006.

Kimball Bailey, who had had a miserable experience there the previous year wrote, 'I determined to give Hampshire a second chance on Thursday. The shambles of leaving the ground even put into perspective the shambles of getting the tickets for which I had paid many months ago … They really haven't got their act together at all. The beer queues were better, though we will draw a discreet veil over the loos …' for which we were very grateful. This and many others like it prompted live apologies on *TMS* to all involved from Hampshire, and promises to improve matters.

During the Headingley Test Match of 2006, an email from a listener sparked a live tea interval investigation when we sent Mark Saggers down to find out about the behaviour of the crowd in the West Stand. It had been prompted by Jill Stringer, who wrote about the boisterous crowd and lack of response to bad behaviour by the stewards. 'The last two hours of the day were awful,' she said, 'The crowd was out of hand … It was impossible to see what was going on; it was impossible to hear anything … As much as I love watching live cricket I think that was my last visit to Headingley.'

That produced a flood of correspondence in agreement and a swift response from the ECB, who said that anyone who found themselves in that uncomfortable a position could ask to be moved to a more peaceful area. And along with the Yorkshire club they took Jill under their wing, giving her and her father seats in the East Stand for the fourth day.

During the one-day international at Headingley in 2006, we heard of the death of Fred Trueman. It sparked a number of listeners' affectionate memories of the great man. Marion Kinns remembered the glowering walk-back of the fast bowler, rolling his sleeve the while, 'Then he turned on his heel and began that long run up with shirt billowing out behind him. The sleeve had always unrolled by the time he delivered his ball! As a five-year-old I found this ritual fascinating.' Douglas Johnstone wrote, 'All of his body strength went into that action. It was amazing that someone so thickset and heavily built could produce something so graceful – poetry

Opposite The scoreboard at Headingley announces the death of Fred Trueman in June 2006 before the one-day international against Sri Lanka. The England team line up to pay their respects.

NatWest Life Insurance

THE YORKSHIRE
COUNTY CRICKET CLUB

Fred Trueman 1931-2006

Protection is our game

in motion.' Michael Clough recalled Brian Statham's farewell in a Roses match, when Fred tore in from the boundary, then stopped and bowled his old mate an underarm ball. Brian Sowerby had a simple message for the England team playing Sri Lanka on that day, 'Win it for Fred!' Sadly, they didn't.

The enlightened decision of the ECB to grant us the rights to broadcast *TMS* on the Internet has opened up a fascinating correspondence from people listening to us in exotic locations. One listener claimed to be listening to us in the Mongolian capital of Ulan Bator and others, during rain breaks, have

Above The *TMS* staff all get involved in dealing with listeners emails – here Vic Marks, Donna Symmonds, Shilpa Patel and Graeme Fowler take their turn at the Oval in 2000.

Opposite Sri Lankan bowler Lasith Malinger, whose bowling action (as well as his name, of course) prompted a number of limericks from *TMS* listeners during the 2006 tour.

told us that it is worse where they are – in a tropical downpour in Brunei or Thailand or wherever. Of course, there is a large audience in Australia, even in the middle of the night, when the ABC are not relaying our commentary. Plenty of reaction also comes in from India, but the largest overseas Internet audience is North America – both in the United States and Canada, where there are a great many expats. And they are not restricted to Britons, but Indians, Pakistanis, West Indians and Australians based in those countries.

Nor must we forget those on the continent of Europe. A desperate Alan Tewson, trying to teach English in Munich, wrote, 'If any of you ever visit Munich, YOU try to explain cricket. Even my Bavarian wife believes if I listen on day two or three it must be a repeat. Germans find it difficult to grasp that a game lasts more than 90 minutes.' And Luke Kadinopoulos has found that practising his bowling action in the corridors of the school he teaches at in Cologne worries the children a bit.

Whenever commentators get something wrong, of course, the emailers are quickly on the case. But they do not always agree. The slinging bowling action of Sri Lanka's Lasith Malinga prompted discussion about what side muscles he might damage when he delivers the ball. Lee Maidment from Nottingham said they were the trapezius muscles;

Simon Lewis from Shrewsbury insisted they were deltoids, while James Pickering, studying such things at Leeds University, went on about the latissimus dorsi, thoracic vertebrae and even the intertubeculat groove. Tricky game, cricket.

Mention of Malinga brings us on to limericks. CMJ is a great one for suggesting that a name might lend itself to that form of verse. The results pose no threat to Andrew Motion's Lauriat position, like Alison Magnuson's:

There once was a man called Malinga
Whom everyone called the gunslinger
His hair was a mess
But his bowling impressed
And for Sri Lanka he was a humdinger

Actually, 'humdinger' appeared a great deal, but Adam Watts, in the midst of A-level revision, managed to avoid it:

There is a young man called Malinga
Who was called a bit of a slinger
He bowls from the side
And can reach ninety-five
But he isn't much of a singer

Adam apologised for the slur – if it was one – on Malinga's musical talent.

Another who prompted the muses was Zimbabwe's Trevor Gripper. 'Nipper', 'slipper', 'flipper', and 'ripper' all featured in the flood of efforts that came in and happily news of them reached the Zimbabwean dressing room, prompting Gripper himself to come to the commentary box to collect all the poetic efforts for the entertainment of his team-mates.

Plenty of listeners are moved to verse, like Bob Ely, after England dropped nine catches in a Test Match. The last of his six verses on the subject reads:

They say that catches win matches
And I'm sure that it's perfectly true,
We must hope that next week
    at Edgbaston
Our England team find some good glue!

Since its inception in 2001, we have broadcast a recording of MCC's annual Cowdrey Lecture on the theme 'the Spirit of Cricket'. These always produce a considerable reaction, generally in support of the celebrated ex-cricketer delivering the lecture.

Richie Benaud railed against match fixing in the first lecture and no one could find fault with that. In 2005, Geoffrey Boycott proposed tough measures for improving over-rate (a constant theme in correspondence from our listeners) and found most people in agreement. And the 2006 lecturer, the former New Zealand captain Martin Crowe, mostly found favour with his sentiments on a number of topics: the dangers of relying on TV replay technology, the reluctance to do anything about suspect bowling actions, standardising tours to three Tests, three One-Day Internationals and three Twenty20 games and his feeling that Bangladesh and Zimbabwe should not be playing Test cricket. Philip Redmond, a regular *TMS* correspondent, after accusing the media of sitting on the fence for too long, was in tune with most of the reaction we received when he wrote, 'Every single point of Martin Crowe's address should be thrust down the throats of those who glory in the comfort and prestige of their ivory tower offices.' Bill Monkau, an umpire in Holland, said, 'This address is the best ever delivered to the benefit of the game of cricket. Every aspect is worth pondering on.'

Mention of the Primary Club, a charity founded – just before *Test Match Special* was first broadcast – as a club for all those who have ever been out first ball, inevitably creates a lot of interest. Brian Johnston started *TMS*'s association with the charity by raising money for the blind at Dorton House School in Kent where the infants' section has since been named after him. Traditionally, we try to remember to give out contact details for the Club for those who want to join during the Saturday's play in any Test Match. But for your information the website address is www.primaryclub.org. That mention will always prompt letters and emails from those who have missed the address and we always have to make sure that the BBC Information Office has those details each season, or we are likely to receive a puzzled call on the lines of, 'The commentators were talking about a club for blind ducks'.

Aggers likes to appeal for correspondence on a subject using the instant power of email to the full.

Several times he has asked where people are listening to us and when we were broadcasting through the night from New Zealand, what on earth they were doing. Nicky said she was operating on a Scottie dog – but it was all right, she is known to us as a vet. One man in Leicestershire was repairing lawn mowers at two in the morning in the middle of winter. There was a huge response from university students, glad of the company as they tried to finish the unforgiving dissertation.

How to get England's 'super-sub', Gary Pratt, out to Australia for the defence of the Ashes in 2006–07, was one topic and another – not entirely unrelated – that produced an entertaining and inventive response was what to do about the increasingly frequent calls of nature which seem to beset the England team. The suggestion that a Portaloo be positioned on the boundary found a lot of favour and produced a great many variations.

More ridiculous than that in 2006 was the tale of Herbert the cockerel in Norfolk. Rachel Fisher told us that her father keeps *TMS* on his car radio while he is working in the garden. When the signature tune starts in the morning, Herbert gets into the car and listens to the commentary from start to finish. 'He gets very excited when a wicket is taken – crowing and growling,' said Rachel. 'He also knows when play for the day is over when the music starts again. He then gets out of the car and returns to his hens in the chicken shed.'

Fascinating books, pictures and old newspaper cuttings are often sent in by listeners for our perusal. This is a frightening responsibility in the cramped and frantic chaos that is the state of most commentary boxes during a Test Match. Judge David Maclaren Webster lent us a remarkable, charming little Victorian book on cricket, from Cassell's Sixpenny Handbooks series. He charmed us even more than his book with the closing line of the letter which accompanied it, 'You are the worthy successors to the Voice of the English Summer. If *TMS* were ever to go or to change too radically – in format or personnel – then we would be in for endless Winter.'

Well, we know he is a judge, let us hope he is a good judge.

Opposite Zimbabwe's Trevor Gripper is another player whose name prompted the would-be poets to send in their efforts.

Above Gary Pratt: folk hero and England's 'super-sub' whose run out of Australian captain Ricky Ponting during the Ashes Test at Trent Bridge in 2005 earned him a place in the hearts of all English cricket supporters.

Overleaf It's not a pleasant sight as England players hold their heads in shame as one of nine catches goes down in the First Test against Sri Lanka at Lord's in 2006.

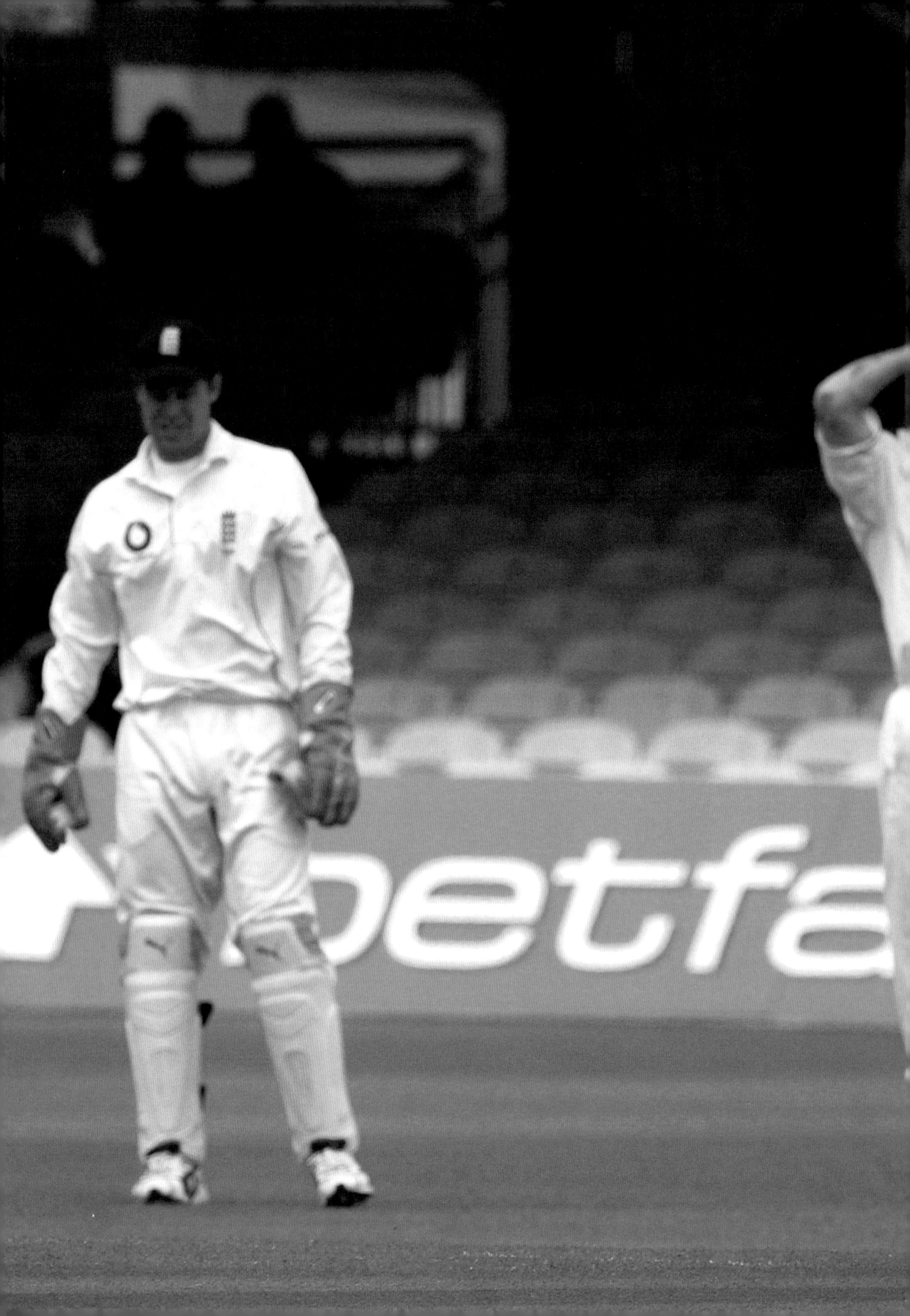

Index

Picture credits

BBC Books would like to thank the following for providing photographs and for permission to reproduce copyright material. While every effort has been made to trace and acknowledge all copyright holders, we would like to apologise should there have been any errors or omissions.

© Action Images page 215; © Peter Baxter pages 58, 63, 74, 85, 96, 99, 101, 104, 106, 108, 119, 120–1, 122, 127, 132, 134 both, 135, 147, 153, 154, 159 both, 160, 161, 164, 165, 166, 168, 172 right, 175, 178–9, 182, 186, 191, 194, 195, 205, 209 bottom, 210 and 216; © BBC pages 7, 12, 13, 27 top, 32, 33, 47, 51, 53, 67, 69, 70, 77, 82, 84, 89, 91, 100, 107, 112, 123, 139, 143 and 155; © Harsha Bhogle page 124; © Colorsport page 131; © Tony Cozier page 172 left; © Cricketpix (Graham Morris) pages 8, 61 bottom, 72, 75, 81, 109, 110–1, 115, 184 and 187; © Patrick Eagar pages 43, 44, 95, 144, 157, 176 and 197; © Empics 15, 21, 24, 29, 30, 50, 57, 64, 92 both, 93, 140, 142, 146, 148, 152, 162, 173, 180, 182, 185, 188, 189, 199, 202–3, 204, 206–7, 209 top, 211, 212–13, 217, 218, 219 and 220–1; © Getty Images pages 13, 16, 17, 19, 22, 23, 35, 36–7, 38, 41, 45, 54, 59, 61 top, 94, 151 and 200; © Mike Keating/*Telegraph-Mirror* (Australia) page 198; © Jim Maxwell page 192; © David Munden pages 170–1; © Popperfoto page 62; © *Radio Times* pages 11, 26 all and 27 bottom; © *The Sunday Times* pages 48–9.

The illustration on pages 4–5 is by John Ireland and is reproduced with kind permission of John Ireland and Not Just A Game Prints, the photo on page 14 was supplied by Peter Wynne Thomas at Nottinghamshire CCC and the illustrations on pages 42 and 138 are reproduced by courtesy of the Lord's Taverners. Cricket ball image © www.istockphoto.com/mousepotato. Microphone image © www.istockphoto.com/scottkrycia.

Selected bibliography

■ Allen, David Rayvern, *Arlott: The Authorised Biography*
HarperCollins, London, 1994
■ Allen, David Rayvern, *Jim: The Life of E.W. Swanton*
Aurum, London, 2004
■ Hudson, Robert, *Inside Outside Broadcasts*
R & W Publications, Newmarket, 1993
■ Johnston, Barry, *Johnners: The Life of Brian*
Hodder & Stoughton, London, 2003
■ Martin-Jenkins, Christopher, *Ball by Ball: The Story of Cricket Broadcasting*
Grafton, London 1990
■ And, of course, *Wisden Cricketer's Almanack*